S0-AFU-244

THE WORLD OF ARCHAEOLOGY

General Editor: GLYN DANIEL

A History of Mexican Archaeology

IGNACIO BERNAL

A History of
Mexican Archaeology

*The vanished civilizations
of Middle America*

with 115 illustrations

 **THAMES AND HUDSON**

Frontispiece: Tarascan copper mask representing the God Xipe. Michoacán. Ht 13 cm

Translated from the Spanish by Ruth Malet

First published in the UK in 1980 by Thames and Hudson Ltd, London
© 1980 Thames and Hudson Ltd, London

Published in the USA in 1980 by Thames and Hudson Inc, New York
Library of Congress Catalog card number 79–63882

Printed in Great Britain by The Pitman Press, Bath, Avon

Contents

To one of the last strongholds of scholarship, Cambridge University and Corpus Christi College in particular where this book largely took shape and where I spent a most enjoyable year, in grateful recognition

Introduction

As with Genesis, so with Darwin, mythologies of the creation of the universe, philosophers of civilization: all these have been attempts to formulate explanations of the origins of the world in general, and of man in particular. In their very different ways all have sought to trace the present back to the very beginning. In this sense both the Bible and the theory of evolution are history. Part of this huge task of rediscovery was achieved by archaeology. While the antiquary of yesteryear adhered in general to the Biblical tradition, the archaeologist of today carries on his work in an evolutionary conceptual framework.

Many and various are the ways in which archaeology has been defined, showing beyond question that the subject has meant different things at different times. But underpinning the changes is to be found a theoretical structure – we could call it the philosophy of the archaeologists themselves – that has changed with them and the period in which they lived and worked.

Archaeology begins with the antiquary,* the pre-archaeologist, who seeks out an object either for its beauty or because it is a strange and interesting survival from the past. He has on occasion served political, religious or simply commercial interests. We might say that the antiquary is an archaeologist before the advent of the strati-graphic method, before the study of the objects themselves came to be replaced by the study of a total culture, and of them within it as one of its manifestations. His finds did not lead him on to study the complexities of a social system or the development of an economy as these related to the possibilities offered by the environment, nor did he make any claims to that effect. The fact is that this kind of antiquarianism, this love of ancient things, began when men first felt curious about their ancestors. The wish to link the present with both the unknown past and the future, into which if possible he would like to be afforded a glimpse, is always there, though a strong theoretical, often mythological, framework of interest may some-times underly it.

The notion of looking at objects and monuments as though they were written records, and attempting to use them to solve historical

---

* I am of course using the word in its dictionary meaning: 'student or collector of antiques or antiquities' (*Concise Oxford Dictionary*, 1976 edn). This is how authors such as León y Gama understand the word. I do not include in the definition the modern antique dealer, trading in objects with an eye only to their value expressed as money.

problems, is a very old one. The well-known incident reported by Thucydides at the beginning of his *History of the Peloponnesian War* is a case in point. He tells us how both Carians and Phoenicians lived on the island of Delos:

'This was proved during the present war, when Delos was officially purified by the Athenians and all the graves in the island were opened up. More than half of these graves were Carian, as could be seen from the type of weapons buried with the bodies and from the method of burial, which was the same as that still used in Caria.' (I.4. Tr. R. Warner).

The Athenians, on the evidence of the grave goods and even of the bones buried there, made precise deductions about whose burials they were, with an estimate as to their date, much as an archaeologist would do today.

Plutarch has a similar example. Cimon, the Athenian general, very much wanted to have the mortal remains of Theseus conveyed to Athens. With the help of an eagle, he dug up a grave. 'There they found a coffin of a man of gigantic size and, lying beside it, a bronze spear and a sword.' (Tr. I. Scott-Kilvert, 1960:41). This 'proved' that he had found the hero's tomb.

Other scholars set about interpreting the ancient inscriptions and so change them into archival records. The great conqueror Assur-banipal of Assyria (he whom the Greeks called Sardanapalus), writes:

'I read the beautiful clay tablets from Sumer and the obscure Akkadian writing which is hard to master. I had my joy in the reading of inscriptions on stone from the time before the flood' (Finnegan, 1959:216).

This same king sent scribes to gather together every tablet they could find in Assyria and Babylon. Many other examples exist to prove the great interest aroused by ancient inscriptions. Such as what Herodotus tells us of Cadmus, or Nero setting his scribes to the deciphering of the documents found at Knossos. These examples will have to do duty for many, impossible as it is to cover in detail the huge mass of information, much of it of absorbing interest, that goes to prove the curiosity felt by the ancients about relics from the still more distant past.

This same feeling inspired a wish to safeguard the monuments themselves. From the middle of the sixth century BC, or a century after Assurbanipal, Nabonidus, last king of Babylon, discovered unfinished the ancient temple at Ur, the Ur of Abraham. By reading the inscriptions cut into it by its ancient builders, he was able to carefully restore the building and to complete it (Woolley, 1950:110, 183). The inscription he added reads:

'Upon the ancient foundations whereon Ur-Nammu and his son Shulgi had built I made good the structure of that ziggurat, as in old times, with mortar and burnt bricks . . .' (Finnegan: 1959:50).

Lastly, the digging up and preserving of objects in their countries of origin, or their removal to the capital cities of conquerors, has been done for a number of reasons: the desire for prestige, as a token of national or dynastic glory, out of an urge to collect, or for purely aesthetic considerations.

Archaeology, though still in its infancy, comes alive in the nineteenth century with the appearance of two kinds of scholar: the archaeologist proper, and the prehistorian.* This seems to me to be little more than a formal distinction, and for this reason I do not go into it here. I understand by archaeology that scientific search which, by discovering and studying the material remains of vanished peoples, seeks to learn about human behaviour through what is left of the fruits of their thinking minds and their shaping hands. An archaeologist should not let himself get bogged down by descriptions of artefacts, nor wholly immersed in their classification, but should explain their use so as to elucidate as far as possible whichever culture it is he is studying.

The post-war period has seen the emergence of the new archaeology. It has enriched the field, but sometimes at the expense of undermining the early vigour of the discipline by concentrating on the minute details of a specialist approach, and so losing touch with the society that gave rise to them. Vaillant, it will be remembered, expressed the fear, some forty years ago, that archaeology might end up as an obscure branch of mathematics.

We are also reminded of Sempronio's words in *La Celestina*, that wise old book by the sixteenth-century Spanish dramatist:

'Leave off, sirrah, leave off these beatings about the bush, leave off these versifyings; speech which is not held by all in common, which all cannot share, which only the few can understand, cannot be good speech' (Rojas, 1913, II:22).

And this is the danger to which Jacquetta Hawkes draws our attention when she refers to

'publications so esoteric, so overburdened with unhelpful jargon, so grossly inflated in relation to the significance of the matters involved, that they might emanate from a secret society, an introverted group of specialists enjoying their often squalid intellectual spells and rituals at the expense of an outside world to which they will contribute nothing that is enjoyable, generally interesting or of historial importance' (1968:256).

* The term prehistory, first defined by Tournal in 1833, can be taken to mean periods lacking written records as opposed to periods having them (Daniel, 1967:24–5 cites Tournal). If this is so, then archaeology concerns itself with cultures that do have writing, even if this is not very advanced. This would explain Piggott (1966:13): 'archaeology is in fact a branch of historical study'. Perhaps when Atkinson says: 'The archaeologist has but little claim to be a kind of historian' (1965:21) he is thinking of prehistory. And yet, as Grahame Clark has pointed out, prehistory is the past common to us all. The earliest stages in human development are everywhere the same. This is the essential difference between history, which is local, and science, which is universal. It opens incredible horizons by contrasting the humanization of man with the static state of the animal, lacking history (1970:XII). If I do not deal with prehistory here it is chiefly because what I am about to say is necessarily a local history, the history of Mexican archaeology. Though much of this history is, if the word is taken in its strict meaning, prehistory.

These strictures apply equally well to those archaeological animists who, forgetting the people who created them, describe cultures in terms of ceramic or lithic types. The three-legged pot, the projectile points, crowd the centre of the stage while their makers are ignored.

Some among us have also come to use a very strange vocabulary indeed, as Glyn Daniel has pointed out (1976:28):

'This new archaeology is bedevilled for non-American workers and particularly for our continental colleagues, by jargon, by gobbledy-gook, by well-meaning scholars who are apparently unable to speak or write in good English or American and use phrases such as "the logicodeductive-evolutionary systems paradigm". I sometimes wonder, to use A. E. Housman's phrase, whether here "confusion of language is masking confusion of thought".'*

New methods offer exciting possibilities. They are already producing results in better-dug sites and will do so increasingly, shedding light on aspects of the past which till now were hardly worth discussing even as a possibility. Theories have been developing alongside these advances, some genuinely far-reaching and sophisticated, others no more than dogmatic.

Modern methodology is an import from the United States, which is not to say that Europe did not make its own important contribution. It is already common practice to make use of data thrown up by other disciplines: geology, geography, palaeontology and many others which are clearly ancillary to the study of man, although they may possibly not tackle the subject directly. The tendency among 'new' archaeologists when looking at the archaeology of Mexico is to give preference to the techniques of the prehistorian, making little use of either the extraordinary wealth of written records both Indian and Spanish, or of the studies in the interpretation of early scripts, or in the history of art. My own view is that Mexican archaeology is best studied along a line that lies midway between the new archaeologists and the prehistorians, an opinion shared by archaeologists of the Middle East and other areas of ancient civilizations in the Old World.

Behind the scientific objectivity there is, of course, a human being at work, which is why it is important, if very difficult, to unravel the archaeologist's motivations. With a few outstanding exceptions, Mexican archaeology is for the foreigner no more than an academic exercise in the satisfaction of intellectual curiosity. But it is part of the Mexican's past, part of his very life.

We all have our theories that we long to test against fieldwork. But I ask myself whether, even when we are doing this, we are not motivated by what Kidder (1946:260) calls 'an incurable liking to

---

* Cf. Rafael Bernal: 'Invariably, when the world of letters shrinks into a coterie and the common reader no longer takes any part in it, pomposity creeps into the style, the language becomes a kind of riddle or word-game, muddled, highly affected, intentionally obscure. This is partly to prevent non-initiates from understanding it. Partly, also, to hide that it is void of content, this strange emptiness of ideas which comes about when the rich flood of popular vigour ebbs away from it. This notwithstanding, the same ideas are handled again and again, trotted out and put through their paces, with only the gleaming harness being brought up to date' (1972, ms.:13).

dig'. Certainly, without taking this addiction into account, it is hard to understand why archaeologists eagerly endure heat, insect bites, poor food and broken sleep.

In the chapters that follow I shall seek to show how, in the minds of certain Mexican scholars of the seventeenth and eighteenth centuries, studies with an antiquarian flavour were closely linked with the rise of nationalism, though still a long way from even hinting at political independence. Independence once obtained, the twin ideas of culture and nation followed separate paths. They became, though alas not in every instance, the two sides of a logical equation which might be formulated as follows: given that Mexican culture is the outcome of an ongoing and as yet incomplete fusion of two worlds, the Indian and the Hispanic, understanding of it can only come from an equal knowledge of both its root-stocks. Hence the absolute need for archaeology to throw light on what is still obscure in Mesoamerica's past.

But however much one tries to be objective and to see things exactly as they were, and however much the artefacts, by their unchanging nature, lend themselves to this treatment, it becomes clear when we study the history of the discipline in Mexico that even the interpretation of artefacts is subject to the dictates of changing fashion. There seems no way of avoiding this; with the result that one vision of ancient Mexico is conjured up by the conquerors and chroniclers of the sixteenth century, another by the representatives of the Age of Reason, another by the Romantics, and yet another by the Positivists of the end of the nineteenth century. Marxist interpretations in use today produce their own, newer dogmatism.

It is impossible to foresee what the next viewpoint will be. As the philosophers follow one another in the march of time they produce changes in the perceptual climate as it affects the different kinds of artefact. Until a few years ago the great monuments received the most attention; prior to that, works of art were the most often studied. Now, the emphasis is on searching out the most apparently trivial details of a people's daily life, and on disparaging every other approach as 'élitist'. This seems to me an absurd line to take, since we ought to be concerned with both palace *and* hut. The way I see the matter, the archaeologist has in the past frequently been guilty of studying the palace and nothing else. But many are now looking at the hut in isolation, oblivious of the study of the ancient world's most notable advances. Without harmonizing all these aspects, it is difficult to get any idea of what a vanished society was really like. Herein lies the importance of taking into account *everything* that has come down to us, and of trying to look at even such aspects of them as are not immediately apparent.

It is generally accepted that history tends to particularize, while anthropology seeks to formulate generalized rules. Though this may be true more often than not, history too must generalize. Toynbee sets a powerful example by generalizing world history in order to try to understand the circumstances that gave rise to civilizations, the courses they took, and the reasons for their fall. He did not set out to write a local history of one nation state, even of one civilization, but of their universal fate.

One of the fundamental aims of archaeology in Mexico is precisely that: to fit its ancient history into a universal framework. In much the same way as the Mexican scholars of the eighteenth century were up in arms against many of the ideas which came out of the Enlightenment in Europe, the Americanist has to refute the standpoint of such eminent archaeologists as V. Gordon Childe, when he brushes aside ancient America as not being 'in the main stream of history'. Here we might mention in passing that he has no difficulty in affirming the leading part played by 'the most ancient near East' as the cradle of all civilization. The late Sir Mortimer Wheeler, for his part, leaves America out of his reckoning altogether.

Pallottino (1968:32) opposes this point of view when he maintains that the shrinking of the world today

'asks us to recognize in every past experience, no matter how separated by time and space, the potential of the human spirit in the light of its extraordinary possibilities of development and conquest in the future . . . Everything leads us to believe that archaeology, this strong and youthful offspring of the historical sciences, can and should make a valid contribution to the working out of a new universal humanism, suited to a scientifically minded age.'

We can bring this about by applying Wheeler's dictum: 'the archaeologist excavates people, not things' (1956:13).

My overriding concern in this book has been, not to write a historical account of the theories and methods current at various times, and used by different researchers, but to pass in review the sequence of accretions to the store of knowledge, while at the same time giving some attention to those errors which often delay this process. Even when archaeology itself has taken a blind turning, mistakes have their uses in that they teach us humility and keep us from the thought that we shall be too clever to repeat them in the future. We have to keep clear in our minds that certain currently fashionable archaeological techniques of field and laboratory work are simply steps towards the acquisition of knowledge, however much some of their devotees may attempt to blur this fact and seek to present them virtually as ends in themselves. This is indeed to confuse technology with social science.

Where Mexico after the Spanish Conquest is concerned, not enough attention has so far been paid to the time of the viceroys from the archaeological point of view, though it has so much to give; the antiquarians of that time illumined the path we are still following, though it is narrower and deeper now. Their writings are our link with the ancient culture, not yet dead, and their work is full of information of importance to the archaeologist. They deal with many different subjects, quite apart from the data they yield on objects and monuments, now lost to us, all of which makes them invaluable. The reader may feel that I have included authors who cannot be thought of as either antiquaries or archaeologists. These conquerors, civil servants or, later still, colonial travellers, were not chiefly noteworthy for their interest in the antiquarian aspect. But when they are describing ruins or archaeological remains, many now no longer extant, they display towards the indigenous culture the attitudes of their time. These attitudes show up even more clearly in the work of the historians – almost professional by this time – who, without themselves doing any excavating, contribute or interpret extremely valuable information. Over and above the intrinsic interest of the old chronicles, they jointly cover the least known period of time. As a result, there has been a tendency to overlook the archaeological importance of the data lying buried in the viceregal manuscripts.

It is on this account that I have divided this book into chapters according to the nature of the interest shown by each period in archaeology or allied subjects. Grouping studies and finds along a time scale allows us to glimpse some of the hidden motives behind the conscious thinking that inspired the work, and to become aware of the ideas on the indigenous culture that were in circulation at any given time. It is true that these stages follow the general course of history fairly closely. Nevertheless, any division into periods is bound to be somewhat arbitrary, given that ideas do not change abruptly from one year's end to another. So it is that the dates given in the various chapter headings are no more than indications of when the ideas described exerted the most influence or were most widely held.

Considerations of space have prevented me from including the biographies of even the most important figures named in the book, very interesting though many of them are. Nor do I claim to mention each and every single piece of work carried out. Within these enforced limits, I have attempted to pay tribute to the achievements of the trail blazers and to the archaeologists whose most recent work has advanced our knowledge to a remarkable extent. Thanks to them, Mexican archaeology can look forward to a brilliant future. I do think, though, that the Mexicanist loses nothing and gains much if he retains some of the old antiquary's interests, while discarding a great deal of the old ways of thinking and all the old methodology.

Ethnography and ethnohistory are both more closely bound to archaeology than any other science or exploratory technique. Despite this, and although the boundaries are often very difficult to draw, I have tried to avoid entering into a discussion of ethnohistory, of ethnography, of ancient history itself and, even more rigidly, the vast literature of the Conquest of Mexico (1518–22). This is why great names such as Friar Bernardino de Sahagún, the sixteenth-century ethnographer, hardly appear, except [24] in regard to the little there is in his work that relates directly to archaeology. The limits I set myself are narrower than might at first sight appear. Certainly until 1750, though also after this date, archaeological themes were handled as though they were ethnography. So most European, and even many Mexican, ideas on the Mesoamerican past have to be left out of account. Nor have I got involved with 'images', whether Aztec or other, as say Keen (1971) has done, since archaeology deals with the reality of artefacts and the inferences we may draw from them, rather than with written texts. It should be borne in mind that this book, as a history of Mexican archaeology, is breaking new ground. It is difficult, if not impossible, to gain a sound grasp of any science with no knowledge of its development through time – of its history, in other words. Nevertheless, I hope that the information contained in these pages will prove to be of some value to the reader.

Most archaeology is funded with public money, in Mexico at least. The state is concerned not so much with the increase of knowledge as with the creation, by excavating and restoring suitable ruins, foci of national pride, of a greater feeling of continuity with the people's own past and, less importantly, the encouragement of tourism. Therefore, in order to dig ruins and preserve them, to 'archaeologize' about them, the authorities holding the public purse-strings have first to be persuaded of a site's attractiveness as an investment (Molina, 1975:72). This, while hardly a science, affects the directions in which the discipline develops and strengthens its links with the public sector. This relationship involves, at the very least, the moral obligation to preserve the finds and structural remains as symbols of the nation's past and as tangible evidence of its history. This is why it seems to me essential that the public be guided and encouraged towards an interest in archaeology. Though it might not be realistic to expect the public to play an active part in the advancement of knowledge, they can exert a very real and valuable influence on a subject which might attain considerable popularity. Without this wide interest from outside, archaeology runs the risk of becoming an esoteric science, limited in its appeal to a small group of scholars. No one can work in a vacuum, without support and understanding; the public must not come to think that archaeology, in the flippant words of Hooton (1938:218),

'implies an iterest in the obsolete paraphernalia of the pas, which to the multitudes stigmatizes its students as unregardful of the necessities of the present – the senile playboys of science rooting in the rubbish heap of antiquity.'

Further, as regards the public and the training of future specialists, the archaeologist has a duty to instruct. However often the Jesuit Clavijero might mention a 'professor of antiquities' at the Real y Pontificia Universidad, the chair had long been vacant when he came to write his *Historia Antigua de México* in 1780. Those concerned with primary and secondary education were even less interested, generally preferring to see Mexican history as beginning with Columbus. The prehistoric world was barely glanced at through a screen of confused legends and tales of the Conquest, which tend to reflect Western more than native history.

Mine was the first generation in Mexico to have the chance to pursue professional studies in archaeology. Even between 1900 and 1940, everyone – with the exception of those few who had studied abroad – devoting his time to it was more or less self-taught. There was no such thing as a training structure, only loosely connected series of courses, such as those taught from shortly after 1900 onwards at the Museo Nacional and, later, at the University.

These limitations explain why a man as eminent as Alfonso Caso himself had hardly a master to teach him his trade. But a state of affairs that put a damper on the discipline also allowed of enormous variety and scope. Nearly everyone had originally trained for another profession, which gave them a wide cultural background. They saw the problems raised by the past with eyes conditioned by their very different origins, training, life-styles and temperaments, all of which imparted variety and richness to their work. Without feeling the need of complicated methodology, they understood their new enthusiasm as simply and directly as Grahame Clark was later to do: 'Archaeology may be simply defined as the systematic study of antiquities, as a means of reconstructing the past' (1968:17). I shall be referring again at a more suitable opportunity to these related aspects of the study of archaeology.

Museums carry out the twin tasks of the conservation of finds and the spreading of knowledge. Public interest has been instrumental in causing them to become research centres, along with universities and scientific societies, and have sometimes been able to exert considerable influence. In addition, their needs have often affected the course taken by research or by excavations. Because of this, one chapter of this book will be devoted to Mexico's archaeological museums and their activities.

Any history of a particular archaeology as local as Mexico's must set itself limits of both time and space. This would hardly seem worth saying; but when we come to look at the idea more closely, we find that it excludes both colonial archaeology and archaeology since Mexican independence. Allowing for this, we might call our subject the history of Mexico's precolumbian archaeology. Yet there is a stumbling-block even here, in that I shall be referring to only part of present-day political Mexico though taking in the whole territory that was once inhabited by the Maya – an area which jointly saw the flowering of a prehispanic civilization. This area is known as Mesoamerica and I shall only incidentally be including any data concerning the area that is loosely called 'Northern Mexico'. My purpose in doing this is to avoid confusing two very different histories.

So far, so good. But where to take up the tale? Were there any antiquaries among the prehispanic Mexicans themselves? We know of a few cases, such as the great collection of offerings from Tres Zapotes, which included a variety of objects from different periods, suggesting a collection of antique *objets d'art* (Drucker, 1955:66). A different though related concept has emerged in many parts of the world as the wish to put up monuments to fulfil the function of historical records, to immortalize glorious achievements by making them indestructible. Of such are the stelae of Piedras Negras, which record the names of the succession of noble lords to rule there. The Stone of Tizoc, almost one thousand years later in date, is also a 95,96 monument of this kind, in that it exalts the conquests of this particular emperor. Precisely because they have this informative function, sculptures of religious and political importance often fell victim to succeeding conquerors wishing to erase the memory of those they vanquished. 'Damnatio memoria', as it affects archaeology, existed in Mesoamerica too.

Sahagún (1956, III:184) took the Toltecs to be the earliest settlers, 24 and uses archaeology to support his assertion. He writes:

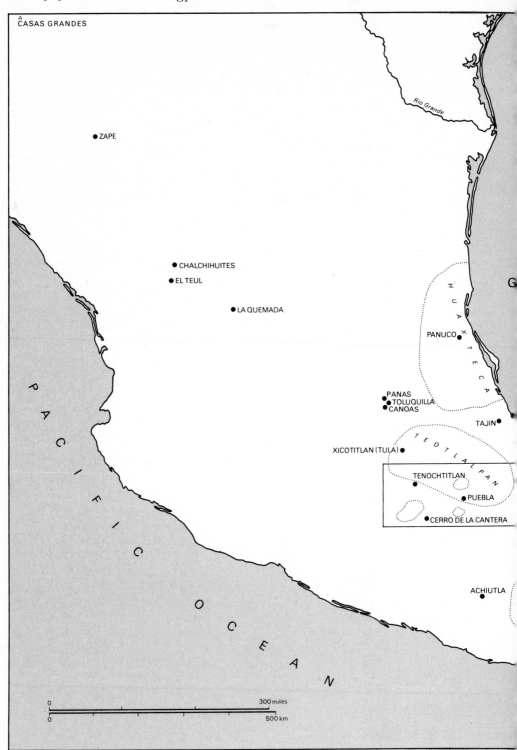

△ CASAS GRANDES

Rio Grande

●ZAPE

●CHALCHIHUITES

●EL TEUL

●LA QUEMADA

H
U
A
X
T
E
C
A

G

PANUCO●

PANAS
TOLUQUILLA
●CANOAS

TAJIN●

XICOTITLAN (TULA) ●

T
E
O
T
L
A
L
P
A
N

TENOCHTITLAN
●
●PUEBLA

●CERRO DE LA CANTERA

P
A
C
I
F
I
C

O
C
E
A
N

ACHIUTLA

0   300 miles

0   500 km

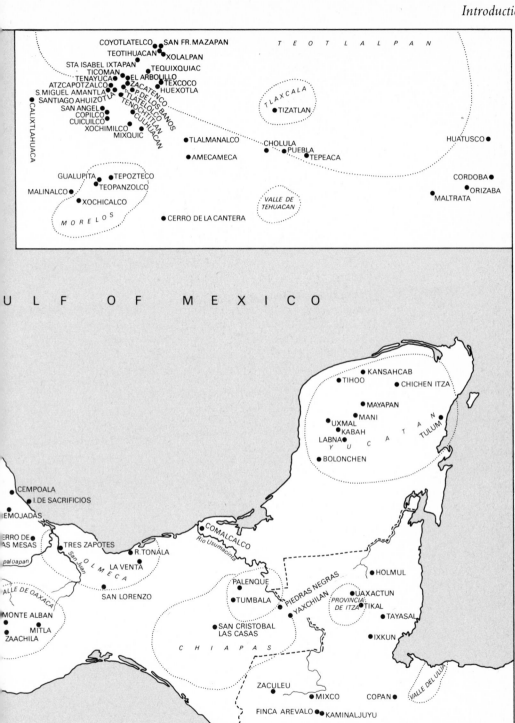

1 Map of Mesoamerica, showing principal archaeological sites

'[The Toltecs] . . . lived first in the village of Tullantzinco, and that for the space of many years, in evidence whereof they left there many antiquities and an idol they called in their tongue Uapalcalli . . .

'And it was from there they spread to the banks of a river near the village of Xicotitlán, the name of which is Tulla. And from their dwelling and living hard by there are signs of the many great works that there they did, and among them a work there which can still be seen today even though they never finished it. They call it Coatla-quetzalli, which is pillars in the form of a serpent, having its head on the ground to serve it in the office of a foot, its tail and the rattles of it being held in the air. Also remaining is a hill or mound which these Toltecs aforementioned began and never finished, and the old buildings of their houses, the plaster as it had been laid on today. Even to this day are also found things of theirs, wondrously wrought, viz: pieces of their pots, or their earthenware, or other vessels, or their bowls and cups. From beneath the earth came also jewels and precious stones, emeralds and fine turquoises . . .' (id.:64).

In spite of these faint indications that the Indians felt an interest in the objects surviving from their past, we cannot properly refer to them as antiquaries. I have, therefore, begun my account of the history of Mexican archaeology in the sixteenth century. I shall bring it up to around 1950, when the subject becomes too extensive for it to be adequately dealt with in a single short volume.

Chapter One

American–Indian Origins: Speculation and Debate

BEARING IN mind the evident fact that every relic of the past is man-made, the basic theological and historical problem facing the conquerors of America and, after them, Europeans in general, was: what, in the final analysis, were the origins of indigenous American man? Immigrants from Europe had to come to terms with the native settlements they found on every hand, and with the countless monuments, ruins and objects which, though often destroyed by them, they sometimes described in their writings. Those who never left the Old World saw the problem less directly, but it was there for them, too.

This question is clearly applicable to the whole of the American continent, not only to Mexico, and therefore oversteps the limits of this book's terms of reference. What distances the question still further is that the innumerable answers given by those many authors who concerned themselves with probing into the unknown were rarely based on archaeological evidence. Their main lines of argument were founded upon Biblical exegesis, ancient legends of the Greeks or other peoples both European and Asiatic, as much as on apparent linguistic or ethnographic similarities such as circumcision, clothing or the lack of it, the supposed fact that men urinated in a squatting position while women did it standing up, tales of migrations, the incidence of religion or its absence, as described by Columbus for the West Indies, and so forth. To this motley catalogue many writers added elements of what now goes by the name of physical anthropology, comparing the native American peoples with various human races according to facial features, or skin colour, or talking of the existence of bygone giants.

Though there is not much in them that concerns archaeology, these ideas will have to be lightly sketched in, as from the end of the fifteenth century they will help with an understanding of how the Spaniards first, and others later, reacted to the ruins and to the mystery of that hidden history to which only archaeology could provide a key.

Some of their ignorance can be explained by the fact that many of the accounts written by *eye-witnesses* of the early American experience were not published until the nineteenth century. Antonio de Herrera and Juan de Torquemada, and most authors who were, like them, published at the beginning of the seventeenth century, suggest several possible origins, often without making a firm choice between them. That there was some highly confused theorizing among those sixteenth-century writers who wrestled with this problem is clear from the writings of Gregorio García (1607). As Huddleston (1943, 13) so rightly says, a strong belief in ethnological comparisons was much in evidence, along with a tendency to accept transatlantic migrations, and the easy promotion of possible into probable origins. García's work teems with ideas and argument. He wanted, not so much to prove a single theory as to prove them all; though it is true that in the edition of García amplified by Barcia and published in 1729, arguments are added in support of the old theories and the whole tends now to the acceptance of the old data. But Spanish power was already in decline, and the end product of this period was to be a deepening gulf between scholars in Spain and those in the rest of Europe.*

At the outset no problems about American origins arose, Columbus being convinced that what he had discovered was part of Asia. He remained firmly of this opinion till his death in 1506 but, already towards the end of the fifteenth century, doubt was beginning to creep in. There was increasing speculation about the true nature of the new lands, particularly the islands, and whether they could safely be identified with Asia. Pedro Mártir de Angleria, that remarkable man who saw it as his duty to spread awareness of the discoveries, ever growing in importance, mentions for example Solomon's Ophir as a possibility, but without committing himself as to whether or not the local inhabitants were descended from these mythical migrants. He refers also to a number of ethnographic traits which might be shared between the Americans and other peoples. This train of thought had its following for two further centuries at least.

In September 1513 Vasco Nuñez de Balboa discovered the Pacific and took possession of it in the name of the King of Spain. This was proof positive that America could not be part of Asia. Magellan's voyage made assurance doubly sure. In 1522 the only vessel of this expedition to survive, that captained by Sebastián El Cano, arrived in Seville. A ship had been around the world for the first time. This deepened the mystery surrounding the origins of American man and lent the problem added urgency; it opened the sluices to a flood of candidates for the role of ancestors of the American Indians.

In this world of revealed religion, over which Genesis held undisputed sway, every man living had to be a son of Adam. Given that these Indians were men, they had in some way or another to be descended from Adam.

The Mexican, Edmundo O'Gorman (1967), has ably demonstrated that the notion of the Indians having been thought of as animals was a canard.** Many did take them to be men. This was the

---

* That Spanish thinkers and those in the rest of Europe saw America through different eyes was apparent almost from the time of the Conquest. We have an interesting pointer to this in the fact that, although some Spanish work on America was translated into other languages, the reverse was never true. Only in the rarest cases did Spaniards write in Latin, then the lingua franca of European intellectuals. This also holds good for the men of the eighteenth-century Enlightenment.

** It would seem that Pope Clement's Bull of 1530 was misinterpreted, as was also the Sublimus Déus promulgated by Paul III in 1537.

2 Bartolomé de Las Casas
(1474–1566)

subject of the famous controversy between Juan Ginés de Sepulveda
and Bartolomé de Las Casas. The Aristotelian, Sepulveda, said in an
oft-quoted passage (1941:109) that certain of the Indians' customs
proved only 'that they be neither bears nor monkeys nor are they
quite without the power of reason, that is to say, they are not
animals; but men, albeit imperfect' (O'Gorman, 1967:LX, n). If they
were not to be men, or near-men, there would be no logical reason
behind the very real and consistently compulsive urge to convert and
baptize them. Animals are not offered the sacraments. So the only
solution was to work out which Old World people could have
furnished the intervening stages between Adam and these newly
discovered men. The year 1520 saw the appearance in England of a
play by one John Rastell, in which the playwright speculates about
how America came by its people.

Little by little views on the subject changed, not only with the
passage of time, but depending also on the author's native country
and to which branch of Christianity he subscribed. Fascinating
though all this is, it is taking me too far from the subject of this book,
and I shall touch on main points only when these refer, however
tangentially, to archaeology. Such references are few, as scarcely any
of the most prolific Spanish authors, or those other Europeans who,
being farther removed from the arena, were of necessity more
theoretical, were in a position to make comparisons or to found their
theories on actual artefacts.

Among those most often credited with siring American man are
the Carthaginians, the Jews (the famous Ten Tribes of Israel), the
Chinese navigators whose traditions of migration are collected in
Antonio Galvao (1555) and, particularly from the second half of the
seventeenth century on, those men of the European north whom we
group together and call Vikings. Just about everyone, in short, with

any claims to being a maritime people, or who had kept alive legends of ancient population movements. Nor was there any lack of hypothesizing about vanished continents, particularly Atlantis, which owed its great sixteenth-century popularity partly to Seneca's celebrated lines in *Medea* and partly to the belief that Plato had referred to it. Agustín de Zárate and Cervantes de Salazar were among those who subscribed to this theory.

In Mesoamerica we must draw a distinction along geographical lines between two schools of thought. The ruins of the ancient Maya civilization were so marvellous that they would have been well beyond the simple skills of the sixteenth- or seventeenth-century Maya. There an antecedent race, which had reached a far higher level of development, would have to be postulated. Only the few who
25 shared the views of the sixteenth-century Franciscan Diego de Landa rejected this theory. The great living cities which Hernan Cortés, the famous conquistador, and his soldiers had seen in Central Mexico furnished proof that indigenous peoples had built them, although here too the fabled Toltecs are brought into account, to say nothing
88 of Quetzalcoatl or the giants lifted from Indian history as it persisted in legend.

Carthage was a favoured source of an already 'civilized' immigration movement. The idea appears again and again, decked out in various forms: it is the more salient for us because it sometimes receives some archaeological support. Lizana (1633) and Pedro Simón (1627) were not alone in thinking that the Yucatán ruins were of Carthaginian origin. The anonymous author of the *Isagoge Histórica Apologética* (1935:77) adds to the confusion by mixing up Phoenicians and Spaniards; according to him, 'statues, buildings and character types' of Guatemala bear out this mixed origin. Among his many theories, Gregorio García points out how closely the American pictographs resemble the Carthaginian, in much the same way as the ruins in Yucatán and Charcas echo their building style. But Calancha (1638), Pedro Cubero (1680) and Zamora (1701) will have none of it.

Another idea which achieved widespread currency gave the Indians Hebraic origins, though few were at the outset prepared to firmly defend this thesis. The most noteworthy among these was Friar Diego Durán who, along with Las Casas, Oviedo, Torquemada and others, mentions the notion as being in the air and as coming under discussion by those interested in unravelling the mystery. It would seem that the idea was engendered in a book by Lumnio, which first saw the light in 1567 and was confused in the extreme. In it the prophets Esdras and Isaiah and the Fourth Book of Kings are cited as proof. Genebrand (Paris, 1567) put this forward with some success. The Ten Tribes thesis seems to have originated in Spain in the work of Suárez de Peralta about 1580, and the Ophir idea launched by Pedro Mártir (see page 20) is taken by Benito Arias Montano in 1572 as referring more directly to the peoples who settled Peru. I can find no argument from archaeology in any of this.

Another myth has Jews appearing in Ecuador, and from here come such unlikely publications as those of Manaseh ben Israel or Thomas Thorowgood, both of 1650. None of this is quite without political significance, implying as it does a Zionism *avant la lettre*. Nor should we forget the disputation in 1642–44 between Grotius, who favoured the Norwegians, Ethiopians and Chinese, and de Laet who came out for the Tartar Scythians.

One theory which never won wide acceptance postulated two independent Creations. This seems to have originated with the unorthodox physician and philosopher Paracelsus in 1520, but does not become of much account till 1655, when Isaac de la Pereyre put forward the suggestion that God created two Adams – a separate one for America. Whether they were contemporaries is not made clear, as he speaks of one Adam whose descendants, the Amerindians, disappear (in the Flood?) and of another, the Biblical one, from whom stem the Israelites. This could also be made to explain why Egypt and Mesopotamia are older than Israel. The idea spread through part of northern Europe, and provided a basis for a number of books in English, Dutch and French. But none in Spain, perhaps because the Inquisition did not allow it. It led to Feyjóo (1945:40:48), for instance, indignantly spurning Pereyre's ideas on the subject of Adam, accusing him of 'vomiting out so noxious an error'. What is interesting in all this is that the polygenesis idea had its backers, and that it may have been a link with the thesis that the first men orginated in America and made their way from there into the Old World.

So we have writers, such as the author of the *Isagoge Histórica Apologética* (1935: 41–48), León Pinelo (1943, I:284) and others, juggling with the idea that Adam began his earthly life in America and that we need to explain how he made his way thence to the Old World.* Echoes of this persisted until quite recently. It is strange that at the beginning of the nineteenth century Galindo – who we should not forget was an Englishman and might therefore have read about these things in languages other than Spanish – thought that the first American civilization had collapsed because of internal dissension; that a century after the fall of Rome, the survivors had become variously the Chinese, the Indians, the Persians and the Chaldees, and that their roots were therefore to be sought in America (1945:218).

Tied in with the various lines of thought about the first Americans, but having clear political overtones, was the work of such as Vicente Palatino de Curzola, Gregorio García, Diego Durán and Fernández de Oviedo: by far-fetched argument they 'clearly demonstrated' the right to the Indies of the Spanish crown; although they accepted other theories too. They thought that if they could prove that the Spaniards were the first to settle the New World, their right to hold on to it becomes clear. Some, like Oviedo (1851, II: Ch. III), basing themselves upon the doubtful authority of one Beroso (whose works I have not been able to consult) and on a number of others, held that in 1658 BC, during the reign of Hesperus, twelfth

---

* There was no limit to what Pinelo (whose works date from 1645–50) would believe in: monsters, Amazons and all the rest. Nevertheless he was interested enough to bring in allusions to monuments, feather-work, silverware, stone-cutting and lapidary work, as well as to stone tools.

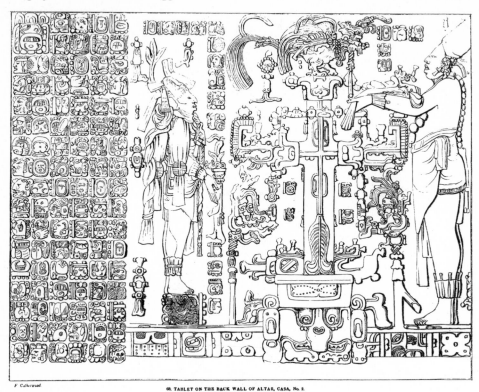

F. Catherwood

68. TABLET ON THE BACK WALL OF ALTAR, CASA, No. 2.

3 One of the so-called crosses of Palenque. Drawing by Catherwood

King of Spain, the Spaniards discovered, conquered and proceeded to rule over certain islands – which is why they came to be called the Hesperides. Subsequently, contact was lost and the memory of the feat persists only in Greek mythology. 'God gave Spain back this overlordship after so many centuries' through the medium of Columbus. We should not forget, however, that the work of Oviedo first appeared as early as 1535. Among some of his contemporaries, such as Las Casas (1951:74), Fernando Colón (1932, Ch. x) and Herrera (1615:314), these ideas were not taken seriously.

For others, such as Gómara (first published in 1552), Spanish rights begin in Carthage, whence they pass to Rome as conquerors of Carthage. On the fall of Rome they pass to the popes as 'heirs to the Roman Empire', who in their turn cede them to Spain by virtue of Alexander IV's famous Bull (1729:137–189).*

There was archaeological 'evidence' around to 'prove' the earlier arrival of the Spaniards. Crosses were found in America, and in Mesoamerica in particular. This group of writers thought their presence could only be explained by a previous visitation of the Spaniards, the great Christian colonizers.

These crosses, fairly widely distributed but with a tendency to

* It would be interesting to know if Galindo (1945:218), in his reference to Palenque was not subconsciously echoing this thought when he speaks of events alleged to have taken place 'a century after the fall of Rome' (see page 23 above).

4 Quetzalcoatl wearing his cloak decorated with crosses. Copied by Ramírez and published in León, *Bibliografia Mex. del siglo XVIII* (1906)

concentrate in Yucatán, might be the starting point of Landa's story (1938:257) that an 'Indian of sound judgment' had told him of the discovery of burials having metal crosses above the bones of the dead. But Landa, more knowledgeable than the (so many) others who did no more than repeat what they were told, remarks: 'If this were so, it may be that some few from Spain did in truth arrive there but, being soon overtaken by death, their memory has not been kept in remembrance'. In other words, though Landa accepts the matter of the crosses and the Spaniards at least as a possibility, he thinks that even if they existed they could not have been responsible for the structures which, as we shall see, he was certain had been put up by the Maya themselves. Román (1575, II:392) takes the view that the crosses and other religious symbols bearing a likeness to the Christian ones are not the result of earlier Spanish settlement. What are called the crosses of Palenque were discovered too late to have 3 had any effect in the centuries immediately after the Conquest; they only became important later.

These hints at a Christian presence in precolumbian America fit in with the idea that St Thomas visited the continent to spread the gospel at the time of the apostles. This makes an early appearance in the literature. Gregorio García mentions the possibility in 1607 and in South America Antonio de la Calancha, shortly afterwards, sets about tracing the apostle's route. In New Spain (as the Spaniards originally called Mexico) it did not take long for St Thomas to become confused with Quetzalcoatl, since he is described as a bearded white man wearing a tunic with a pattern of crosses. This piece of syncretism between paganism and Christianity, which cannot have been a solitary example, was to be studied by the writer and scholar Carlos de Sigüenza at the close of the seventeenth century. Both he and Becerra Tanco (1675) thought that St Thomas had visited Tula, and linked him in this fashion with Quetzalcoatl. For a number of reasons which have come under recent scrutiny by Lafaye (1974:256) there existed a spiritual link with the Virgin of Guadalupe, a circumstance that also leads Boturini to make some mention of the apostle in his work on the Virgin. Mariano Veytia (see page 57) devotes a great deal of space to this tradition. Borunda, a lawyer who I can only hope knew more about law than he did about history, decided when he saw the newly-discovered (1790) solar calendar stone (see page 81, below) that the hieroglyphs cut into it must refer to the foundation of Mexico by St Thomas. A quaint Dominican friar, Servando Teresa de Mier, took up the twisted thread of these ideas. In a celebrated sermon he preached on 12 December 1794 he suggested, among other things, that the image of the Virgin of Guadalupe had been miraculously imprinted not on Juan Diego's blanket, according to the tradition, but on St Thomas's cape. Thus he sought to show that the Virgin had been present in 'Anáhuac' (ancient central Mexico) well before the Conquest, so that the country's conversion could not have been due to Spanish efforts. In 1862 José Fernando Ramírez summed up current opinion on the true magnitude of the event: 'Noteworthy as a flight of fancy, though totally devoid of historical or philosophic merit.' (367). The whole affair has no immediate connection with the subject of this book, but is interesting as pointing in another context to the interest awakened by an archaeological find, and in the turning of scholars' attention towards ancient Mexico and its ruins at the end of the colonial period.

But, to return to the subject of the birth of America, what were the Indians thinking? The religious, philosophical and other discourses which so heavily engaged European attention were of no interest to the Mesoamericans; so long as they remained unaware of the existence of 'old' continents, the matter did not constitute a problem for them, nor did they feel any need to see themselves as having arrived at their present habitation from elsewhere. This may well be why Sahagún pays the matter so little attention: his Indian informants had no opinions about it. They thought of the Creation in terms of cosmological myths offering a variety of explanations.

They did, however, have an idea that America had been inhabited by giants before ordinary men; it was even said these gathered fruits and roots rather than cultivate the ground. This is the legend of the *quinametzin*.* By the sixteenth century, Mendieta is calling this a 'sure thing' and even giving examples of exceptionally tall men living in his own time (1870:96). Simón (1627:30–32) writes of the ship found in the Andes and dating from before the Flood, in which the giants all perished by drowning. Even as late as the end of the seventeenth century the English doctor-pirate, Lionel Wafer, is repeating this traveller's tale of New Spain, told to him by a ship's captain who was also a friend of his. He says, 'There is in this country an ancient belief that there were giants dwelling in Texcoco,   16 a little city five leagues distant from Mexico. In the time when the Duke of Albuquerque was viceroy, I myself saw bones and teeth of a prodigious size, and a tooth there was three inches wide and four long among them. The viceroy commanded his ablest philosophers, doctors and surgeons to give a medical opinion. They were of one mind that from the size of the tooth, the head must have measured in height at least a yard and a half . . . The Duke commissioned two portraits of this enormous head, one to send to his king and one to be kept for himself as a curiosity' (Wafer, French edn, Paris, 1706:384–5).**

When a question of outsize bones comes up, it is usually taken to imply that these have been confused with the remains of prehistoric animals. This is a very possible explanation, but it is interesting that no less a figure than Landa thinks that some Indians 'were persons   25 greater in stature than those now living and much the stouter in both girth and strength . . .' (1938:210). Torquemada asserts that

'in these regions there were certainly [men] with bodies such as have appeared in many different parts of the globe; we have seen their bones, and so unlike were they to our own, and of such great size, as to reflect thereupon did strike terror into us' (1723, I:34).

Human bones in a burial often do strike an unfamiliar observer as being larger than they actually are, and perhaps the mistake grew out of this.

Save in the most general sense in that, as I have already said, it presumed that before the Spaniards' arrival there had been men who were either more highly civilized or simply bigger, this type of thinking was not to affect the few archaeological ideas circulating from the sixteenth century on. It did, however, mean another lead into the past of America, and inspired work in comparative anatomy as well as the more scientific studies undertaken by Linnaeus at the beginning of the eighteenth century.

All these early suppositions spawned a vast literature which is sometimes interesting and sometimes merely amusing as illustrating the incredible lengths to which absurdity can go. 'It seems that the

◄ * In Toltec mythology, a race of giants who inhabited the earth during the second of four eras.

** Confusion surrounds Wafer's voyage and its dates. It is my belief that he never visited Mexico, and he himself says that his account of New Spain is taken from a notebook given him by a friend, a Spanish captain whose name is not quoted. It would be interesting to find out if these drawings still exist. It might perhaps be worth searching among the Albuquerque family papers. We must not forget, however, that the giants were not always thought of as men, but rather as 'fairylings' and connected in some way with the stone axes and other tools.

manifestly impossible has a greater appeal to the imagination than the merely improbable' (Spinden, 1933:220). Reasoning based on the ancient relics, on comparisons with and links between them, is almost never used. As already mentioned, the explanation lies in the scarcity of publications and the almost total absence of archaeological studies before the second half of the eighteenth century. Nor was there any material, either in America or in the Old World, with which fruitful comparisons could be made. Consequently, where Mesoamerica is concerned, say for the Maya area, I can find only fleeting speculations as to who might have built the structures; these I shall come to later but without always alluding to the first American settlers or to the land whence they came. A further complication is that racial and cultural argument are often allowed to become entangled.

There are various general books on the subject which can be consulted (Winsor, 1887, Wauchope, 1962 and particularly Huddleston, 1967), and many more could be named whose authors supported this theory or that. I have regretfully to give up the idea of teasing out the extremely complex history of these ideas and their development as they were perceived by Western and even by Chinese intellectuals, but to follow up their lines of reasoning would take me beyond the confines of this book.

Amid all this confusion, however, one paramount figure stands out, that of the Jesuit José de Acosta. Beginning in 1590, he published
5 in full his most important work, the *Historia Natural y Moral de las Indias*. Despite the then almost total lack of data, by discarding frivolous comparisons and theories built on air, he succeeded in arriving at the right answer, however incomplete, thanks to his common sense and his ability to argue a case:

'And this we do surely know, that for ages past men have dwelt in these regions, nor can we deny the plain teachings of Holy Scripture, that all men are descended from one man, and he the first; so are we the more certainly constrained to admit that men came here from distant Europe, from Asia or from Africa, but how they came, or what road they took, we have still to seek out the knowing thereof' (1940:61).

He sets out most clearly the problems surrounding not only the presence of man, but of animals, which could hardly have got there in boats, for 'to embark them along with men is mere folly' (1940:321) '. . . so must we then, for the beasts as for men, discover the path they followed in the journeying from the Old World into the New' (1940:75) '. . . for it has to be that they came, not sailing upon the ocean, but walking upon the earth' (id.:77). Using geographical explanations although the American North West was still unknown, he sees that there must have been a land bridge to account for the animal distributions. He it was who fathered scientific thinking on this subject.

Followers without number saw the truth of his ideas as they freed themselves from the slough of confused ignorance, to become the salvation at least of Spanish thought. We have already mentioned Herrera and Torquemada. In the first half of the seventeenth century

5 Title page of José de Acosta's *History* of 1608

Calancha and Solorzano also reached what Huddleston (1967:101–102) calls the inescapable conclusion that the problem surrounding the arrival of men and animals in America can only be solved by presuming the former existence of a land bridge between America and the Old World across the *estrecho de Anián* (i.e. Bering Strait) already mentioned by Martínez (1606:104–5). Ignorance of the geography of the northwest corner of the continent prevented them from being any firmer in their judgments. Some of the English, and Johannes de Laet in the 1640s, also seem to be of the same mind as Acosta. Broadly speaking, the idea of an influx from North East Asia was widely shared in the seventeenth century.

The motley throng who took up the study of the coming of the Americans to America (many of whom I have of necessity omitted to mention) produced a multiplicity of theories of which I have picked out those most widely accepted before the eighteenth century. By then Feyjóo was writing:

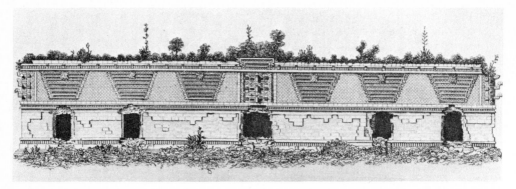

6 Uxmal. East facade of the Nunnery. Drawing by Catherwood

'Long study and careful scrutiny of so many and so varying opinions have convinced me that in none of them does there reside that proof necessary to the serious mind, and that many of them do not even have the virtue of probability' (speech 25).

Some nineteenth-century writers discard them totally, as quite without merit. Bancroft (1886, I:2–5) does this, without giving them the benefit of careful consideration, and without having noticed that in one form or another they persisted well into his own day.

In pleasing contrast, a few authors with a real knowledge of the Maya zone were tireless in the reiteration of their belief that the monuments were erected by the Maya, even if they fall short of making an ideational link with the origin of man in America.* When Landa (1938:69) asserted that 'these buildings were put up by the Indians and by no other nation, which is to be seen in the stone statues of naked men bound about with long ribbons which they call *ex* in their tongue and other devices such as the Indians use', he was almost three centuries ahead of John Lloyd Stephens. In the succeeding paragraph he refers to the discovery of a vessel buried in 'a building which they pulled down'; it was found to contain, among other things, 'three strings of fine stone beads of the kind the Indians used for money. All this can be taken for signs that the Indians builded them' (id.:210).

Though without the same degree of firmness, Friar Antonio de Ciudad Real, who wrote the official account of Father Ponce's survey of the Franciscan establishments of Yucatán in 1588, holds the same opinion. Thus, when in his very fine description of Uxmal he refers to the statues adorning the façade of the Nunnery, he echoes

---

* It is indeed strange that Landa and others in the middle of the sixteenth century were reasoning more clearly than the mass of the Mexican public for whom, even today, the essential difference between two problems – the general one of the origins of American man, and the particular one surrounding each region – still remains blurred. The second is concerned with such local movements as, say, where the Mexica came from, and whence precisely they launched themselves into the Valley of Mexico. Many mix this up with the origins problem without giving a thought to the many centuries that elapsed between the two events, apart from their having had differing causes and their having produced different results. Similarly, in times past the problem of man's origins was often confused with the matter of who may have put up the buildings.

Landa by saying 'there are figures sculpted in high relief showing naked Indians with their loin cloths . . . from which it would indeed seem that they were builded by Indians' (*Relación*, 1873, II:459). About their age he thinks that according to what he had been told by 'an Indian of ripe years and in full possession of his wits' – how close to Landa this is – 'that more than four score years and ten had passed since their building' (id.II:461). He does not mention the origin of the various other sites which he describes very briefly.

Writing in 1576 about Copán on the outskirts of the Maya area, Diego García de Palacio also takes the Maya to have put up the buildings.

'They do say that in ancient times had come there and built these palaces a great lord from the province of Yucatán . . . of the fables they recount this looks to be the nearest to the truth' (1866, VI:39).

Considering when it was written, his account of Copán is so outstanding that Maudslay is perfectly justified to say of it: 'It might have been written by any intelligent visitor within even the last few years' (1889, Vol. I of text: 7).

The various *Relaciónes de Yucatán*, which often copy from one another or plagiarize Landa's manuscript, comment from time to time on the origin of the Maya. For instance, in the report of the village of Kansahcab, dated 20 February 1579, we read:

'the natives are of the lineage of those who built these buildings aforesaid and in the land which is theirs there be yet some who descend in the line direct from these their ancient forefathers . . .' (*Relación de Kansahcab*: 196).

7 Uxmal. Part of the Nunnery wall showing man in a loin cloth. Drawing by Catherwood

8 Copán. Stela L. Drawing by
Catherwood in Stephens 1841,
Vol. 2

88   Possibly these writers are hinting at Quetzalcoatl and the Toltecs in
their accounts, as does García de Palacio.
37,38,17,19   Referring to the mighty ruins of Uxmal, Chichen and others in the
20,109,112   area, the Franciscan friar López de Cogolludo writes in 1688, a
century on:

'Some have said that they are the work of the Carthaginians or
Phoenicians: but this is commonly refuted on the general grounds
that no sound histories exist to show that people of any such nations
ever set foot in these regions' (1867, I:285).

He also rejects the assertions of Sánchez de Aguilar (1892:95) 'by
which it is agreed that they are the work of Mexicans, not of
Carthaginians as our people thought'. By 'Mexicans' he means
Toltecs. Quetzalcoatl again. The quotation from Cogolludo is
interesting as showing how, in the seventeenth century, the earlier
conviction that the ruins were Maya work was weakening its hold,

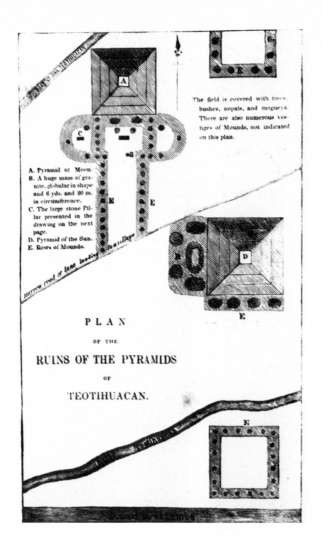

A. Pyramid of Moon.
B. A huge mass of granite, globular in shape and 6 yds. and 20 in. in circumference.
C. The large stone Pillar presented in the drawing on the next page.
D. Pyramid of the Sun.
E. Rows of Mounds.

The field is covered with trees, bushes, nopals, and magueys. There are also numerous vestiges of Mounds, not indicated on this plan.

PLAN

OF THE

RUINS OF THE PYRAMIDS

OF

TEOTIHUACAN.

9 Plan of Teotihuacán. After Maler

and this author was clearly being made uneasy by what he has read in other sources. It is now that the fables about European or Asiatic origins grow in insistence. Let us remember that Aguilar was writing in 1635 or thereabouts. It is also interesting to see that the line between 'Mexicans' (of the central valley) and the people of Yuçatán is already clearly drawn.

In Central Mexico at this period there were no opinions as clearly formulated as Landa's on the subject of the ruins and their builders. Influenced perhaps by the finds of large bones, or perhaps by Indian legends, people thought that Teotihuacán was the work of giants while the other cities, already historic, had been built by Toltecs or Mexicans. The truth of the matter is that in Central Mexico interest in the ruins was so much slighter than in Yucatán, that no one felt any need to make up his mind about who put them there.

The archaeologists and historians who in the nineteenth century held ideas similar to those of the wildest colonial writers were legion.

Kingsborough is an example. It is even odder that in our own day the mania for explaining the origins of American man and his culture by excursions into fantasy shows few signs of abating. Many are the so-called explanatory texts to appear, airing the most far-fetched notions. The (also recent) studies claiming to establish intercontinental diffusion are different in kind. They are concerned less with the physical origins of the Amerindians than with calling attention to similarities between cultural traits. Although their ancestry can be traced back as far as the nineteenth century, the best work by archaeologists of standing belongs more surely to the years after 1950. It would be interesting to look at the most important work to be based squarely upon archaeological studies, but this is not feasible within the compass of this book. There is no point whatever in referring to those whose sole aim is to take advantage of human gullibility.

Chapter Two

'Proud Mansions' and the Men who Discovered Them (1520–1670)

IF WE TAKE as our yardstick the level of antiquarian interest shown in the local Indian cultures, we can usefully divide the three centuries of viceregal rule into three unequal periods. The first and longest phase begins with the fall of the Mexica Empire and lasts until 1670. The second takes us up to around 1750; it bears the imprint of the outstanding figure of Sigüenza (see page 49, below), and of the new breed of scholars who followed close upon his heels. The third and last period begins with the Age of Enlightenment and takes us up to Mexican Independence.

28,30

Clearly it would be too much to expect archaeological investigation to have been carried out during the one hundred and fifty years prior to 1670, but these years did not even yield antiquarian research of a kind already becoming familiar in Western Europe.* Although the many valuable studies of ancient Mexico written at this time are ethnohistorical, ethnographic or linguistic, they are none the less of vital importance to the modern archaeologist. Their authors brought widely differing backgrounds to their descriptive task: conquerors, churchmen, civil servants, Indian intellectuals, travellers.

The earliest of them, including Hernan Cortés and Bernal Díaz del Castillo, describe, at length and sometimes marvellously well, Tenochtitlán and other cities. No Indian author's description of his country's capital has come down to us. Although still functioning cities are their subject matter, which makes them not strictly speaking archaeological, a knowledge of these accounts yields unique insights into the Mesoamerican world on the eve of the Spanish Conquest. Often, and above all for Mexico City, these descriptions are the most reliable guidelines we have in the search for understanding what the capital was like, archaeological exploration now being only possible in very exceptional circumstances. Such few modern urban studies as exist make it clear how little remains of the ancient city's ruins, confirming at the same time the accuracy of the data given in the first-hand accounts of the sixteenth-century chroniclers.

93,95,97

* Here Mexico is very different from, say, Scandinavia, where we see the emergence of the serious antiquary from the sixteenth century onwards (Klindt-Jensen, 1975). Where Italy is concerned, the resurgence of interest in antique art can be seen in Petrarch. The movement takes on political overtones with Cola di Rienzo, that extraordinary adventurer, who sought to restore the Roman Empire.

Despite their having produced by far the fullest accounts of what they saw, the religious missionaries were not as rule appreciative of either ruins or antiquities. Quite the contrary; when they do refer to them, it is more likely to be to demand their destruction on the grounds that they are idolatrous and hinder conversion of the Indians. They were totally convinced of the need to demolish all visible remains of a past they wished to obliterate. Conversion to Christianity was, after all, the friars' mission, however much we may today regret some of the things they did.

Let us look, for example, at Bishop Zumárraga's letter of 12 June 1531 to the Chapter of the Franciscan Order:

'Know ye that we are much busied with great and constant labour to convert the infidel . . . five hundred temples razed to the ground, and above twenty thousand idols of the devils they worshipped smashed and burned . . .' (García Icazbalceta, 1881:311).

9 We have many similar contemporary reports, those on Teotihuacán for example. Among the few sites then known, this was the most visited, presumably because it is dramatic in appearance as well as lying near the capital. Mendieta writes (1870:87):

10 'Portrait' of Nezahualpilli, king of Texcoco. From the Codex Aubin

36

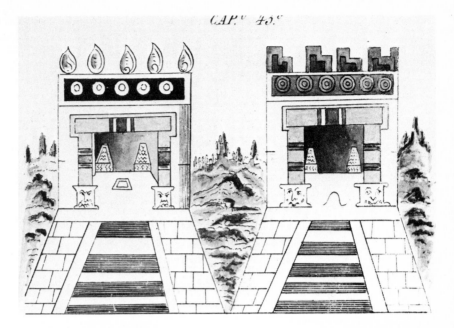

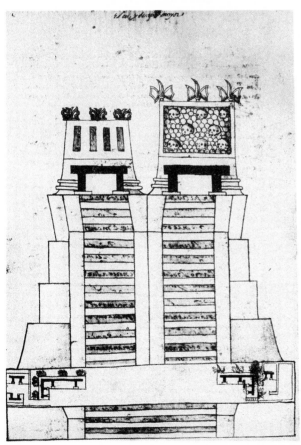

11 The Great Teocalli (Temple) of Mexico. From the Codex Aubin

12 The Great Teocalli (Temple) of Mexico. After Durán

13 Mexican scenes representing war and commerce. Detail from frontispiece of Herrera's *History*

14 Moctezuma en route for the temple. Detail from frontispiece of Herrera's *History*

'About the village of Teotihuacán lie many temples . . . and one in particular of marvellous size and height and at the crown of it stands there still a stone idol the which I have seen. Because of its great size no means have yet been found to bring it down from there and put it to some use.'

Mendieta, in other words, felt so little antiquarian curiosity that he saw in the statue that crowned the summit of the Pyramid of the Sun an object fit only for breaking up. Torquemada (1723, II:138) mentions the two great pyramids and the more than two thousand temples, adding that the area is held sacred to the gods. He is not certain why the buildings were placed there but, given that the idol-worshippers were in the habit of dotting their countryside with dwellings for the sun and moon, he supposes the same to have happened at Teotihuacán, a theory he makes fit in with a series of examples: Egyptian, Greek, Roman, which he goes on to quote. Mendieta sees no reason to destroy the site, but neither does he describe it in any detail.

29

Burgoa and Durán cut much deeper. The former recounts, in his customary clumsy style, the tale of one Friar Benito, a monk who, having undergone many dangers and paid many a ritual courtesy, finally attained the cave in Achiutla of a pagan idol known as The People's Heart.

'. . . It was an emerald great as one of those swollen peppers they grow in these regions. Carved on its crest was a chick or little bird, marvellously well wrought, the whole entwined above and below with a little serpent carven with the same power of art. The transparent stone had a glow like that of a candle in its inmost depths; it was a jewel so ancient that none could call to memory the beginnings of the worship of it' (1934, I:332–3).

Then he ground to dust what must have been a fabulous jade. Friar Durán went further still in his zeal to stamp out the memory of the old-time religion; he suggested nothing less than the destruction of the newly-built (sixteenth-century) cathedral, for no better reason than because many of its pillars rested on the carved serpents' heads which bordered the central courtyard of what had been the great temple. For him, everything tainted with idolatry must be smashed, even to the Stone of Tizoc, still visible in his day in the Plaza Mayor in Mexico City, and now on show in the Museo.

Possessed by a like ardour was Archbishop García de Santa María who, in the first years of the seventeenth century, ordered the destruction of the sculptures then to be found everywhere in Mexico City (Torquemada, 1723, III:208). The chronicler adds that, even then, it was too late since 'the Indians now living, not only do they hold them in no esteem; further, they mark not where they stand, neither know they for what purpose came they there'. Nevertheless, two hundred years later we have León y Gama reporting the survival of many of these statues, whether visible, or buried, or incorporated in the fabric of colonial buildings (1832, Part Two:80). Lastly, we should not forget that, on Landa's instructions, many Maya manuscripts, as well as the Texcocan archival records, were burnt.

15 Early indigenous carving adapted as capital of a pillar in Mexico's first cathedral. National Museum of Anthropology, Mexico City

That this passion for the smashing of idols has in fact been greatly exaggerated is partly the churchmen's own fault. They proclaimed their missionary fervour by overstating the extent of their destruction, often beyond the limits of the possible. Part of the blame must also fall on more recent historians who, for different reasons, sought to discredit the process of converting Indians.* The fact is that, though the clerics might fulminate about the need to destroy the relics, the study of the pagan past concerned them deeply, and not infrequently they carried their researches into it beyond the line of their religious duty. The struggle for souls called for knowledge of the heathen world, knowledge as the driving force of change. Thus we have those splendid ethnographic studies, the ethnohistories and, along with them, all the grammars and dictionaries of the Indian languages, without which the voice of God would have remained unheard.

52 Nothing more exalted than the greed for gold drove Grijalva to the looting of Indian burials, both on the Isla de Sacrificios and on the Rivier Tonalá (Juan Díaz, 1858:298, 304). Many of these robberies took place at the time of the Conquest, but later similar episodes included the one involving the ill-starred Figueroa in Oaxaca who, after gathering together a goodly store of gold lifted from graves, suffered shipwreck in which he lost not only his goods but his life (Díaz del Castillo, 1939, III:127). Searches of this kind must have been of frequent occurrence, and that they sometimes received government authority is shown by the licence granted in 1530 to the Count of Osorno, President of the Consejo de Indias, to seek out and open graves, the permit to run for two years. Six years later the crown claimed rights over all finds and in 1538 Osorno goes so far as to grumble at this hardship. Many other documents exist which refer to these conditions, such as the licence granted in 1587 by the then viceroy, the Marquis of Villamanrique, and the custom was kept up until 1774 at least.** Grave-robbing is still going on today; it destroys historical evidence and makes it more difficult for research to gain ground.

This period produced few descriptions of the Central Mexican ruins, and no excavations having as their aim the advancement of knowledge were undertaken. The clerics, the public servants and the most interesting Indian authors pay them passing attention. Ixtlil-xochitl (II:173 et seq.) paints for us a fairly complete picture of the 16 palace at Texcoco, referring to the map of it which appears in the Codex Quinatzin. But the chronicler adds 'as it can clearly be seen in these our days by the ruins thereof'. He saw them then, and thought of them, as part of the stuff of history.

Things were different in the Maya zone, where Friar Lorenzo de Bienvenida (1877:71) held office at Tihoo, present-day Mérida, from 1548 on.

* Cf. J. García Icazbalceta on the destruction of Indian antiquities as recorded by Friar Juan de Zumárraga, Mexico 1881.
** Cf. Bulletin of the *Archivo General de la Nación*, VI:418–19, 1935 and XXII (missing), 1951.

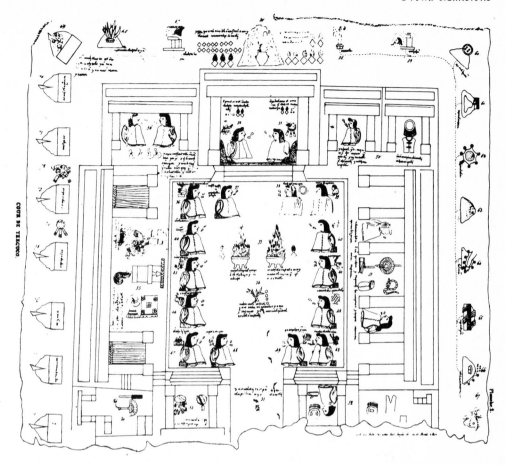

16 Courtyard of the palace at Texcoco. From the Codex Quinatzin

'They [the monks] called it thus on account of the wonderful structures which are thereabouts; of all the discoveries in the Indies there are none so fine; mounds of stone neatly dressed, and the stones right large, with no record to tell us who placed them there; seemingly they were made before the coming of Christ into the world, seeing that the trees growing out of them were as tall as those upon the earth around: they are in height five *estados* [35 feet], of drystone, and crowned with the dwellings, four rooms like unto the cells of friars, in length twenty feet and in width ten and every portal of tall stones as high as the door itself, and vaulted, and there is great wealth of these in this region. The people are not used to live in them, but only make for themselves houses of wood and thatch, there being more dressing of plaster and stone than in all the discoveries. We the friars took space in one of these dwellings for the chapel of St Francis . . .'

The documentation begins to be important with Diego de Landa (1542–79). His *Relación de las Cosas de Yucatán*, written in Spain in 1566, ranks among the very best accounts. Apart from its descriptions of various sites, one can extract a mass of valuable detail strewn throughout its length. So far as we know, it was the first to include drawings of Maya buildings. The most interesting of these is the one

25

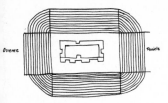

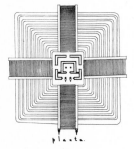

17 Plan of the Castillo at Chichen Itzá. After Landa

18 Plan of the Castillo at Chichen Itzá. After Marquina

19 The Nunnery at Chichen Itzá. Drawing by Catherwood

showing the Castillo at Chichen. Although Landa's sketch plan of the Castillo, as well as his description of it, is not without a fair degree of error, it also includes much accurate information on such items as the nine recessed structures, the ninety-one stepped levels, the serpents' heads at the head of the main stairway to the north, the precisely dressed stone revetment. . . . We do not know when Landa made his drawings but, if they were done in Spain and so from memory, this would explain the most serious of the errors, as, for instance, the shape of the base and of the main temple, shown as rectangular instead of square.

Without perhaps being fully aware of it, Landa and those like him were using ruins and occasionally artefacts to emphasize historical points, much as might a modern archaeologist.

Though things fell out differently in Central Mexico, in the Maya region the ruins aroused keen admiration right from the start. We have only to read Landa's description of Chichen with its 'gallant' buildings. Again,

'Yucatán should be given the name and repute that are its due for the multiplicity, grandeur and loveliness of its buildings. . . . For in this it is so . . . the most notable thing of those discovered in the Indies till this day, because they are so many and stand in so many regions, and are so well builded of stone, in their fashion, as to strike terror into the heart' (1938:209).

6,7 The 'very numerous' buildings of Uxmal also excited great admiration in Antonio de Ciudad Real. García de Palacio speaks of 'Proud mansions . . . such skill, such a richness . . . stone cut with exquisite nicety'. Beginning in 1575 with the first recorded visit, Copán casts

20 The 'Church' at Chichen Itzá. Photographed by Maudslay

21 Copán. Hieroglyphic stairway. Reconstruction drawing by Proskouriakoff

22 Maya archway at Labna. Reconstruction drawing by Proskouriakoff

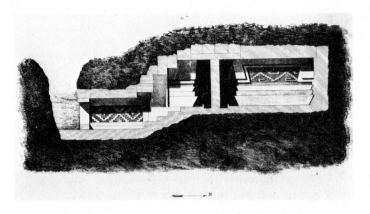

23 Mitla. Cross-section of tomb. Drawing by Castañeda, reproduced in Dupaix

its spell. Las Casas himself falls beneath it: 'buildings deserving of praise had they, which can today be clearly seen . . .' (1967, I:278).

The vaulted arches and the wonderful precision of the stonecutting of the Maya are often mentioned admiringly. Lizana speaks of 'mansions so splendid, freely adorned with sculpted figures . . . having nicely executed portals' (1893:3). Similarly, Sánchez de Aguilar refers to 'famous, great and awe-inspiring palaces' (1892:94). Cogolludo goes some way towards summarizing these views and others like them at the end of the seventeenth century.

I wonder whether the difference in the level of appreciation of the Maya and the Central Mexican ruins might not be due to nothing more than the vaulted arches and the rich sculptural ornament of the first, contrasting favourably with the stylistic severity of the second. (If I do not bring in the enthusiastic descriptions of, say, Tenochtitlán, it is because of my expressed intention to exclude living cities). In those days the Maya façades and their sumptuous ornament were plain for all to see, while the great stark masses of Teotihuacán and Monte Albán, impressive though they are now, then had the purity of their lines obscured by earth, and overgrown with brushwood. Might not this be why Mendieta (1870:87), for instance, remarks on the immense size of the pyramids at Teotihuacán but is not struck by their beauty? Burgoa does not mention Monte Albán. However, his description of Mitla reads: 'two clusters of the utmost size and multitude that there are in this New Spain . . . truly a thing of wonder', which might lend support to my idea that the decoration at Mitla is elaborate enough to recall Maya architecture. Motolinia (1858, I:170) says that Friar Martín de Valencia found there 'certain buildings more worthy to be seen than in any other region of New Spain'.

24 Bernardino de Sahagún (1499–1590)

On the one hand these studies often give an indication of the condition in which the structures were found, leading to speculations concerning their age. On the other, there seems not to have been the remotest interest in their conservation, the passion for collecting being apparently quite unknown. It first became evident in the second half of the eighteenth century.

The Maya script and the Maya calendar are subjects of no lesser importance. But in this context there would be no point in dwelling

El Yllmo. Sr. D. Fr. Diego de Landa, natural de Cifuentes, España, Obispo de Yucatan. Siendo Guardian de este Convento de S. Antonio, 1553, fabricó el primitivo clausfro y esta Yglesia y Santuario de la Inmaculada Concepción Ntra Sra. de Izamal, cuya milagrosa imagen inauguró trayéndola de Guatemala, costeada por el Pueblo Izamalense, año de 1559. Trajo a la vez otra igual que dejó en Mérida, y habiendose aburado la una despues de 380 ... en el incendio de esta Yglesia, el 17 ... la otra.

25 Diego de Landa
(1524–1579)

10,11,16,44,61

upon the cardinal nature of Landa's observations, since they belong to a later date. Others write of the codices, with descriptions of how they were made up. What is more, they had evidently become aware of the existence of writings incised on stone. Landa himself reports the finding in Mayapán of stelae 'bearing certain characters such as they use' (1938:78–9); and 'with certain characters and letters of those that in ancient time the Maya Indians did use', writes Ciudad Real (1873, II:459). 'Certain letters which we wot not of', adds Garciá de Palacio (1866:37).

It goes without saying that the Spanish colonial administration was hardly concerned with tourist promotion, any more than it took kindly to the presence of foreigners in its American possessions. For this reason travellers were few, especially in the years we are now dealing with. Such English as did come were merchants, pirates or those in league with so lucrative a profession. Some of them, while far from being interested in archaeology, do mention a ruined site here or there; Robert Tomson, for example, who came to Mexico in 1555 (1869:212), or the famous Thomas Gage who travelled through parts of Mesoamerica after 1625, smashed an idol in a cave in Mixco,

26 Maya hieroglyphs engraved
on stone, found at Copán.
Drawing by Catherwood

27 Maya hieroglyphic script.
From Dresden Codex, drawn
by Humboldt

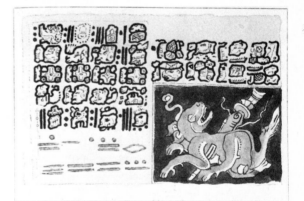

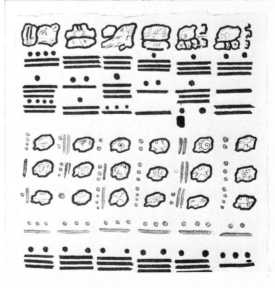

and refers among other things to certain sculptures in Mexico City. The Italian Francesco Carletti, at the end of the sixteenth century, and the Spaniard Pedro Ordoñez de Cevallos *'el clérigo agradecido'** (1614) have also left records but tell us nothing of archaeological interest. There would be no point in mentioning them, seeing that they give us so little pertinent data, were it not that they may be regarded as the precursors of later travellers whose works will be of great importance.

To sum up, in this century and a half no excavations having so much as antiquarian objectives were embarked on, but there were descriptions written, often in splendid prose, of sites and monuments, sometimes even of isolated finds. Upon occasion these were envisaged as documents, disclosing something of the native past and its chronology. In the Maya area the ancient culture was not attacked as violently as it had been in Central Mexico, so that with the exception of isolated incidents – however appalling – the friars did not proceed to the destruction of the sites or of the occasional find. On the debit side of the ledger, this area lacked the bulging storehouse of historical chronicles, both native and Spanish, which emerged in Central Mexico. Because of the differing effects of the two conquests perhaps? The fall of Tenochtitlán, which meant the

14,31 end of the Mexica Empire, and the tales surrounding Moctezuma, his precious stones, his life style, became transformed into a legend known to all. But the conquest of the Maya was short of showy exploits and lacked the epic grandeur of the occasion when Cortés and Cuauhtémoc confronted each other. In some ways the cycle of great writing on the precolumbian world ends in 1615 or thereabouts

13–15 with the publication of the works of Herrera and Torquemada. Once the great days of Santiago Tlatelolco are over, we enter the new political climate created by Luis de Velasco, viceroy from 1590 to 1595, and high culture is closed to the indigenous population. Publications dealing with the ancient civilization or written in Nahuatl were curtailed where they were not expressly forbidden. By 1670, memory of the Indian world and its conquest had long grown dim; the colony turned in upon itself and lost most of its previous interest in ancient Mexico.

* Literally 'the thankful cleric'.

Chapter Three

Research in the Archives (1670–1750)

THIS SECOND of the three stages into which I have split the colonial era may seem to have somewhat arbitrary boundaries, since in some ways it is hard to draw a distinction between it and its predecessor, but beneath the surface important things were taking place and indications of what was to be characteristic of the third period put in their earliest appearance.

Under the influence of the philosophy of Descartes and some of his contemporaries, new subjects of interest began to be taken up. These had not attracted much attention in the first half of the seventeenth century, but they would lead to the concept of a new cultural type, the Mexican. This gave an impetus to the need to study the old histories again, and a revival of the wish to understand them.*

The leading light of this movement was Carlos de Sigüenza y Góngora (1645–1700). A typical creole, son of Spaniards though born in Mexico and resident there all his life, he became a member of the Society of Jesus; expelled while still quite young, he nevertheless remained on the best of terms with the Society. Sigüenza divided his life's work between his priestly duties, his functions in a viceregal department, his chair at the University and his private research. Among those who thought in the modern Cartesian manner, he was beyond doubt the most erudite man of his time in Mexico and echoes of his fame crossed the Atlantic; Louis XIV himself invited him to Paris. He left us a legacy of several published books and manuscripts. These, unhappily now lost, would have been of the greatest archaeological interest.**

In Sigüenza's antiquarian approach, which in his work has to be disentangled from his other interests, I discern three strains.

In the first place, he conducted the initial investigation in the true spirit of archaeology, in that it attempted to use a monument to

* This frame of mind belongs particularly to the creoles, who were at odds with the Spaniards from 'the old country' clinging to a monopoly of power. Creoles were also keenly interested in the practical questions of rights over forced Indian labour, as well as the wealth they believed to be due to them as descendants of the conquerors.

** For Sigüenza's life and work see: Carlos de Sigüenza, *Obras*, with a biography by Francisco Pérez Salazar, Mexico, 1928; Irving A. Leonard, *Don Carlos de Sigüenza*, Univ. of California Press, 1929; José Rojas Garciadueñas, *D. Carlos de Sigüenza*, Mexico, 1945 and numerous other relevant titles, which are listed in the works cited above.

28 Don Carlos de Sigüenza y
Góngora (1645–1700).
Posthumous drawing made at
the turn of the seventeenth
century

29 Teotihuacán. The Pyramid
of the Sun, photograph taken in
1963

throw light on a problem in history. Whether or not he wrote up this
piece of research is not known because, as I say, most of his historical
and antiquarian papers have not come down to us. Luckily however,
a successor of his, the Italian Lorenzo Boturini, in a reference to the
Pyramid of the Sun at Teotihuacán, recorded the following:

'I had a map made of the pyramid which I have in my collection and
on circumambulating it I observed that the celebrated Don Carlos de
Sigüenza y Góngora had attempted to breach it with drills, when he
met with resistance; the centre is known to be hollow' (1746:143).

The idea that the pyramid was hollow and contained a tomb has
never been either fully confirmed or refuted. Later on, though
Alexander von Humboldt based his opinion on Boturini's account,
he interpreted Sigüenza's investigation differently. He took it to
mean (1811, II:65) that it had been designed to reveal whether the
pyramid was entirely man-made or had simply been the shaping up
and facing of a natural mound, which would detract from its
importance. 'Don Carlos de Sigüenza thinks it immensely ancient,
only slightly less so than the Flood' (Gemelli, 1927:195).

The second reason why Sigüenza and his circle of friends and
followers are so important to the field of prehispanic studies, is their
abiding passion for collecting manuscripts and relics from the past.
For the first time in Mexico an important accumulation of books and
papers on the subject was gathered together. Sigüenza began the
study of the Indians of New Spain at the age of twenty-three and
persevered in it throughout his life. His source materials were his

PARAYSO OCCIDENTAL,

PLANTADO, Y CULTIVADO

por la liberal benefica mano de los muy Catholicos,
y poderofos Reyes de Efpaña Nueftros Señores
en fu magnifico Real Convento de

JESUS MARIA

de Mexico:

DE CUYA FUNDACION, Y PROGRESSOS,
y de las prodigiofas maravillas, y virtudes,con que exalando
olor fuave de perfeccion, florecieron en fu claufura
la V. M. MARINA DE LA CRVZ,
y otras exemplariffimas Religiofas

DA NOTICIA EN ESTE VOLUMEN

D. Carlos de Siguenza , y Gongora
Presbytero Mexicano.

CON LICENCIA DE LOS SVPERIORES
En Mexico:por Juan de Ribera, Impreffor, y Mercader de libros.
Año de M. DC. LXXX. IIIJ.

30 Title page of Sigüenza's
Presbytéro Mexicano

own important collections of manuscripts, later to be vastly enriched when his friend and protégé Don Juan de Alva Ixtlilxochitl bequeathed to him what was left of the great archive of Texcoco. Ixtlilxochitl was the son of the famous historian of the same name, and a descendant of Nezahualcoyotl. His noble forebears had for a long time been lords of Teotihuacán and this may perhaps have sown the seed of Sigüenza's interest in the site. Not without reason did another savant of the time, Ignacio Castorena y Ursúa call Sigüenza 'the treasurer of the most original literature in America' (Sigüenza, 1928: LXXXVI).

The fate of Sigüenza's library is a rather sad one. It passed on his death to the Society of Jesus, but the volumes began to go astray when the Order was dispersed in 1767.

A century later we find Clavijero, with whom we shall be dealing 50 in the next chapter, writing:

'Carlos de Sigüenza y Góngora, Mexican of renown, professor of mathematics at his nation's university. This great man was one of Mexico's most deserving sons, since at great expense he created an extensive and select collection of manuscripts and old paintings, and set himself with the utmost diligence and perseverance to depict the antiquities of that kingdom. Among his many works . . . he wrote: 1. *La Ciclografia Mexicana*, a work of great labour, in which by the calculation of the eclipses and of the comets shown in the historical pictures of the Mexicans, he adjusted their measurements of time to ours and, using sound sources, explained the method they used to calculate the centuries and the years and the months; 2. *La Historia del Imperio Chichimeco*, in which he set out what he had found in the manuscripts and Mexican pictographic writings concerning the first colonies to pass from Asia into America and the events that befell the most ancient nations to establish themselves in Anáhuac; 3. a long and very erudite dissertation on the publication of the Gospel in Anáhuac, carried out, he believed, by St Thomas the apostle, making use of the Indian tradition of the crosses found and venerated in Mexico and of other relics; 4. the genealogy of the kings of Mexico, in which he traces back the line of descent to the seventh century of the Christian era; 5. critical commentaries on the works of Tor-quemada and of Bernal Díaz. All of these learned writings, which could have been of the greatest assistance to my History, were lost through the carelessness of the heirs of that wise author, and there have remained only some fragments of the works of some of his contemporaries, such as Gemelli, Vetancurt and Florencia.'

Clavijero does not believe it was Jesuit carelessness that brought about the loss of the papers, but that this took place later, when the Company to whom they belonged went into liquidation.

The third reason why Sigüenza is so important – and this explains the foregoing – is that he regarded himself as a Mexicanist. He looked ahead nearly a hundred years to events around the middle of the eighteenth century, and in his work is a foretaste of attitudes to be taken up later by Clavijero and his contemporaries. Over and above simple academic interest and his desire for knowledge, Sigüenza sought to show that the Mexico of his times was already a blend, though as yet incomplete, of Spaniard with Indian, and that from their fusion would emerge Mexican historical sensibility. Hence his desire to advance the claims of both strands of inheritance which, interwoven, would make the long thread of his nation's history. Since Indian history and its achievements were the lesser known, they would have to be studied, dragged back from oblivion, if they were to be understood. Let us remind ourselves that, in his day and age, a few of the great chronicles, but precious little else, had so far been published. The great bulk of the documents mouldered in the archives in Spain. Sigüenza had no means of access to them, and indeed almost nobody bothered to study them.

His wish to advance ancient Mexico's claims to glory shows itself in many ways, and had for its final object the fostering of the nationhood of the new Mexico of mixed blood. We can see this in his work again and again. One instance: when the viceroy, in the person of the Count of Paredes, entered Mexico City, a triumphal arch was thrown over the road according to tradition. Sigüenza objected to the usual adornment of figures lifted from classical mythology: 'the love which we owe our country enjoins us to cast aside fables and to search out more convincing subjects with which to adorn this so

31 Seventeenth-century
painting, believed to be a
portrait of Moctezuma, in the
Museum of Ethnology,
Florence. (Formerly in the
Uffizi Gallery)

triumphal portal', he writes, using the baroque style he always
favoured (1928:12). With this aim in mind, he had the arch decked
out, not with classical gods, but with Mexican emperors. There
being twelve niches and only eleven sovereigns to fill them, he made
up the number with Huitzilopochtli. He went so far as to append to 43
his name in one of his books, *El Paraíso Occidental* (1684), the title
'Presbytéro mexicano' ('Mexican priest').

Perhaps this is why Sigüenza was alone in thinking of Mexican
history as a continuity with its beginning before Columbus. He
differed in this not only from those who had gone before but also
from many who would be working in the field much later. In his
view there is not that complete break at the Conquest which makes
history seem to begin with Cortés, or with Columbus at the very
earliest. This idea, which is only now gaining general acceptance,
seems to me to be of the most essential importance.

These Mexicanist implications in the work of Sigüenza and the
best of his notable contemporaries and followers in the first half of
the eighteenth century carried no hidden overtones of Independence,
still less of a break with the Spanish crown. 'Love of country'

demands that they delve as deeply as they can into the indigenous half of Mexico; this is why this theme seems to me to be closely linked with the development of archaeological studies. Once begun, it had to go on, as Mexican patriotism saw itself as a cultural and not as a political matter. These writers equate culture with nationality. Take, for example, Bernabé Navarro:

'. . . in building a culture, they built it for their country and through her, and when they came to create their nation, they created within a specifically Mexican framework . . . with its good qualities and even with its bad . . . The Mexican thus formed was a product not of his race, not of his environment, but of his culture and his culture alone' (1964:60).

These Mexican-oriented attitudes which first manifested themselves in Sigüenza's day gathered force in the second half of the eighteenth century. They were shared, though with a difference, by Sister Juana Inés de la Cruz, one of Sigüenza's best-known contemporaries who had the additional distinction of being his close friend. The celebrated nun even composed a poem in his honour: 'O sweet and melodious Mexican swan'. When death came to Sister Juana, Sigüenza delivered her funeral oration.

The great Nahuatl scholar, Agustín de Vetancurt, a Franciscan born in 1620, died in the same year as Sigüenza. He does not appear to have taken any interest in artefacts; his importance lies in his use of maps, books and original Indian records and sources

'which were shown to me by my countryman and friend Don Carlos Sigüenza y Góngora . . . curious searcher in the ancient records, and anxious that the grandeurs of this New World should be known and published throughout the globe, and this has he said in divers papers and books he has had printed' (1698: last page of catalogue preceding text).

Apart from sounding the same incipiently Mexicanist note, Vetancurt produced an interesting bibliography of the written source materials he used, which was an unusual thing to do at that time. The Mexican interest in bibliography, which was happily to persist, may owe its earliest beginnings to him.

In his book *La Estrella del Norte*, Francisco de Florencia, a Jesuit born in the same year as Vetancurt, undertook, with Sigüenza's approval, to substantiate the miraculous apparition of the Virgin of Guadalupe, an event which, as we have seen, is tied in with Mexicanism, and which is still the subject of lively discussion. When he was preparing his manuscript and searching for a pamphlet which in the event he never found, he went through Sigüenza's papers with care, looking

'among the many and most curious papers and the most ancient of maps which from every part and at the cost of much labour and gold he has gathered together, to hold them, and to understand them, Don Carlos de Sigüenza . . .' (1688:94 verso).

I want finally to mention one who was an exact contemporary of Sigüenza's, the Neapolitan Juan Francisco Gemelli Carreri, a great traveller who spent almost the whole of 1697 in Mexico. His book

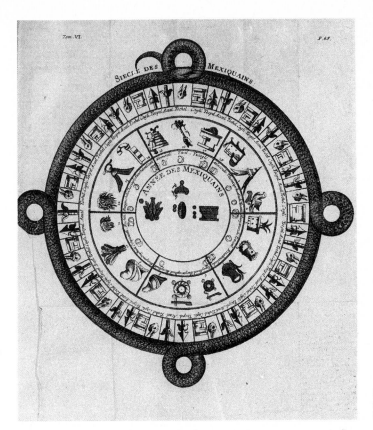

32 Conjectural Mexican calendar, published by Gemelli Carreri (1645–1700)

Giro del Mondo is an account of his travels. Of its nine volumes we need only look at the sixth, which deals with New Spain. Although Gemelli is fondest of describing religious festivals, theatrical presentations, hunts and so forth, he *does* become a friend of Sigüenza's.

'So comes it about that the calendar stone of Mexico* and other ancient things left by the Indians which are to be seen in this my book, are owed to the labours of Sigüenza and the kindness he did show to me in making me free of such exceeding rare curiosities' (1927:67).

He goes into some interesting detail on the ruins and associated finds, which prove his interest in what I believe to be the ideas stemming from Sigüenza and his group, although clearly, as Gemelli was a foreigner, there was no question of nationalism in his case.

Let me quote a few examples from among many:

'At a little distance (from San Angel) a mound is to be seen, called *de los ídolos* because in other days the Indians offered sacrifices on it. In the hollow of a low, ancient wall** can still be seen certain little idols

---

* To be included by Veytia a hundred years later in his *Calendarios Mexicanos*.

** It may have been similar to the wall at Tlalmanalco illustrated by Dupaix (1824, 2nd expedition, plate XIV).

33 Figures on a wall at Tlalmanalco. After Dupaix

fashioned of clay, and Indians not standing overfirmly in the faith there do place their abominable offerings' (1927:160). 'I did go to Atzcapotzalco to see if there did not yet remain traces of the palace of the king of that place' (id.:65). 'I went to Santiago Tlatelolco that I might furnish myself with drawings of the garb of the Indians but I was constrained to return empty-handed because that . . . the Viceroy had caused the destruction of an ancient painting which there had been on a wall there' (id.:171). 'Being on the ninth day of August gone into the college of San Ildefonso some objects of antiquity for to see, on the east side of the same did I perceive sundry ancient stones, and into one of them were there cut figures and hieroglyphs, and among them an eagle with cactus leaves about it; and on another stone I found set into a wall appeared circles and other figures' (id.:185).

This quotation is particularly interesting to me because it seems to point to the beginnings of a museum at the great Jesuit college. Finally, he pays a visit to Teotihuacán and describes it briefly, establishing links between it and Atlantis (id.: 195–8).

I have come across a great number of other references to antiquities in the work of scholars writing at this period. To refer to them all would take up too much space. I have had occasion earlier to mention the name of the Italian, Lorenzo Boturini, and I shall take him as my final example. Scion of a noble house, Boturini came to Mexico in 1736 at the age of thirty-four. His original purpose had nothing whatsoever to do with archaeology, being in fact an attempt to collect a pension which the viceregal administration was committed to paying to a descendant of Moctezuma, the Countess of 14,31 Santibañez. What the outcome of his representations might have been I do not know as, fortunately for us, he soon turned his attention to other things. In a strange amalgam of devotion to the Virgin of Guadalupe and curiosity about precolumbian Mexico, he wished both to confirm the truth of the apparition and to write a work of history. In pursuit of these objectives he dug into the archives in Mexico City, at the University and elsewhere and, presumably, became acquainted with the Sigüenza papers. This was the start of what he called his 'museum' and which ended up as a magnificent collection of ancient documents. We know this from the catalogue appended to his work, and from the judicial inventories drawn up when the viceregal administration confiscated his papers. This was a catastrophe for the Boturini collection and for us too, as in the comings and goings attendant upon it, part of the collection went astray.

His enthusiasm for this particular Virgin led him to embark upon a fund-raising campaign with the object of providing her with a crown. The government viewed this project with disfavour, declaring Boturini not to have the necessary permits to live in Mexico, still less to carry out his designs. The viceroy, Count of Fuenclara, ordered an investigation into the Italian's activities, and in 1743 he was thrown into gaol and had his museum confiscated. Not long afterwards, although found innocent, he was expelled from the colony and took ship for Spain early in 1744. The vessel in which he was travelling was captured by pirates and when at last he arrived in

34 Illustration from Boturini
1746, with 'portrait' of author

Spain he was penniless and, according to his own account, without clothes to his back. At that time there was living in Madrid a rich creole from Puebla, Mariano Fernández de Echeverría y Veytia, who took the Italian into his home, while at the same time helping him to seek redress from the king. At the close of the usual formalities, Philip V appointed him *historiógrafo de las Indias*, but on condition that he return to Mexico to continue his studies. Boturini could not fulfil this condition, the pittance he was to receive being inadequate for his passage. He continued to live with Veytia until his death in 1751. Veytia himself produced an ancient history, which was published posthumously. It contains little new, and its author seems not to have understood the ideas of his Italian friend.

Apart from his highly-coloured life and his museum, Boturini is interesting by virtue of his book *Idea de una Nueva Historia de la América Septentrional* and his *Catálogo del museo histórico indiano*

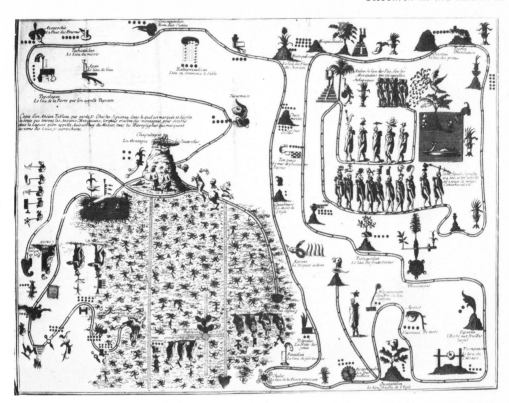

published as an appendix in Madrid in 1746. Plainly at least the raw materials for the catalogue had come with him from Mexico.

35 The Aztec migration. From the Codex Boturini

The *Idea* is an outline derived from the *Scienza Nuova* of his famous countryman Giambattista Vico (1668–1744), the father of historiography. Boturini divides the development of ancient Mexico into three parts, along the dividing lines set out by Vico, whose example he does not acknowledge in his study of Roman law from the twelve tablets down to the *jus gentium*. He thinks of these three developmental stages as essential to universal history: the divine world, the heroic world, and the world of men. When Vico undertook the extrapolation of his conclusions from Roman law to universal history, he embroidered fact with fancy. By taking him for model, Boturini not only fell into the same trap, exaggeration, but in doing so produced a piece of Mexican historical analysis which, while in some aspects entirely modern, is in other respects totally unacceptable. His book is in a class of its own within Mexican historiography.

Boturini divides the Amerindian past into three ages. In the first, Noah's descendants invent the gods. As men were living in caves having a single aperture – which were, so to say, one-eyed – he calls this age the Cyclopean, but asserts that it was above all things theocratic, oracular, in that while it lasted men obeyed the wishes of the gods. Living in fear of omens and idolatry, men turned to religion and the virtuous life. In those days only such chiefs could rule as the gods

36 Mariano Veytia (1718–1789)

59

regarded with favour. Frugality and sobriety held sway over these natural sages in an age without malice or ambition, simple and happy. They were, by all accounts, nomads and immeasurably poor. They were 'wise men, priests and kings'. Boturini illustrates these conclusions by descriptions of thirteen major Indian deities, while mentioning many minor ones.

During the second age the heroes gather together the hungry wanderers of the preceding epoch and group them into families in the Roman sense of the word. The heroes make up the élite. They are to be compared with the planets, and here a very garbled version of the legend of the creation of the suns at Teotihuacán is introduced, although the famous site is not mentioned by name. Boturini deals with the calendar and with the far-reaching changes that are then brought about. Arguing from natural law, he makes the heroes conquer lands so that they may work them, and enslave nations that oppose their just ends – a 'just cause' for making war, then as ever. The heroes are not tempted by the pleasures of the world, but boast of their mighty strength and prowess in the profession of arms. This is the *guerra florida* in embryo, not to develop till the succeeding age. They are still essentially demigods, if in practice already agriculturists, with a society composed of two social classes.

In the third age, men shake off the yoke of the heroes. The erstwhile serfs begin to assert themselves and at last to grasp the fact that they are the equals of the heroes. What is even more unfortunate for the élite is that these formerly humble folk begin to question divine origins, on which they had for so long prided themselves. The people at large wish to know the law and to have things explained to them in the language of everyday speech. These heady new ideas hasten the demise of the old heroic aristocracy, making way for the monarchy. Arguing against his general thesis, Boturini points out that the customs of the Mexican Indians of this time have no connection with those of any other peoples. He also reveals himself as a rabid geographical determinist as, according to him, it is climate that decides both physical constitution and behaviour patterns in humankind.

The plethora of errors that flaw Boturini's work do not invalidate its central idea, deriving from Las Casas, of regarding Mesoamerican civilization as part of the history of mankind as a whole, however much, as I mentioned in the introduction, some archaeologists of standing may have taken exception to it. In thinking of precolumbian history as having no bearing on, nor any links with, Old World history, they forget the importance of studying the American civilizations for their own sakes. It is because, and not in spite of, their separateness, that they have much to tell us about the development of a human culture isolated from other civilizations. Further, as Daniel has said (1975:278):

'American archaeology teaches us . . . that what really has happened in human history is not necessarily just what happened in the Near East and Europe.'

Boturini's blemished publication met with something less than complete success. Various of his successors, such as Clavijero or

Prescott, criticized it, but it found an eventual defender in Hamy in
1885. The book's value resides in its attempt to place the development of ancient Mexico within the framework of world history, and
to tackle the general problem of the rise of civilization. He was a
Toynbee two centuries ahead of his time.

An unlooked-for effect of Boturini's work is worth a mention,
bearing as it does upon future avenues of investigation. When the
hearing of his case in Spain was over, the Consejo de Indias advised

'the founding in the capital of New Spain of an *Academia de Historia
de México* . . . To this institution the Boturini papers were to be
entrusted . . . The plan failed to be awarded the Royal seal of
approval. There might perhaps have been whiffs of suspicion already
abroad about the dangers inherent in giving encouragement in
America to studies with a possible nationalistic cast . . . . It seems
enough to remember this precedent, while adding that, when the
Academia de México was first seen as a possibility in 1746, it was in the
context of a wish that the documentary sources, and probably also
the archaeological remains of the indigenous cultures, should be
investigated in terms of a search for their meaning in the light of
open, universal history' (León Portilla, 1970:167–8).

It seems to me that this particular precedent, as well as the founding
of the Academia and other related events, herald what is to come
about under Charles III, and which we shall be discussing in the next
chapter.

As to historical work in the Maya zone, not only was there much
less of it, but it was in the main restricted to restatements of
previously-known sources, though new elements did appear there
from time to time. The fine descriptions of monuments of which I
gave an idea in the preceding chapter hardly appear any more.

This period's most important figure is Diego López de Cogolludo,
a Franciscan whom I have already mentioned (page 32). Though he
is in essence writing colonial history, he does sometimes include data
of archaeological interest. While he injects into his work a few
observations of his own, the bulk of his facts are taken from previous
work. Long though they are, I shall quote two passages to
illustrate the kind of writing then being produced in Yucatán
(1688:176–77):

'When that this land was discovered and conquered, there were
found in it ruins that called forth powerful feelings of admiration in
those authors having knowledge of them, as they continue to do
today in those who behold what is left. They are manifold in the
fields and on the wooded hillsides, some are vast structures especially
those at Uxmal, Chichen Itzá and others which are they say to be
seen to the east of the high-road from Bolonchén to Tikul and in
them is fairly to be seen which of them were used as temples, the
form of which it remains for me to describe. Hard by the temple
itself there is upon occasion another building wherein dwelt maidens
as they might be nuns . . . In Uxmal is there a great court with many
separate apartments in the form of a cloister where dwelt these
maidens. . . . It is a structure truly to be admired, the walls being, as
they all are, of carven stone, bearing in half-relief figures of men in
arms, a diversity of beasts, birds and other things and who was the
craftsman who made them we know not, any more than we know

37 Uxmal. The Nunnery and Temple of the Magician. Reconstruction drawing by Proskouriakoff

who worked the land. All the four walls of that great court (a town square it might be called) are girdled with a serpent worked in the same stone as the walls, and having the tail ending beneath the head, the whole being of circumference four hundred feet.

'Due south of this building lies another, wherein they say dwelt the lord of this region; it is not in the form of a cloister but is yet of stone carven with the figures described for the other, and round about do stand many another such, but smaller, which were they say the dwellings of the captains and great lords. In that to the south there is a wall to the inside upon which (exceeding long though it be) runs a cornice at a little more than half the height of a man, and for its whole length. This cornice is very smooth and is finished at the corners with the greatest nicety, very equal and perfect, where (I recall) they had cut out of the stone and left outstanding there a ring so fine and seemly as could be, a work of high beauty: clearly manifesting that they were the work of the hand of a craftsman of no mean skill. We know not who they were, nor have the Indians it in their tradition. . . .

'Dr Aguilar does say in his report that it was the Mexica Indians who made them; but yet can I find no other to say any such thing, and so I think it an opinion privy to himself. The truth was not known even at the very beginning of the conquest; and there seems now no way to seek it out; but the certitude of their magnificence is plainly to be seen and it does lead . . . Las Casas to reflect thereupon. Some of them are high enough to need stairways having a hundred steps and more, a little wider than six inches each. I once climbed up the one at Uxmal, and regretted it when I had to descend; because as the steps of the stair are so narrow and so exceeding numerous the

building rises up right sheer, and as the height is nothing inconsiderable the vision turns faint and it is not without its danger.' (id.: 193).

Guides today frighten tourists with the danger, telling them of the serious accidents which some have suffered in the descent of the House of the Dwarf at Uxmal.

It is well known that the last outpost of Maya independence, called the Province of Itzá by the Spaniards, did not fall to them till the last years of the seventeenth century, though Cortés had visited it as early as 1525.

Playing no part in this struggle, Juan de Villagutierre Sotomayor – happily for us a man of intelligence – wrote a very full *relación* in which he described something of Tayasal. From it I have taken the following few paragraphs:

'Of the twenty-one *cues* or temples of idols found by General Ursúa and his men of the island, the principal and greatest belonged to that most totally false priest Quincanek, first cousin to King Canek. It was in shape square, on nine stepped levels with beautiful breastworks, the whole of the finest stone, and each facing wall about 20 *varas* [16.70 metres] wide and very tall.

'And on the highest step or level, as one went in, was there to be found an idol, squatting as it might be, in human shape, ill-favoured. And within the temple towards the front, there was another idol representing war: of the size of a jewel, and this General Ursúa kept for himself. Above this was there another of plaster, with a visage like unto a sun, surrounded by rays of mother-of-pearl, and outlined with the same and the mouth all stuffed with teeth drawn from the mouths of Spaniards they had killed.

38 Uxmal. The Governor's Palace. Reconstruction drawing by Proskouriakoff

39 Fuentes y Guzmán's impression of a wooden stela, based on information derived from Luis Xirón of Nicaragua

'In the midst of this temple, which was builded like a castle, there dangled from its crest, held up by three ribbons of fine cotton thread of different colours, a half-rotted shin bone, and this they do say had been that of Cortés's horse. . . .

'The other temples or places of worship were common to all the folk of the village . . . and in them idols without number, made in forms and materials, and having names, all various and all abominable . . . in none of these did they perform that most cruel sacrifice of tearing out the living heart, save only in that principal temple. . . . Nor were such infidels as wished to enter always allowed to pass freely into any of these temples, except it were in the countryside, in the caves or in the woods, in the forest caves did they worship their idols. . . .' (Villagutierre 1701:500–502)

On an earlier page (362) he mentions a great city a mile in circumference with stone foundations and covered with ruins. According to Morley (1938, I:41), he might have been thinking of Yaxchilán.

One of the region's conquerors, Avendaño, describes what Morley supposes to be Tikal. His account, still not fully published, reads:

'In the midst of these tall forests through which we passed there is a great variety of ancient buildings. Save some in which I could see them still dwelling, and even those were exceeding tall, although I was without great strength, I climbed (albeit laboriously) up to them. They were like unto a convent with their little cloisters, and many dwelling-rooms, all of them thatched, *con vuelta de coche* [with space enough for a coach to turn in], and whitened within with plaster, of which there is an abundance, all the hills about being made of it. Thus it is that these buildings are not like those hereabouts in the Province, in that they are of stone and of stone only, particularly as regards their arches, whereas these others are of limestone and stone and then dressed with plaster' (Avendaño, MS. p. 159, quoted by Morley, 1938, I:55).

Shortly after the conquest of the Itzá and the Lacandones, Fuentes y Guzmán was to write his *Recordación Florida del reino de Guatemala*. Among much that is of no interest to us we find relevant paragraphs, some of which are clearly eye-witness accounts and are accompanied by maps, such as that of ancient Guatemala (1932, I:353) or Zaculeu (id. III:107). The description of Copán is a little fanciful (id. II:210–215) and his study of the Pipil script is also curious in the extreme (id. II:107–112).

As it is not my intention to produce a catalogue of the period's publications, those already mentioned must serve as an indication of what had been achieved by the middle of the eighteenth century. In the eighty years summed up here, apart from Sigüenza and a few others, some of whose findings are of doubtful value, no one was interested in excavating ruins or looking for finds. The period is much more noteworthy for assiduous collectors of manuscripts; these, though unfortunately not often published, were frequently used as raw material for the writing of chronicles which, though lengthy and confused, are yet not without importance precisely because their authors *did* make use of the original documents so many of which have since been lost. At the close of this period the warp

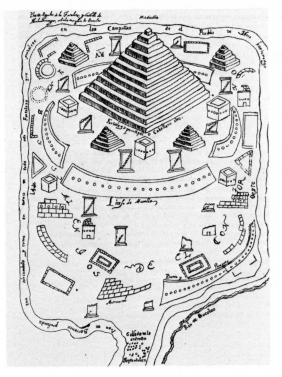

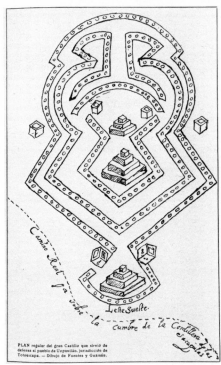

threads are already on the loom and the figures are beginning to be woven into the tapestry. Certain of the lines of argument, seen at first as scattered and without bearing one upon another, now begin to manifest their interdependence and to make some sort of pattern. The birth of Mexicanism, coupled with its interest in the mother-figure Guadalupe-Tonantzin, the pride it took in being a new member of the human race, the wish for recognition and the indignation unleashed in the next period by criticism of the American continent, these are some of the occasionally hidden driving forces which called for a fresh look at the Indian past and an even more urgent need for an understanding of it in order to include it in the new cultural nationhood. People's minds were awakening to an interest in the material remains of this past. This was archaeology in the making, which we shall see growing to man's estate in the final stage of the colonial period.

40 Layout of Zaculeu. After Fuentes y Guzmán

41 Layout of the Castillo at Uzpantlan. After Fuentes y Guzmán

Chapter Four

The Age of Reason (1750–1825)

THE END OF the colonial world, clearly influenced by the ideas of the Enlightenment, owed much of its intellectual success to its fresh conception of man and his culture. The Enlightenment is no different from any other school of philosophy in displaying various facts, not always harmonious. These discords come to the surface even in the handling of matter relating to Mesoamerican archaeology and provide the starting point for many an acrimonious dispute, to say nothing of an infinite variety of accounts of the Indian and his past. So wide was the range of conflicting arguments that, whatever the stance adopted by any one thinker, it was bound sooner or later to be refuted by another. These were not just personal differences of opinion between individual figures of the Age of Reason, but had a tendency to group themselves along national lines. Even where the basic ideas are much the same, the question of the American Indian is treated differently in France, Germany and England; for religious and historical reasons the position is different again in Spain. Italy is chiefly notable for the writings of those Mexican Jesuits who took refuge there and who set themselves to oppose the anti-American ideas of the rest of the *philososophes*.

This attitude, which may be said to have had its faint beginnings in the sixteenth century with, say, Cárdenas (1591), who describes the degenerative effects of a tropical and, according to him, unbearable climate upon the Indians who were weaker than Spaniards (1913:154–163), or even with John Donne's *To the Countess of Huntingdon* (1597), continues to be adopted by various Italians such as Porcacchi (1590:377–378), Botero (1596:157–160), Magini (1597–8:203) and Zappullo (1603:377–378) who catalogue Indian beastliness and filthy habits: all seem to be foreshadowing the great debate of the eighteenth-century Age of Enlightenment. This concerns not men alone, but plants, animals and even geology. Although Buffon was later to tone down somewhat his unfavourable opinions of America, he did describe how the animal species of that continent were not only peculiar to it, but were also often inferior to or weaker than those of the Old World. Thus, for example, the lion is superior to the puma and a whole series of large mammals do not exist in America where, among domestic animals imported from Europe, the pig is the only one to flourish. (An odd twist is that in Mexico even today the pig is thought of as the only domesticated animal of foreign origin whose meat is more savoury than that of its Old World counterpart.)

42 (*opposite*) Cannibals' banquet beside a temple. After Philipono, 1621

43 (*opposite*) Huitzilopochtli. An early engraving

Under a 'hostile Nature' the American Indian underwent the same changes as the fauna.

'They shrink under that miserly sky; in that empty land man, with his paucity of numbers, lives widely scattered and wandering. Far from being lord of these regions, he exercises no dominion over them. Never having subdued either the elements or the animals, neither does he rule the seas, nor channel the rivers, nor work the earth. He is no more than a high-ranking primate, and exists for Nature only as a creature without importance, a kind of automaton, powerless equally to improve upon her or to help her. Nature had treated him more like a stepmother than a mother, denying him the emotion of love and the urgent desire to be fruitful and multiply. Though it is a fact that the savage of the New World is more or less of the same stature as the man of our world, that is not sufficient to make him an exception to the general rule of diminution in size in all natural beings inhabiting his continent. The savage's organs of generation are weak and small. He has no body hair or beard and lacks ardour when with his female. Though, thanks to his habit of running, he is more agile than the European, he is nevertheless very much less physically strong. He is far less sensitive yet, despite this, he is more timid and cowardly: he is totally without liveliness and activity of mind. Bodily motion is for him action more determined by essential necessity than a voluntary movement or exercise. Free him from hunger and thirst, and you would simultaneously destroy the driving force behind his every movement. He would remain crouching dully, or stretched at ease upon his back, for days together' (Buffon, 1825–8, XV:443–6).

Its learning and its splendid style made Buffon's book vastly popular, to the point where Darwin, much later, was to take up this branch of study, so typical of the eighteenth century. Buffon's immense work *Histoire Naturelle, Générale et Particulière* in forty-four volumes, commenced publication in 1749.

David Hume's *Of Natural Characters* had come out the previous year. Toynbee says of it:

'Thus Hume not only ignores Race but, for practical purposes, rejects the Physical or Climatic Environment into the bargain as a possible cause of the actual difference in cultural achievement between one human society and another. The social environment is the differentiating factor to which Hume ascribes almost exclusive, and at the same time almost unlimited, potency' (1935, I:470).

He is Buffon's opposite, therefore, in that he is not a geographical determinist.

In the same year Montesquieu also published a famous book, *L'Esprit des Lois*. A determinist, he believed that tropical conditions gave rise to tyrannical regimes in America (Mexico, Peru), while free peoples were all to be found nearer the Poles.

Among the many other writers who touched on this topic, the Dutchman Cornelius de Pauw, author of *Recherches Philosophiques sur les Américains* (Berlin, 1768), is of some importance because of the spitefulness of his work and the fury it evoked, not only in Mexico but also in Europe. This odd *abbé* was the most extreme of the *Encyclopédistes*. For him America and everything in it, including its human inhabitants, could not be considered anything but degenerate. Zavala (1949:142) sums up Pauw's ideas as follows:

'Indolence and laziness together make up the character of the American peoples. They are simple and lack ambition, they do not seek to see the future; they eat, dance and sleep; their memories are short which may be the fault of tobacco; they have no growth of beard; they secrete from their nipples a kind of milky substance; display little ardour in love; their women give birth without pain . . .'

In his desire to distort, Pauw goes so far as to quote Las Casas, who had for so long urged the necessity of according the Indians protection as a weaker people. Many writers, among them Clavijero whom I shall return to later, infuriated by Pauw and his fellow anti-Americans, felt impelled to counter-attack. In the United States, men as eminent as Thomas Jefferson rose up against so great a slander (see his *Notes on the State of Virginia*). In our time the controversy is of no more than historical interest, but its importance lies in the contribution it made to the creation of the nationalist-archaeological spirit in Mexico, and this is why I have summarized it.

To complicate matters, there circulated abroad those romantic sentiments best expressed in Jean-Jacques Rousseau, the 'discoverer' of the 'noble savage'* It is true he exalted the American Indian's way of life, but always as essentially primitive, never dignifying it to the level of civilization. This was essential to Rousseau's argument, since he was claiming to show the degenerative effects of civilization upon man, and how virtue was to be looked for only in his notional 'noble savage'. It is true that Rousseau's model takes its inspiration largely from his own vision of the Iroquois and the Hurons, and that he intended no reference to Mexico. Unlike other *philosophes*, Rousseau and those of similar mind, looked kindly upon the Indians, which enabled them to severely criticize what Europeans, and particularly Spaniards, had done in America.

William P. Robertson is exceptional in his admiration for the conquerors and does not really believe the so-called 'black legend': 'he exposed to full view the senselessness of taking for historical truth what was no more than a tangle of distorted fairy tales' (Carbia, 1944:227). However, Robertson is fair in his criticisms of the cruelty of much that was done by the Spanish soldiery. His view of prehistoric Mexico is in general more balanced, and he goes as far as to praise the local civilization, but he does it as a mouthpiece of the Age of Reason and with the ethnocentricity which was as common in his time as it was often to be later. This comes across strongly where he says:

'. . . if the comparison be made with the people of the ancient continent, the inferiority of America in improvement will be conspicuous, and neither the Mexicans nor the Peruvians will be entitled

---

* Hardly a discovery: in one form or another writers of the calibre of Ronsard, Montaigne or Rabelais had been using this and similar ideas since the sixteenth century, to point a contrast with the civilized evils rife in a decadent Europe.

to rank with those nations which merit the name of civilized . . . they can hardly be considered as having advanced beyond the infancy of civil life' (Robertson, seventh edn, 1796, VII: 150, 152). '. . . these boasted efforts of their art are uncouth representations of common objects, or very coarse images of the human and some other forms destitute of grace and propriety . . .' (id.:174).

'Even their cities, extensive and populous as they were, seem more fit to be the habitation of men just emerging from barbarity, than the residence of a polished people. A number of low straggling huts, scattered about irregularly, according to the caprice of each proprietor, built with turf and stone, and thatched with reeds, without any light but what they received by a door, so low that it could not be entered upright . . . (id.:188) . . . the other celebrated temples of New Spain exactly resembled that of Mexico. Such structures convey no high idea of progress in art and ingenuity; and one can hardly conceive that a form more rude and simple could have occurred to a nation in its first efforts towards erecting any great work' (id.:189).

Zavala points out

'there is no unanimous agreement. Not only about the noble savage idea as opposed to the idea of the uncivilized brute, but at other limits of the then prevalent areas of preoccupation: for example, feelings of satisfaction with, or pessimism about, the century's advances' (1949:19).

This feeling of optimism is another characteristic of the Age of Enlightenment. In the words of Ortega y Gasset (1932:625): 'The spirit stands open to all the winds that blow, fired by a great optimism and faith in man's destiny.' Certainly the end of the colonial era was a time of hope, later to be overtaken by great change, as Alamán was to note:

87

'In the Republic of Mexico we have gone from overblown notions of power and wealth to a despair equally without foundation and, because earlier we hoped too much, there seems now nothing to hope for' (1852, V:952).

It looks to me as though these swings between hope and despair affected perception both of prehispanic Mexico and of those archaeological studies which were becoming so much more common in the last years of the colonial era, to diminish later, and then to increase in volume once more towards the middle of the nineteenth century.

The 'black legend', an idea widely accepted in France and England, has a sixteenth-century ancestor in Las Casas and, curiously enough, among his contemporaries, the disgruntled creoles. It interests us here because, in order to disparage the Conquest and the Spanish victories in America it resorts to an exposition of the low level of the indigenous cultures, thus weakening the merit of their overthrow and colonization.

2

Few of the European writers of the Age of Reason had set foot in America, and they based their opinions on published sources which varied in value over a wide range and which they often misinterpreted. Determined as they were to win adherents to their beliefs,

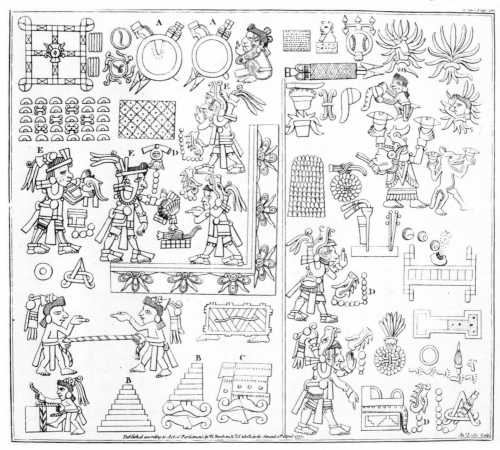

Published according to Act of Parliament, by W. Strahan, & T. Cadell, in the Strand, 1st April 1777.

44 Details from the Codex
Vindobonensis, as reproduced
in Robertson 1777, Vol. 2

their 'philosophical histories' reached such a fever pitch and degree
of disregard for truth, that they may have been a contributory cause
of the reaction that was, in the ensuing century, to bring into being
documentary history, which struggled so hard to be impartial, and
to base its conclusions on none but *documentos irrefutables*.

Juan Bautista Muñoz, appointed by Charles III *Cronista de Indias*
and charged with the task of writing their history, was a major
forerunner of this movement. Muñoz immediately applied himself
to the Herculean labour of reorganizing the Spanish archives, an
undertaking of such magnitude that by the time of his death he had
managed to finish no more than the first volume. Nevertheless his
collections of unpublished papers provided material for many
nineteenth-century studies and are still important today. Like
Charles III he was a Spanish-style Enlightenment figure, assailed by
historical rather than religious doubts. He writes:

'I have done what I could to lay the facts in evidence, and to quote
them in all truth and simplicity' (1793:a3). 'I brought myself into a
state of universal doubt as to everything up till then written on the
subject, founding the firm resolution to extract the pure truth from
the facts and the circumstances, as far as possible on the strength of
true and incontrovertible documents' (id.:V).

As we shall see later, it was Muñoz who, without ever having seen America, on being given the first news of the discovery of Palenque, persuaded Charles III to decree that exploration be carried out at the site. Thus the Age of Reason received the support of the Spanish throne and the State for the first time took a hand in promoting archaeological investigations. The king's interest in this type of research dated from his years of rule at Naples.

There have been thinkers like Ortega y Gasset who believed the Age of Reason never existed in Spain. He thought of Spain as that European nation which 'skipped a century for which there was to be no substitute . . . the great century of education passed us by' (1932:625). Gregorio Marañon disagrees with this, however, saying with regard to Feyjóo and his times,

'As a nation, Spain perhaps stood somewhat apart from the *encyclopédiste* movement, which was élitist everywhere but, as always, there were among Spaniards those . . . concerned to prevent a break in the thread of continuity of civilization' (translated from the French of Sarrailh, 1954:709).

But Feyjóo, the Benedictine friar, had written as early as the third decade of the eighteenth century: 'Experience is always to be preferred to reason'. This is the source of his tremendous admiration for Newton and his obsession with the idea that science should free itself from the weight of Aristotle's authority, and distance itself slightly from orthodoxy to do so. He preached the development of experimental science, rationalism as a philosophy, a belief in progress and popular philanthropy. He urged educational reforms such as the casting off of priestly dogma, speculative, legalistic and theological study, to make room for learning with a practical purpose; natural science, physics, mathematics and the technology that was just then being introduced. Feyjóo's philosophy made its influence felt in Mexico, though one can doubt that it was considered required reading by the ecclesiastical canons, or by the viceregal government.

But be that as it may, neither in Mexico nor in Spain did the Enlightenment engender that anticlerical and antimonarchical violence characteristic of it, above all among French writers.

One development deriving from this body of ideas was the formation, first in Spain and later in the main American cities, of *Sociedades económicas de amigos del país*. The earliest was founded in the Basque provinces at the beginning of 1765. The Guatemalan one at least became important because of the interest it showed in the excavations at Palenque.

Another consequence of the *sociedades económicas* and of the royal patronage was the development of botanical gardens and out of these grew, in 1790, the first garden and museum of natural history in Mexico. This was in some respects the ancestor of the Museo Nacional. Years after Linnaeus, these gardens seem to have been directly derived from the ideas of Buffon. In the same spirit a museum was founded in Spain, which Robertson heard spoken of:

'Many of their [Mexican] ornaments in gold and silver as well as various utensils employed in common life, are deposited in the

45 Animals of America. After Clavijero

magnificent cabinet of natural and artificial productions, lately opened by the king of Spain' (1777, II:285).

Yet a further by-product was the creation in 1808 of a *Junta de antigüedades*. All these will be considered in Chapter Six.

So it came about that ideas launched in Europe by Descartes and Locke and already partly accepted in Mexico by Sigüenza and in Spain by Feyjóo were, with the collaboration of the Mexican Age of Reason, gradually to break with the medieval Spanish line of continuity; they would awaken fresh curiosity and promote the renewed interest in the Mexican past, an interest which was already assuming an archaeological character.

The reaction of Mexican intellectuals to the criticism of the Enlightenment was to reconcile various differing views they had held. I shall not be concerning myself with the political ideas, whether social or religious, but with the archaeological and the nationalistic ones, which in Mexico were one and the same.

Among those who are loosely termed historians, and whom I shall try to keep separate from those more accurately called archaeologists, there is a good deal of variety, but almost invariably it was attacks from the Enlightenment that provoked their replies. Some of them do not even refer to archaeological subjects, but they do partake of this nationalism which is intimately linked with the study of archaeology or ethnohistory, and which leads them to produce important bibliographies or biographies. Among these scholars, an outstanding group centred on the dissolved Society of Jesus which had taken refuge in Italy, though outside the Papal States; it is for this reason that much of their work appeared first in Italian or was translated into that language, to give them a Europe-wide distribution. The sadness of exile combined with indignation at the slanders of the Age of Reason to rekindle love for the long-lost country and an

46 Fighting apparel of the Mexicans. After Clavijero

47 Hieroglyphs of the names of Mexican towns. After Clavijero

Armadure messiccane

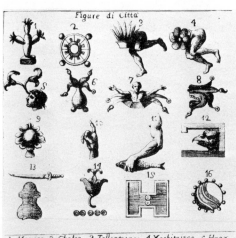

Figure di Citta

1 Messico. 2 Chalco. 3 Tollantzinco. 4 Xochitzinco. 5 Huaxjacac 6 Atotonilco 7 Ahuilizapan. 8 Atenco. 9 Tchuillojocan. 10 Nepohualco. 11 Michmalojan. 12 Quauhtinchan. 13 Tlacotepec 14 Macuilxochitl 15 Tlachco. 16 Terorauhtla.

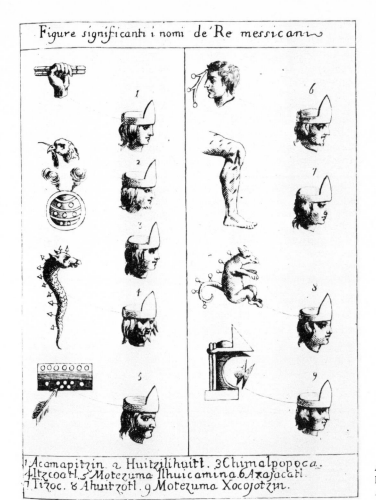

Figure significanti i nomi de'Re messicani

1 Acamapitzin. 2 Huitzilihuitl. 3 Chimalpopoca.
4 Itzcoatl. 5 Motezuma Ilhuicamina. 6 Axajacati.
7 Tizoc. 8 Ahuitzotl. 9 Motezuma Xocojotzin.

48 Names of the Mexican
kings and their hieroglyphs.
After Clavijero

ardent desire to establish its greatness. 'The ancient history of Mexico which I have undertaken . . . to serve my country . . . and to restore to its true splendour the truth now obscured by the unbelievable rabble of modern writers on America', writes Clavijero in his preface (1945:25).

Born in Veracruz in 1721 and, along with the rest of the Jesuits, exiled to Italy in 1767, Clavijero died there twenty years later. Besides the *Historia Antigua de México* of 1780, he wrote the *Disertaciones* in which, with wide learning and a great array of facts, he rebuts the Enlightenment criticisms. He is concerned as much with the physical world of America as with prehistory, history and culture. Perhaps because of his absence from Mexico, Clavijero found the materials for his history in books, papers and Indian paintings, and not in monuments or archaeological objects; which does not mean that he is unaware of their importance, simply that being unable to study them in person he was obliged to use others' descriptions of them. He cannot emphasize too strongly the need for their conservation: 'I pray my fellow countrymen to guard what little is left of the military architecture of the Mexica, so many fine antiquities having already been allowed to perish' (1945, II: 263). We should also take note of how in his preface he addresses the following words to the professors at the University:

'I hope that your worships who are the custodians of knowledge in this kingdom will try to preserve the remains of our country's ancient past, creating in this same magnificent building at the University a museum as essential as it would be interesting, in which to house those ancient statues already known to exist, or those yet to be found in excavations, as also arms, mosaics and other antiquities of this nature, Mexican paintings of all kinds now widely scattered and, above all, the manuscripts, both those of the missionaries and those of the Indians themselves, now lying in the libraries of certain of the monasteries, so that copies of them might be taken before they are eaten away by moths, or lost through some other misfortune. What was accomplished a few years since by an interested and learned foreigner, Boturini, is an indication of the way that might well be taken by our countrymen . . .' (1945, I:22).

The nationalistic side of the movement initiated by Sigüenza got a powerful boost from Clavijero. His defence of Mexico stresses the physical world, but in his descriptions of the ancient grandeur of the Indian civilizations, he does point out the error of supposing the indigene to be incapable of great things. I believe Clavijero's importance lies in his having written the first history of Mexico to

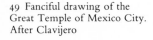

49 Fanciful drawing of the Great Temple of Mexico City. After Clavijero

broach a variety of different aspects of it, rather than a straightforward chronicle.

The basic idea of raising these written monuments which would make it impossible to doubt the value of Mexican culture, both then and as it had been in the past, and in so doing to forge a new nation, was also the driving force of two others who devoted their lives to the service of the same ideal. The first, Juan José de Eguiara y Eguren, another fierce critic of Pauw, devotes almost half his preface to a eulogy of ancient Mexican culture and demonstrates, by means of a quite exceptionally full bibliography, the quantity and quality of work written and printed in Mexico up until that date. At the end of the eighteenth century we find Beristain commenting,

'love of his country and tender concern for the honour of Americans, especially those of New Spain, set both his heart and his pen against lightmindedness and lack of respect, worse than insult . . . It was to vindicate our honour . . . that Sr Eguiara began to form his library' (1816–21, I:448).

50 Francisco Javier Clavijero (1731–1787)

In our own time Millares Carlo writes (1944:32–33):

'For the first time someone undertook the task of cataloguing the literary and scientific productions of Mexico, the unpublished along with the published. . . . Nowhere else in America had anyone then begun to do any work like it.'

The second, Juan Luis Maneiro, a friend and fellow Jesuit of Clavijero's, published while in exile his *Vidas de los Mexicanos Ilustres*. He does not so much set out to destroy the arguments of the Age of Reason as to describe, in his typically eighteenth-century style, his dreams of certain Mexican glories and the sadness of exile: 'I am writing, a Mexican banished from Mexico for full twenty-two long years, in which time it has not yet been granted to me to pay my country the debt of love I owe it . . .' he writes in his preface.

If I have mentioned these men who had no direct connection with archaeology, it is because in Mexico in its early stages the discipline is, as I have already explained, so clearly linked up with incipient nationalism. Following the traditional line taken by Sigüenza, who equates culture with nation without paying heed to what the biological origins of different Mexicans may have been, they recognize none the less the need for a knowledge of precolumbian culture.

The case of another priest, José Antonio de Alzate (1737–89), was very different, in that he was not a Jesuit and therefore not exiled to Italy. He had been a student of Clavijero's at the Colegio de San Gregorio in Mexico and his interests had ranged over many disciplines in the Enlightenment manner. Either as a result of his own studies or of his master's teaching he produced dissertations against Pauw and Robertson and, on the subject of American Indians, thought that

'the black and vile colours in which they are usually depicted for us by Foreign Authors, moved me some years past to enquire into their origin, their habits and customs and, in a word, everything that concerns their Arts, Sciences, etc. . . .' (1791, page I of the dedication).

51 Reconstruction drawing of the temple at Xochicalco. After Nebel

With this object in view he deals with

'Monuments of Architecture . . . A Building lays bare the character and culture of a people. . . . The study of antiquities has always been highly esteemed. . . . We know that many a historical fact has been confirmed or denied in consequence of the finding of a Medal or of an Inscription. . . . If the unbounded zeal of some and the greedy ignorance of others had not destroyed the Mexican Monuments, we might have collected a great store of antiquities with which to have established the true descent of the Indians, their customs . . .' (1791:2–3).

These ideas gave rise to the beginnings of his interest in archaeology which was already clearly demonstrated in his *Antigüedades de Xochicalco*. Not content with hearsay evidence, he twice visited the famous site, drew a map and made drawings of certain details. For the first time, a book about an ancient city is published and illustrated with prints. It is no longer a matter of a passing reference or two in an alien context, but of a work dealing exclusively with an archaeological subject. Though Alzate's description may be inaccurate and his interpretation fanciful, this in no way lessens the value of some of his data.

On 12 July 1785 Alzate also published a descriptive article on Tajín. As in the case of Xochicalco, it is a first mention of this site, which had apparently not been noticed before. It is also of interest as being among the first publications of the antiquities of Veracruz; '. . . at the end of March in this year 1785', writes Pedro José Márquez,

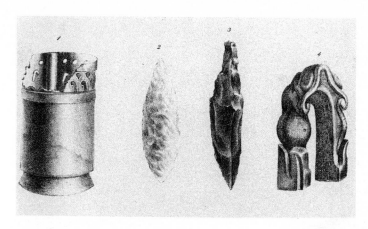

52 Implements found at the Isla de Sacrificios. After Góndra

'Diego Ruíz . . . found in a thick wood a pyramidal structure with one part lying upon another as it might be in a tomb, up to its peak or crown. On the eastern face it has a stairway made of ashlar, as is indeed the whole building, laid in lines or on the square, and this stair is made up of fifty-seven visible steps, and it is known that another large section of the stairway is buried underground, having subsided naturally under the weight of undergrowth and brush of the area' (1967:185).

There follows on from this a short and passable description of the pyramid.

Alzate's work breaks new and fruitful ground. From the sixteenth century up to the nineteenth, outside the central valleys and the

53 Low reliefs at Xochicalco. Drawings by Alzate, published by Márquez

54 The pyramid at Tajín in the eighteenth century. Reconstruction drawing by Gualdi (1841)

Maya zone, there is almost no description of the sites, and the data on ancient artefacts are few and far between. Nor was any attention paid to such regions as Veracruz, Oaxaca and the like, except for an occasional reference to Mitla. That other areas now entered upon the archaeological scene was thanks first to Alzate and later to Dupaix (see page 93, below). The old state of affairs, which took the central valleys and the Maya zone to be the only important focal points of culture in ancient Mexico, was to linger on into the first decades of this century. But the first break-through comes now, although the results of studying areas previously unknown and coming to see them as equal in importance to those already described, came to be fully understood only very slowly. Certainly areas of the greatest significance such as Oaxaca, the Valley of Teotihuacán or the Olmec zone have been recognized as such only in recent times, while others such as Guerrero are still relatively unknown quantities.

But here it is necessary to go back a bit in time and introduce Antonio de León y Gama (1736–1802), who has been called the first Mexican archaeologist; of him José Fernando Ramírez wrote in 1845 (II:LX) that he undertook 'the first and only strictly rigorous archaeological investigation that Mexico can lay claim to'. I am not too sure that such high praise is justified, as the very themes he dealt with had already been handled by others, but he did go to the trouble of searching through a mass of documentary evidence and had the opportunity of examining newly discovered pieces of the highest quality. His training had given him a fondness for astronomy and physics and he was for many years professor of Mechanics at the School of Mining. But he was a man of wide interests: his writings

range from a slight work on the lizard as a cure for cancer to a description of Mexico City before and after the Spanish Conquest. For the prehispanic part of this last, he was obliged to make use of information set down by those who had seen the city before its destruction, or who came to it very shortly afterwards, when its memory was still green in many minds.

55 The pyramid at Tajín prior to its restoration

The most important of León y Gama's books for archaeology is the *Descripción histórica y cronológica de las dos piedras.* The sculptures of the title are two famous monoliths, the statue of Coatlicue, the mother goddess, and the Stone of the Sun, often and inaccurately called the Aztec calendar. They are now the showpieces in the Mexica room of the Museo de Antropología. They were found by accident beneath the Plaza Mayor in Mexico City in 1790, during the course of drainage and reconstruction work. But if their discovery was fortuitous, the change of attitude in the viceregal administration was not. The viceroy the Count of Revillagigedo ordered them to be kept intact, not destroyed as they would have been only a few years before. The change shows the influence of the thinking of Charles III and a few of his advisers.

León y Gama describes the statue of Coatlicue carefully in his book, taking it to represent a goddess he calls Teoyamiqui, a correlation which is not entirely incorrect. The difference in the name can be ascribed to the immense confusion that reigns where the names and attributes of the Indian divinities are concerned.

The Stone of the Sun is more complicated; Gama carried out a long preparatory study before interpreting its meaning in accordance with his knowledge of Indian calendars. He had had the good

56 Colossal statue of
Coatlicue. National Museum
of Anthropology, Mexico
City. Ht 2.57 m

57 The goddess Coatlicue.
Drawing by León y Gama

58 The Stone of the Sun. The
surrounding heads depict ones
found at Teotihuacán. Drawing
by Nebel

59 The Stone of the Sun, as
drawn by León y Gama

60 The actual Stone of the Sun.
National Museum of
Anthropology, Mexico City.
Diam. 3.60 m

fortune to be able to consult the Boturini papers, as well as the various archives: he refers to 'thirty-six years of sorting papers' (1832, Part 2:5). He falls into the error of attributing to the stone a calendrical significance, though he never claims that it was used as a calendar. His work on the Indian methods of measuring time and also on their chronology, is without a doubt superior to anything previously done, and corrects many a misunderstanding not only on the part of his immediate predecessors in the seventeenth century and the first half of the eighteenth, but also among the sixteenth-century chroniclers, who did not understand how the calendar really worked. They ventured to compare it with, and to make it work along the same lines as the European, which was an impossibility.

León y Gama points out, clearly and for the first time, that the Indian and European calendars are responses to very different concepts. This insight meant that he frequently hit the mark, despite occasional errors in his hypothesis – errors which were to be corrected slowly and piecemeal throughout the course of the nineteenth century by such as Fernando Ramírez, Manuel Orozco y Berra and later archaeologists. Nevertheless, areas of doubtful interpretation did remain. What is important for archaeology is that Gama's work is not based on written or pictorial documentary evidence alone, but on the direct study of so incontrovertible a monument as the Stone of the Sun.

Shortly after the publication of the book we know today as the first part of León y Gama's work, Alzate turned against him and published in his famous *Gaceta* a series of criticisms and attacks upon his conclusions. The Alzate-Gama controversy may have struck a contemporary observer as very one-sided, as the latter gave it out that he would not reply to the attacks. He did however prepare for his own purposes replies which Carlos María de Bustamante published in 1832, along with descriptions of other sculptured stones, in a volume that makes up the second part of Gama's book.

We need not consider in detail the rights and wrongs of the dispute, but some of the points at issue are interesting in that they give an insight into how those matters were regarded at the time. An important plank in Alzate's platform of rather crude criticisms is his disparagement of Gama's interpretation because he cannot accept that it might be possible to extract from a monolith all the data he presents on the native calendar. Angrily, Gama replies that he learned sixteenth-century Nahuatl to enable him to read and interpret such unpublished manuscripts as were available at that time; the task took him twelve years. In answer to another, later attack by Alzate, calling upon him to explain the general rules governing the workings of the old chronology, Gama replies that such fixed immutable rules do not exist, as the calendars vary from area to area according to the epoch in which they were used. Alzate also mercilessly slates Gama's mineralogical classification of Coatlicue and challenges him on sundry other minor points (León y Gama 1832). For us it is clear now that most of Alzate's arguments were faulty and that Gama was in the right.

The same thing happened with his descriptions of other sculptures found in the same plaza; Gama includes in the second part of his

book a commentary on a very important one, the great cylinder
bearing representations of the triumphs of the Emperor Tizoc. He   95,96
believes, mistakenly, that he is dealing with a god because the ruler
appears clad in the vestments of a deity. Fifty years were to pass
before this statue would be correctly understood. To his other
studies of the sculptures, Gama adds a very interesting list of the
monoliths in the Mexico City of his day and even in his own home,
with details of how they were sited and their meaning. Certain of
them have survived, and the list points up the exaggeration of saying
that everything had been destroyed. Clavijero pleading for the
creation of a museum of antiquities had yet to be heard in the land.

As I have just been referring to the statue of Coatlicue, I think it   56
would be pertinent to look ahead at this point and briefly outline its
subsequent history, because to do so is to throw a little light on
eighteenth- and nineteenth-century ideas of the value of Indian art. It
was found on 13 August 1790. On 6 September, the viceroy, in
response to the urging of the corregidor Bernardo Bonavia, ordered
that the statue be conveyed to the University where its preservation
would be assured. With great labour they got it moved, placing it
first in front of the second gate of the viceregal palace, and then at the
University, as the 'most appropriate place to take custody of this
curious example of American antiquity'. This was the first state
action and it led, almost unintentionally, to the setting up by stages
of a museum. Once it was installed, Gama did a drawing of the   57
statue. The professors of the Real y Pontificia Universidad did not
wish to expose it to the gaze of Mexican youth because, as they saw
it, the Mexican goddess was unworthy to be seen alongside the
Greek and Roman copies already exhibited there, and which were
the gift of Charles III, a keen amateur archaeologist. The motive
adduced by Humboldt (which William Bullock was later to repeat),
that they were afraid of rekindling in the Indians the slumbering
ashes of the ancient religion, seems a more likely one. Be that as it
may, the stone was re-buried. When Humboldt in 1803 asked to see
it, as he knew it only through Gama's drawing, he had to enlist the
powerful influence of the Bishop of Linares in order to get it dug up.
But no sooner had Humboldt turned his back than underground it
went again. There it remained until 1824, where Bullock saw it after
its third and final exhumation, though Meyer claims that this took
place in 1821 (1852:110). It was not shown to the public even then,
but stowed away in the corner of a corridor, almost buried under
planks and old furniture, probably for chauvinistic reasons. If the
various nineteenth-century travellers who visited the museum did
not describe it, it was for the good and sufficient reason that they did
not get to see it; included among them was the marquesa Calderón
de la Barca, who has left us extensive descriptions of the other pieces
in the museum. The truth is that, until about 1880, Coatlicue was
considered to be a hideous monster. Alfredo Chavero was later to be
one of the first to attempt to rectify this impression. Today the work
counts as one of the Mexica stone-mason's greatest triumphs.

An earlier and far less important commentator than Humboldt
was a fellow Jesuit of Clavijero's, Pedro José Márquez, who translated León y Gama's book into Italian, and edited in Rome a work

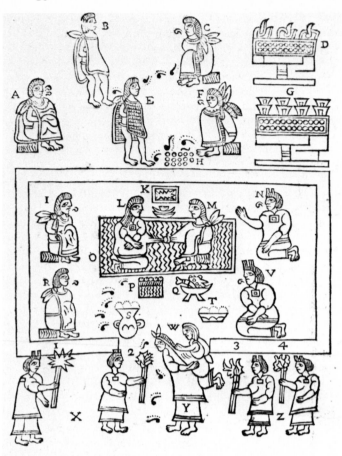

61 A page of the Codex
Mendocino. Published by
Thevenot 1672

based on Alzate's two slim volumes. As a Mexican intellectual, he
expresses his views on its ancient art with the obvious intention of
establishing a parallel with other cultures and substantiating its
importance. He criticizes 'the ugly pictures some writers have
painted of Americans both past and present, and this without proper
examination . . .' (1804: II–IV), and calls for a serious study of these
matters, to show 'the not negligible level of good breeding and
culture to which those peoples of Mexican origin had attained long
before any European ever visited them'.

The study of the pictographic writings that we call codices was
always a subject of interest, though they were interpreted in many
different ways. The first important publication of them that I can call
to mind was that of Samuel Purchas of 1625, when he published in
London the plates of the Codex Mendocino, later republished in
Paris by Thevenot (1672 or, more likely, 1696).

As early as the period we are now discussing, an unlikely person to
be doing work of this kind prepared an edition of the only three
letters of Cortés then known, to which he added plates from the
codex called *Matrícula de tributos*, plus some annotations and a
preface. This was none other than Francisco Antonio de Lorenzana,

Archbishop of Mexico until 1772, and one of the most prominent churchmen of the time in his native Spain as well as in Mexico. Later he would become a cardinal, but whilst in Mexico he travelled widely in his see and interested himself in ancient history. Though he does not often mention monuments, he notes the ruins of Texcoco and Huexotla (1770:189) as well as of the house that had belonged to Moctezuma's brother (id.:194); there can be no doubt that his work contributed to that vast missionary endeavour, the rescue of the Mexican past.

Meanwhile, in the Maya area the first archaeological project ever to be undertaken in Mexico was carried out – namely, the excavations at Palenque. It was in the southeast that the archaeological aspect was dominant, activities in the heartland being more documentary-based. Whether for this reason, or whether because the beauty of the buildings appealed more directly to the Western aesthetic sense, they were admired from the start, in contrast to the views held about Mexica art in general. Quite apart from this, Maya art was never directly attacked by the European *philosophes* of the Age of Reason, and so eighteenth-century Mexicans were never called upon to rush to its defence.

Work undertaken at this period owes little or nothing to the authors previously mentioned, as few of them had thus far been published, and were only to be read by people who, like Muñoz, were prepared to bury themselves in the confused immensity of the Spanish archives in order to study them.

The saga of Palenque built up from very small beginnings. Around 1740, Antonio de Solís, curate of Tumbalá, was granted the priestly living of the village of Palenque, and duly presented himself there, with a train of brothers and nephews.

The family began to look about for land to cultivate, and it was not long before they came across 'stone houses'. The incumbent of the benefice and his family were astonished at their architecture. One of the boys remembered them clearly and when, years later, he went to study at Ciudad Real (the modern Ciudad Las Casas), he told one of his fellow students of the wonders he had seen. This student, Ramón Ordoñez y Aguiar, when he grew up and in due course was ordained, became passionately interested in antiquities. Years later still, he was to write a strange and ridiculous book, *Historia de la creación del Cielo y de la Tierra conforme al sistema de la gentilidad Americana. Teología de las culebras* . . . In 1773, he organized the first small expedition to visit the site. It is very strange indeed that, before the visit by Father Solís, nobody seems to have mentioned the existence of so extraordinary a place. But Ordoñez did more: he told José Estachería, thirty-ninth governor of Guatemala, of the existence of Palenque and he, a cultivated intellectual, ordered José Antonio Calderón to prepare a report. Calderón duly visited Palenque, spent three days there, and on 15 December 1784 handed in an interesting descriptive study accompanied by some wretched drawings. He lists 215 houses, most of them in ruins, and speaks of the palace which 'from its size and style could have been nothing less'. Though unassuming, this is the first solely archaeological report we know of. Calderón, who though intelligent was fairly ignorant, believed

62 Stela from Palenque. Taken to Spain at end of eighteenth century. Museo de las Americas, Madrid. Height 70 cm

Palenque to have been a Roman construction, since sandals decorated with half-moons similar to those we know from Rome were found there: 'they do say that Plutarch concedes that half-moons were worn in their shoes by the noblest of the Romans' (1946:23–24).

Estachería was dissatisfied with Calderón's report and, shortly after receiving it, sent out a second expedition, led this time by an architect, Antonio Bernasconi. As might be expected from one of his calling, his report is rich in architectural details, as well as containing a brief discussion of the 'somewhat Gothic' overall style. 'Its architecture', he adds, 'does not fall within any of those orders known to me, neither ancient nor modern' (1946:39). The August

63 Palenque. Stucco relief.
After Dupaix

64 Palenque. Detail of
stucco reliefs.
Photographed by Maudslay

1785 report went off to Spain and, very soon thereafter, on 1 March 1786, Charles III gave his approval to what had already been done, and ordered that more extensive exploration be undertaken.

Now enters one who, though he did not reside in Mexico, was yet of major importance to its history: Juan Bautista Muñoz, a leading chronicler of whom I have already spoken (see page 71, above). Widely read in the mass of as yet unpublished manuscripts, not only was he immediately aware of the importance of the site, but he also, on 7 March 1786, asked José de Galvez, the newly created marquis of Sonora, to arrange for a series of explorations, to distinguish between

'doors, niches and windows, looking carefully at what may be found to be of ashlar, as well as those of what is called rough stone and mortar, and to the mortar in these; making careful descriptions and drawings of any figures, the sizes and method of cutting of stones and bricks or adobes with particular attention being paid to what are called arches and vaultings. And bring away pieces of plaster, mortar, stucco, bricks both fired and unfired; postsherds and any other utensils or tools to be found; making excavations where it seems best.' (Muñoz, 1946:43).

Muñoz was of the opinion that the ruins 'might illustrate the origin and history of the ancient Americans' (id.:42), and vindicate the old sixteenth-century chroniclers who had sung the praises of the 'grandeur and beauty' of those in Yucatán and Guatemala. Echoes of Landa, or of Ciudad Real! Muñoz believed these ruins to date from long before the Conquest, and that their builders were 'superior in culture and knowledge' though still not the equals of the Europeans (id.). This is a resurrection of the idea that there had at one time existed an ancient folk superior to the sixteenth-century Indian.

65 Palenque. Courtyard of the Palace. Photographed by Maudslay

66 Palenque. Stucco reliefs from the patio of the Palace. After Dupaix

The report drawn up by Antonio del Río, the captain sent by Estachería in accordance with the royal command, is much better known, as it was published – though the edition is hardly a good one – in 1822. It claims to have left no 'window nor adobe wall, no chamber great or small, passage, courtyard, tower, chapel or basement where we have not dug and delved' (id.49). Happily for the splendid ruined city, this is wildly exaggerated, and his report does contain better drawings and some fresh ideas. He thinks it possible that

'some one among the nations (Phoenicians, Greeks, Romans and others), pressed their conquests as far as this country, in which it is known they stayed no longer than the time it took for these Indian

67 Palenque. The Palace. After Dupaix

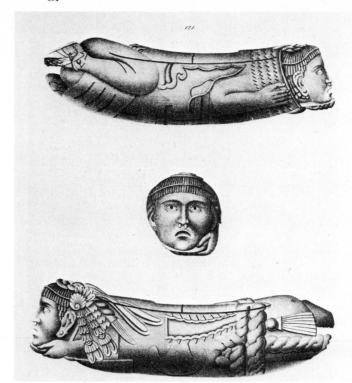

68 Wooden musical
instruments from Tlaxcala.
After Dupaix. The length of
the drum (bottom) on which
Dupaix based his drawing is
60 cm

69 The Pyramid of Huatusco.
After Dupaix

people to rework their inventions and crudely imitate such of their arts as they were prepared to teach them' (id.:65).

This is to suggest a fusion between the idea of an early and more highly developed people and that held by Landa and others; namely, that the Maya were responsible for the presence of the ruins.

A study of the manuscript prepared by Father Tomás de Sosa on Uxmal and other sites led del Río to the conclusion that the Maya people of Yucatán and Palenque at least were one and the same, and to sense that the ruins were very old indeed (id.:51). But del Río kept at least one foot on the ground and did not wish to take wing into 'purely fanciful discourse', but to base his opinions upon a study of the ruins themselves. I myself think that del Río is important chiefly because of the effects his report had on others. Attention came to be drawn for the first time to Palenque, and to Maya ruins in general. This was the spark that kindled Stephens and Catherwood. Another consequence was that some pieces from there were sent to Spain and placed in the new Gabinete de Historia Natural; these were the first finds to be taken from a Mexican excavation for preservation in a museum.

Charles IV had the same cultivated tastes as his father Charles III, whom he succeeded in 1788, and gave orders, not just for excavation to be carried out at any one particular place, but for a complete survey of New Spain, to seek out sites where ancient ruins, objects, statuary and other like things were to be found. After due deliberation Guillermo Dupaix was appointed to direct the work. Of Austrian descent, Dupaix was a simple, very truthful man with some knowledge of history and archaeology; Humboldt points out that he had studied in Italy. What this official proceeded to do was to confine himself to recording, factually and without fanfare, all the discoveries he made. The result was a descriptive itinerary, arranged in short sections explaining his activities; it is almost a journal of his travels.

The first thing he did, very properly, was to find himself a draughtsman. He appointed Luciano Castañeda, who lived in Mexico and who accompanied him throughout his travels. Dupaix was

71 Urn from Zaachila, Oaxaca. After Dupaix

72 Low relief from Zaachila, Oaxaca. After Dupaix

20 Varas _____ ou 60 pieds.

Plan et coupe du Caveau.

54

5 Varas ¼ _____ ou 22 pieds ¼

73 Burial mound of Chila. After Dupaix

not so painstaking in the matter of his bibliography. When he visits Xochicalco, for example, he does not even mention what Alzate had by then published; presumably he did not know of it. Dupaix's first voyage begins at Mexico City on 5 January 1805. He went through Puebla, Tehuacán, Orizaba, Córdoba, and various other places, but when they got to the Huatusco area of Veracruz, Castañeda became ill and they were forced to turn back. Not, however, without having seen most of the State of Morelos.

On the second journey, which began in February 1806, they visit Xochimilco, Tlalmanalco, Amecameca, Mixquic, and do in fact find a number of highly interesting things and various secondary sites in the Valley of Mexico. Then they double back, again by way of Morelos, towards Oaxaca, passing through Acatlán y Chila. A magnificent cruciform tomb there with its great stair is described and a drawing of it made. It had already been opened; with the exception of Mitla, this is the oldest account we have of a Mexican prehistoric tomb, accompanied by an accurate drawing. The expedition travels on through a series of Mixtec sites, coming at last to the Valley of Oaxaca. They go into ecstasies at the sight of Monte Albán, and theirs is the first description of these ruins in the literature. With a fair degree of care and a generally reasonable degree of accuracy Dupaix discusses the architecture of the site, although the marvellous general lay-out of the Great Plaza could at that time scarcely be guessed at, so covered was it with top soil and vegetation.

77 From there, they go on to Mitla, where they make a careful, detailed study of the palaces and tombs, accompanying their commentary with plans and excellent views. After passing through a series of other settlements in the Valley of Oaxaca, the travellers
68 return via Tlaxcala, visiting Tizatlán on the way.

In December 1807, the third expedition takes them once again through Puebla to Oaxaca, but with the intention of pushing further on. To visit the huge ruins at Quiengola, near Tehuantepec, which had also never previously been visited and described, they climb to the top of the hill on which it stands. They also go to Ciudad Real, where the aged Ramón Ordoñez y Aguiar was still living. He makes them a gift of two archaeological pieces. In the words of Dupaix, they think of him as a 'lover of antiquities'. But the authorities here take Dupaix for French.* He is thrown into gaol and endures many hardships but is eventually released and continues his journey to Palenque. When he comes to describe its architecture, he brings to the task considerably more understanding of the matter than had previously been shown by Antonio del Río. Without actually digging, he lists the materials used in the buildings, discussing, for instance, the treatment of stone, how it was cut, dressed and used. He notes the absence of bricks, the structural use of wood, and the beauty and quality of the stucco, making – which is perfectly correct – a clear distinction between the two types. Some he calls

74 (*opposite*) Stucco reliefs from Palenque

75 (*opposite*) Palenque. Relief named Le Beau by Waldeck. Drawing by Castañeda

76 (*opposite*) 'The Cross' at Palenque. Drawn by Castañeda, published in Dupaix

---

* It should be remembered that at this time Napoleon was in the process of invading Spain, so that it was hardly the most propitious moment to be travelling about in the hinterland of New Spain.

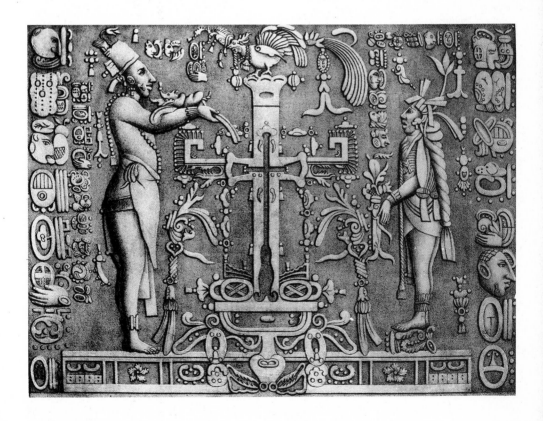

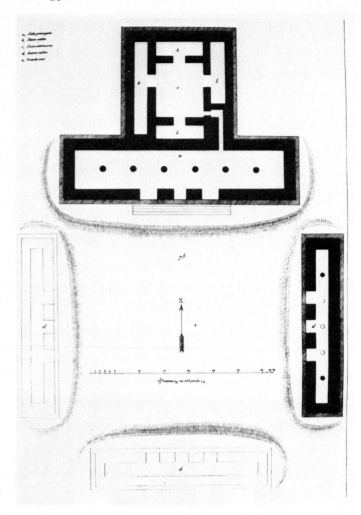

77 Ground plan of a palace at Mitla. Drawing by Castañeda, published in Dupaix

'level' or 'flat', meaning that the stucco is simply applied to the wall, making a low relief; to others he gives the name 'skeletons', meaning that they have a central core which when stuccoed stands out in high relief. Both of these are described. He regards with admiration the numerous hieroglyphs, mentions and even draws the bridge over the Oztolun streamlet, which is still standing today. He decides that it was not the Egyptians who built Palenque, but the citizens of Atlantis, and in support of this contention he draws parallels between Palenque, El Tajín and Monte Albán. He concludes with this remark; 'I have not tried to falsify this description; free of passion as I am, I have tried to tell the truth as far as in me lies' (1834:35). He brought with him on his return a goodly number of original pieces, several of which are now in the Museo de Antropología. Whether he compiled a catalogue which would tell us which objects derive from which journey, I do not know.

78 (*opposite*) Monte Albán. 'Danzantes' in low relief. Height about 1.20 m

In Castañeda's drawings, as retouched for their republication in Paris (1834) and London (Kingsborough 1830), the same faults

appear as in those Antonio del Río's expedition produced. They are accurate as long as they depict buildings, as for example at Mitla, but when it comes to the human figure they are altered and 'embellished' to suit the aesthetic fashion of the time. This weakness can clearly be seen in the rendering of the five dancers of Monte Albán, the only ones then visible, as well as on various urns; this deprives the drawings of some of their documentary importance. But Castañeda's original drawings have recently been found (Alcina, 1969), and these, if clumsier, are much more accurate.

Dupaix concentrated on two main themes: one is the art, an interest which is typical of his period, as we see for example from Humboldt or other travellers of the time. These all asked themselves: 'Is the ancient native art in any way fit to be placed alongside traditional European art, Greek or Roman art in particular?', and they answered their own question in the negative.

The other theme is closely related to the first: it is what we might call cultural progress, the attempt to see how far, compared with, say, the Egyptians, Persians, Chinese or Hindus, the precolumbian Indians had advanced.

With Dupaix, whose book I shall return to later, and the year Humboldt spent in Mexico, we come to the end of important archaeological activity in what had been New Spain and was soon to become Mexico. The latter landed at Acapulco in March 1803, and left from Veracruz a year later. He had come straight from South America where, in the course of his immensely long travels, he had gathered vast quantities of data and made the acquaintance of the scholars of those countries. Simón Bolívar, general and statesman and hero of the South American independence movement, was his friend, and he came armed with letters of introduction from the most influential people in Spain. From the time of his visit to Mexico, when he was barely thirty-five, one could foresee a brilliant future for the illustrious baron and the impact his work was to have.

On his return to Europe Humboldt set himself to the writing of his books on America, two of which are particularly concerned with Mexico. Less useful to the archaeologist is the two-volume *Essai politique sur le Royaume de la Nouvelle Espagne* accompanied by a magnificent atlas, published in Paris in 1811. The other, *Vues des Cordillères et monuments des peuples indigènes de l'Amérique*, published in Paris and London in 1810, is a large album containing sixty-nine freely annotated plates, thirty-two of which deal with Mexico. Five depict archaeological monuments – Cholula (two views), El Tajín, Xochicalco and Mitla. Curiously enough, during his journey Humboldt only actually visited Cholula. He illustrates the other sites with prints taken from Alzate or Márquez, accepting any errors they might contain. It seems astonishing to us that this man, so keenly interested in everything, did not even visit Teotihuacán. A further seven plates are devoted to then newly discovered monoliths, or to those still standing in Mexico City. They are the three famous stones studied by León y Gama, a Mexica goddess from the Dupaix collection and other figures including the wrongly named 'relief from Oaxaca' which is in fact from Building A of the palace complex at Palenque. It is strange that this is the only one that Humboldt

65–67

considered beautiful, seeing he had a mind unusually open and receptive to a wide range of styles in art. 'From the close of the last century', he writes,

'a happy revolution has allowed us to change our way of perceiving the civilization of other peoples . . . my studies of the natives of America are appearing in an age when we no longer take to be without merit whatever does not conform to the style of which the Greeks have left us such perfect examples' (1816:11–12).

But, despite these protestations, he never describes an object without calling it 'primitive', or 'on the long road that leads to art', so that he does not entirely renounce the restricted view adopted by his predecessors and contemporaries. If he admires the 'Oaxaca relief' it is because Maya art lies closest to that of Europe. But this has gone on being a common reaction from the Conquest up to our own day.

The remainder of the plates in his album on Mexico illustrate pages, or details, from the pictographic codices. He made an in-depth study of such of these as he could find, including the Codex Borgia which he calls the Codex de Veletri. Many of Humboldt's conclusions were mistaken, but his learning and feeling for objectivity place him far in advance of the other travellers of his time. He might be likened to Muñoz, except that he did see something of the world instead of staying locked up among the archives. Such errors of fact as his works contain were due to his accepting the conclusions of others where he has not visited the places he describes.

Humboldt was careful, however, not to come to finite conclusions except on firm premises, as, for example, when dealing with the problem of the origins of American culture. He was a diffusionist, like most Europeans, but when he is playing with Egyptian and Roman similarities he does not define them, and when he talks of 'distant peoples' he is not too precise about them. He knew how to arouse the interest of European scholars; this was to be his great gift to Mexican archaeology. His books, skilfully edited in French, then the language of scholarship, met with such success among the intelligentsia of the day that from them arose a renewed desire to become acquainted with things Mexican, and this not only in France, but in England and Germany as well.

In the preceding chapters I have tried, however briefly and inadequately, to sketch in outline the advances made in the field of Mexican archaeology in the colonial centuries. Up till the end of the eighteenth century we can hardly consider that there was any real interest in local antiquities other than in exceptional cases, which were for much of the period unhappily very rare. I have also attempted to show what were the motives and ideas that were impelling scholars and travellers to find out more about the ancient precolumbian world. Humboldt in his introduction to his *Vues des Cordillères* (1816:8–12) had already pointed out some of these stages. He claims that there was great interest in the American monuments from the Conquest till the seventeenth century, giving this as the reason for the appearance at this time of so much important work. Certainly much more had been written than published, so a good deal remained that Humboldt did not know about.

Later on, interest diminished because, according to Humboldt, the Spanish colonies closed their doors to foreigners. Whilst I can quite see the truth of this, it was not the only reason, and chief among the others was the then near-total proscription on the publication of work dealing with the Indian past, and the playing-down of these subjects, because of the ever-present fear of arousing religious doubt and provoking attacks on Spanish domination.

This was the state of things that Sigüenza began to break down. By the eighteenth century Humboldt was already thinking in terms of the European Age of Reason. He belonged, after all, to the previous generation, a genius who scrutinized things closely and saw the fundamental errors of his predecessors. But all his judgments are made from the point of view of a Europe where, he tells us in talking of Clavijero's book, its contents were scarcely believed, as they were assumed to be far, far too lenient with the then so disparaged Indian culture. He, on the other hand, quoted from it freely.

He comments that European writers 'more struck with Nature's contrasts than with her harmonies' described an America sunk in wretchedness while he, who had visited it, found it singularly interesting and attractive. He notes how at the end of the eighteenth century Europeans were becoming aware of the high civilizations of Egypt, but it was Humboldt himself who disclosed America to them.*

For all Humboldt's optimistic account, the publication in Italian of Clavijero and Márquez, the numerous translations of a variety of authors, the spate of Enlightenment theories, Robertson's history, and much besides, very little was known about Mexican archaeology in the Old World. It is strange to find, in the *Biblioteca Americana* published in London in 1789, how few references there are which are not from Robertson or from Clavijero, to whom the editor refers his readers. He takes Clavijero's history (published in English in 1787) to be a 'curious, entertaining and valuable book', which is already an advance on the adverse opinions to which Humboldt refers. All in all, I think that by the beginning of the nineteenth century interest in Mexican archaeology was already alive in European academic circles, though to what extent it is difficult to say. The United States, later to be so active in this field, had not yet begun to launch out into prehispanic studies. In Mexico, however, curiosity about the country's past did exist, a curiosity often mingled with the other concerns I have mentioned and which, after a falling-off probably caused by the War of Independence and its aftermath, was to revive among the scholars, the editors of manuscripts and the travellers of the nineteenth century.

---

* Humboldt's global scientific vision is in marked contrast with European ethnocentricity which shows, for example, in one of the greatest of his contemporaries, Goethe, who writes: 'The antiquities of China, India or Egypt are curiosities and nothing more; it is very well that they should be known to the world, and that in their own surroundings an appreciation of their beauties may be made, but this will never bear more than a very little fruit.'

Chapter Five

Historians and Travellers (1825–1880)

THE YEARS OF the Wars of Independence and after, up to the middle of the nineteenth century, with all the accompanying disorder both within the country and beyond its borders, could hardly have been favourable ones for archaeological studies, particularly where field-work was concerned. Nevertheless, interest held up well. As we shall see, scholars continued to work on the documentary materials, as well as on what was brought to them by travellers, particularly from the Maya area. The latest focus of interest, the establishment of the museum of archaeology which was also to be the nursery of a number of publications, is the subject of the next chapter. In addition, by the end of this period, scientific societies and some universities began the publication of journals, among them some very valuable ones, which occasionally publish matter of archaeological interest. The division I am making is a little on the arbitrary side, as obviously the work of one helps the work of others, and often the same individual takes part in a wide range of studies.

Among the historians who did their research without leaving their studies there were those who produced more or less original work and those who preferred to edit unpublished manuscripts. While this distinction can likewise not be a very rigid one, we make use of it so that we can look at both branches of activity more clearly.

With few exceptions, the historians of ancient Mexico have all been overtaken by the nineteenth century, which of course does not mean that their works have not on occasion been essential to those who came after them. On the contrary, these early manuscripts, now published in full for the first time, are thereby ensured continuing life.

The first editor at this period was Carlos María de Bustamante, an active politician who from 1821 was responsible for the publication of a series of manuscripts, some of them of the first importance for ancient history, such as Sahagún (chapters on Ixtlilxochitl), Beaumont (whom he calls Vega), and the second part of León y Gama's book, of which he has this to say: 'It is an admirable work and one that meets with great approval in Europe' (1832, note). His publications are designed above all to prove his political theses. Bustamante inherited from the Mexican Age of Reason the wish to enhance the grandeur of his country by recalling the ancient Indian glories, as he points out in, for instance, his preface to Sahagún.

Thus he is to some extent at least in the line of the eighteenth-century Enlightenment and his interest in ancient history remained constant even as to detail. For instance, when he read in the newspaper *El Sol* of the discovery made by Ranas y Toluquilla in Querétaro he wrote off for information on the 'king who built them' (*MS. Archivo INAH.* Vol. 477). He never ceased cutting and altering manuscripts, adding notes which were often impertinent, all of which made him one of the least faithful editors imaginable. In his time documentary historians did not regard absolute fidelity to the texts as a necessary attribute of their work.

Impelled by publications such as Antonio del Río's report (1822), and others like it, as well as by the growing success of the works of Humboldt, the Geographical Society in Paris organized in 1825 a competition, in which the prize was to go to the best contribution to archaeology, to geography, or to an account of a journey in Central America. In 1828 Abbé Baradère visited Mexico, and on 7 November he managed to get hold of the text of one of Dupaix's 75–77 diaries, the drawings by Castañeda and half of the objects collected during the expeditions mentioned in the previous chapter. The copies of the diary did not reach Paris till 1832, which is why the work that won the Geographical Society's competition bears the date 1834, although it did not appear until later. The Kingsborough collection had already been published in England (1830–31), appearing there as it did in France with the much-retouched drawings by Castañeda. In fact these had been known and partly made use of before this. Dupaix's text was to have better luck than those of all his predecessors, even if it did come somewhat late. The publication aroused considerable interest, and in the French version was supplemented by work from a number of other writers. Most of these articles consist of hypotheses originating in Paris, lacking factual foundations and not to be taken too seriously. Even Lorenzo de Zavala's piece on Uxmal, for all the writer's high standing, is inferior to Ciudad Real's description of 250 years before, which may be due to the contempt he habitually felt for everything native. Only Lenoir (1834:73) sums up skilfully prevailing ideas about the various periods of the monuments, offering us chronology of a kind. He claims that many believe, as he does, that Palenque might be as much as three thousand years old. 'Thus', he goes on,

'there are in Mexico: *1*. the Mexican antiquities properly so-called, that is to say, those belonging to the Aztec people, founders of Mexico, and who go back to the twelfth century; *2*. pre-Aztec antiquities, for example, products of the Toltecs and other nations who trod Anáhuac soil around the sixth century; *3*. the antiquities of Palenque, and others of the same kind scattered throughout Guatemala and Yucatán and which, though considerably more ancient, are of totally unknown origin.'

It was Orozco y Berra and others in the latter part of the eighteenth century who began to change these ideas concerning the chronology. Then, in our own century, traces of peoples earlier than the Toltecs began to appear, and before long it became clear that the Maya were in fact contemporary with the Toltecs. So Lenoir made at least a small advance along the road to knowledge, which is more than his colleagues can claim.

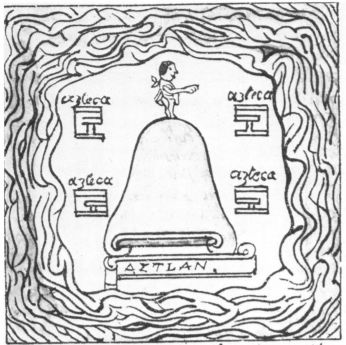

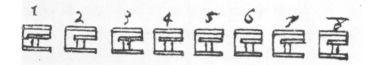

79 Aztlán, place of origin of the Aztecs, from the Codex of 1576

The report on this work drawn up by Walckenaer, La Renaudière and Jomard in 1836 for the Geographical Society, and the prize it won, are worthy of note. As Pollock writes (1940:184):

'Extraordinary is the modern note that it strikes. . . . These men plead for an end to unfounded speculation, for exact recording and for adequate plans, drawings and observations, that should thus allow comparative work.'

This is precisely what Dupaix had been trying to do.

The French and English, presented for the first time with drawings, ruins and objects, all hitherto unknown, began to take American antiquity seriously and to think of it as a cultural entity worthy to be compared with ancient India and Egypt. It is hardly to be wondered at, therefore, that in those same years 1830–48 the enterprising Lord Kingsborough published the nine huge volumes in which are reproduced a number of codices from Central Mexico,

80 Departure from the island
of Aztlán, from the Codex
Boturini

10,11

various other antique pieces and a great deal of documentary
material. Volume IV includes the Dupaix expedition. Kingsborough's work is an important milestone even if its basic thesis was
that the Americans were descended from the lost tribe of Israel.

Between 1837 and 1853, Henri Ternaux Compans published in
Paris twenty volumes of important manuscripts translated into
French, dealing not with ancient Mexico alone but with the whole of
America. Another Frenchman, J. M. A. Aubin, had from 1830
onwards accumulated a marvellous store of documents, including
some that had belonged to Ixtlilxochitl, Sigüenza, Boturini, Veytia
and Gama. As he tells us (1885:5–6), during the years of his stay in
Mexico he saw, in the capital alone, between three and four thousand
archaeological objects housed in collections. That indicates that
interest in these things was spreading. After 1849 he published his
Mémoires sur l'écriture figurative et la peinture didactique des Méxicains
which, along with José Fernando Ramírez's work did a great deal to

SIGUESE SU A B C.

Signos.	Valor fonetico.	Signos.	Valor fonetico.	Signos.	Valor fonetico.
1.	a	10.	i	19.	p(1)
2.	a	11.	ca	20.	pp
3.	a	12.	k	21.	cu
4.	b	13.	l	22.	ku
5.	b	14.	l	23.	x#
6.	e	15.	m	24.	x
7.	t	16.	n	25.	u(2)
8.	é	17.	o	26.	u
9.	h	18.	o	27.	z

81 Landa's Mayan alphabet, arranged by Brasseur

advance the deciphering of the Aztec glyphs. His somewhat unusual character led Aubin to forbid Ramírez access to his papers, which remained unpublished except for those that the latter succeeded in dragging out of him. To finish the story of the Aubin collection, it was bought in 1889 by Eugène Goupil who, in an entirely different spirit, got Boban to publish the *Documents pour servir à l'histoire du Méxique* in 1891. They were left to the *Bibliothèque Nationale* in Paris on his death.

On 27 February 1864, on the occasion of the French intervention in Mexico, Napoleon III set up the Commission Scientifique du Méxique, in imitation of Napoleon I in Egypt. Of all the work published by this Commission, we are of course only interested in what refers to ancient Mexico. Its life and soul was an eccentric abbé, Charles Etienne Brasseur de Bourbourg, who had been on voyages of exploration in Mexico and Guatemala and in 1859 published the fourth and final volume of his *Histoire des Nations Civilisées du*

Méxique et de l'Amérique Centrale. He did, however, carry on with his work until about 1886. All Brasseur's work is a weird pot-pourri of sound sense, great learning, absurd theories, groundless fantasies, and proof that is no proof, the whole in a spirit as remote as possible from the scientific. From that point of view the strange curé of Rabinal did not leave us much of any use; but the great traveller and bookworm followed his nose to one good thing: he made available Landa's account of Yucatán, unpublished till then, and the most important book on the Maya world to come down to us.

Brasseur was also aware of the importance of the Quiché book known to us as the Popol Vuh. Friar Francisco Ximénez had unearthed this in Chichicastenango in the seventeenth century and translated it into Spanish with a wealth of notes and a welter of confusions. The Spanish translation was published by Scherzer in Vienna in 1857, but thanks to Brasseur we have, together with a French translation, the original Quiché text for the first time. These two publications are sufficient to earn for him our eternal gratitude.

There were other, less eye-catching members of the Commission Scientifique du Méxique, however, who played their part: men like César Daly, who had glimpsed something of the future of archaeology, as he reveals in the following observation:

'In order to clarify the history of ancient Mexico and Central America generally by means of a study of their monuments, it is to my mind insufficient to look only at those buildings which are the most harmonious from the artistic point of view; it is necessary on the contrary to begin by drawing a general plan of all the ruins of these regions, with a view to later comparisons between them according to their geographic, political, religious and artistic similarities, as also along the lines of the techniques employed in their construction, the materials used, the skill of their populations, and so on' (1865:155).

This quotation proves that, well over a century ago, someone was thinking about archaeology along relatively modern lines. I shall be referring later to Charnay, who was more of an archaeologist than any other member of this group.

Active around this time too was Don José Fernando Ramírez (1804–71) who, unhappily for us and in common with so many lawyers of his day, wasted part of his life in political concerns, letting himself be dragged down into the whirlpool which was nineteenth-century Mexican government. The extraordinarily unstable conditions prevailing at the time are certainly the reason why some of Ramírez's own work is still unpublished, and has never received the recognition which is its due. This brilliant man had talent and rare skill in finding his way about in the labyrinth of the pictographic writings. There still remain today, fortunately housed in the library of the Museo Nacional, more than twenty volumes of partially unpublished manuscripts which have been much quarried by later researchers.

Despite the unfavourable circumstances, Ramírez published the *Cuadro Histórico-Jeroglífico de la Peregrinación de las Tribus Aztecas* with prefaces, and annotated; it contains, in addition to the *Tira de la Peregrinación*, the Sigüenza map, as well as a series of codices from the

82 José Fernando Ramírez
(1804–1871)

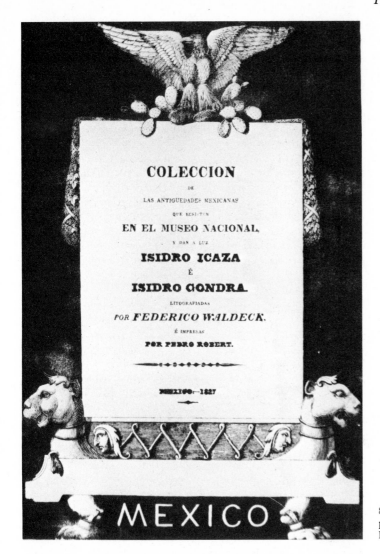

COLECCION
DE
LAS ANTIGUEDADES MEXICANAS
QUE ECSISTEN
EN EL MUSEO NACIONAL,
Y DAN A LUZ
ISIDRO ICAZA
É
ISIDRO GONDRA
LITOGRAFIADAS
POR *FEDERICO WALDECK.*
É IMPRESAS
POR PEDRO ROBERT.

MEXICO 1827

MEXICO

83 Page from the first publication by the Museo Nacional

Aubin collection, such as the Tonalamatl, the Tlotzin map which he calls *Historia del Reino de Aculhuacan*, the Quinatzin and Tepexpan maps, the Codex Aubin 1576 and – perhaps his most important publication – Friar Diego Durán's *Historia*, the first volume of which appeared in 1867; the second did not come out until 1880, after Ramírez's death. 10,11

Publication of Ramírez's 'notes' on Prescott (see pages 115–116, below) began to appear in 1884, and three years later his *Descripción de 42 objetos del Museo Nacional*. This ends up by being an archaeological study, to which he devoted the rest of his life. While accompanying Empress Carlota as Maximilian's Secretary of State for Foreign Affairs on a voyage to Yucatán, he found time to record in his journal some notes on Cholula, and to make a drawing of Uxmal. In Yucatán itself he examined the Dupaix and de Waldeck papers lodged there.

Living in Mexico at around this time and somewhat later, was another publisher of important works, Joaquín García Icazbalceta. In direct contrast to Ramírez and others, García Icazbalceta never meddled in politics and devoted all the spare time that looking after his family and fortune allowed him to the study and editing of part of his own extremely valuable collection of manuscripts. These included Motolinia, Mendieta, El conquistador anónimo, the fourth letter of Cortés, the *Relación de Texcoco* by Juan Bautista Pomar, Zurita, the *Historia de los mexicanos por sus pinturas*, and many more. The editions cannot be faulted, not only for their fidelity to the text, but also for their printing which he always supervised personally when he did not actually do it himself. His bibliographic and philological work, important though it was, falls outside the field we are concerned with here.

The heir to this long tradition was Manuel Orozco y Berra, engineer and lawyer (1816–81), author of works on geography and linguistics, though his most important contribution lay, not in these and other valuable studies, so much as in the gathering together of a great deal of scattered data in the preparation of his weighty *Historia Antigua de México*. This book is as coherent as it was then possible for such a work to be, and is the first great history to be written since the death of Clavijero. With all its subsequent emendations, it is valuable still, and well worth consulting. Much fuller than either Prescott or Bancroft, it tries to be documentary and objective, seeking 'truth and fairness', as its prologue affirms, though its author does not always succeed in this, admitting as he does to some highly fanciful beliefs. Throughout the four volumes archaeological objects 'which I have before me' are constantly discussed; he is not perceiving them quâ objects but as proof of his contentions.

84 Manuel Orozco y Berra (1816–1881)

He either refutes outright many of the conclusions previously reached, or perceives them afresh, his eyes trained on the extensive bibliography he used – virtually everything then available. He describes and discusses sites from all over Mexico, from Casas Grandes to the Maya area (II:320–431), basing his views manifestly on Stephens for the latter. He considers the Maya to be the most ancient in point of historical time (II:498), an idea which in one form or another persisted down to Morley; he sees them as having gone through four separate stages, divided one from another by savage invasions. With this hypothesis in mind, he condemns Clavijero's schema (II:350 et seq.). Opposite is a table which represents an attempt on my part to summarize Orozco y Berra's chronological ideas and indicating the stages he postulated though I must confess to finding his four volumes sprinkled with assertions which frequently contradict one another. He followed the long-standing custom of devoting much of his work to the Maya and Central (Mexica) areas, but runs counter to it in not forgetting the existence of the other regions whose monuments point to their prehistory. He does not, however, define Mesoamerica as a single civilization.

I think that his notion of the greater age of the Maya is a lingering echo of the old ideas about an earlier and more civilized race than that first seen by the Spaniards. This recurrent need among so many writers, even at the time of Orozco y Berra, to presuppose an earlier,

CENTRAL ZONE	MAYA ZONE
The Aztecs and their immediate predecessors	Buildings in ruins
661–1116 Toltecs. Written history begins	Decadence Mayapán (inferior to Chichen) (1000–1500 – Kukulcán)
III Tajín – Strongholds of Veracruz II Teotihuacán – Cholula I Xochicalco – Monte Albán-Zaachila Certain of these sites have two or three phases	70 BC – AD 1000 Chichen AD 528 Palenque, Uxmal. Notable advances. More powerful chiefdoms. Brilliant architecture. Certain Asiatic influences: Buddhistic religion. No Toltec control
Cultural decline. Collapse of the preceding peoples	697 BC – 400 BC Izamal

Prehistoric era   IV Ranas, Canoas, Strongholds
 	
    III Zape, La Quemada, Pillars
 	
    II Zape, Agriculture. Embankments
 	
    I Casas Grandes, Tumuli	

America is first populated

more advanced culture belonging to a vanished people appears in the United States too, and is exemplified by the Mound Builders.

On the other hand Orozco y Berra is not so aesthetically attracted to Maya art, possibly because he never saw it. He says:

'Two classes of pieces have always attracted our attention. For their beauty, certain masks of clean, clear lines, polished and finished with a painstaking care that is truly artistic; drilled with holes in the upper part, they served to cover the faces of the gods in certain solemnities, or those of a certain category of the dead; and, because of the difficulties involved in their manufacture, those we call bobbins because of their close resemblance to the wooden ones used to spin thread. The glassy, brittle material is ground away to the thickness of thin pasteboard. Its evenness leads one to suspect that they were turned on a lathe and not made by hand' (I:299).

He is referring, I suppose, to the Teotihuacán masks and to the earplugs, which were never used 'to spin thread'.

By contrast,

'the images of the gods are hideous. Totally devoid of artistic feeling, they are further disfigured by being overloaded with fantastic symbolism, which imbues ugliness with terror. The statues inspire

85 Stone mask in the Teotihuacán style. National Museum of Anthropology, Mexico City. Height 21 cm

fear rather than respect. . . . In the Aztec pantheon, conceived of by peoples who were moral if barbaric, the gods are decorously chaste; no male goes naked, no female displays more than custom permits; they bear the stamp of an austere and harsh imagination, which is far indeed from the impudent effrontery of what are absurdly called the refinements of civilization' (I:139).

'All the same, one does find pieces that show great artistic advancement. The seated statue in the Museo Nacional, if it is far from resembling Greek or Roman work, does have strong features, touches of vigour and displays a sound knowledge of human anatomy. A head in hard stone, also exhibited there, is the work of a skilled hand. The masks are outstandingly perfect in form; some of the small clay figurines do not leave much to be desired when it comes to pure artistic modelling; one wooden mask is magical, as regards the expression of its draughtsmanship' (I:354).

86 (opposite) Seated idol, of the type mentioned by Orozco y Berra. National Museum of Anthropology, Mexico City. Height 45 cm

From now on, researchers from the United States play a large and active part in the field of study we are dealing with. The first, as well as the most outstanding among the historians is William H. Prescott, who does not publish documents so much as accumulate a great

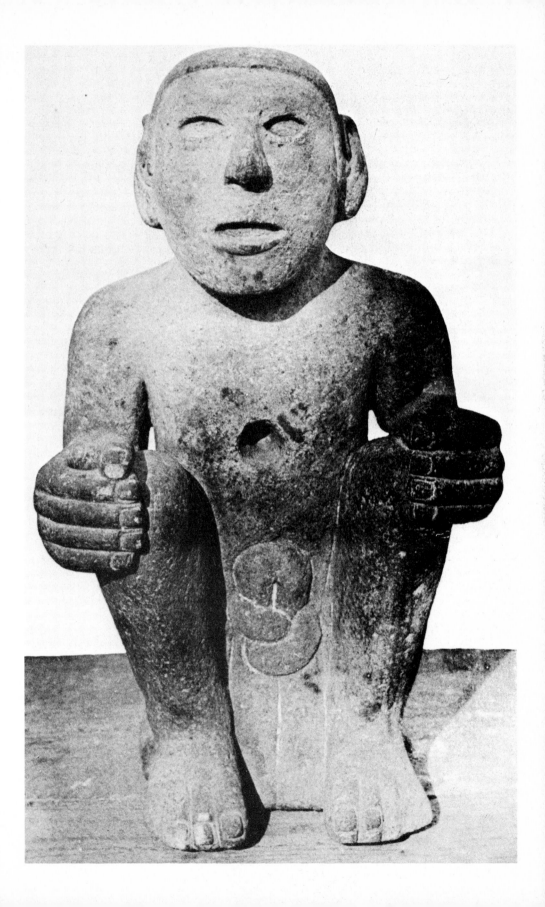

87 Lúcas Alamán (1792–1853).
Portrait with inscription for
Joaquín García Icazbalceta

mass of them drawn partly, thanks to his friend Pascual de Gayangos, from those collected in the previous century by Muñoz (after whose death they had been deposited with the Real Academia de la Historia in Madrid), and in greater part from various Mexican friends, among them Lucas Alamán, whom I shall come to later when discussing other foreign writers: Italian, English and French.

Prescott's sources are perhaps the best, if not the only example of the gruelling labour then involved in collecting the basic raw material without which writers of those days could not begin serious work on a history. They had to copy out manuscripts, make friends, even if only by correspondence, with an endless number of people who might be able to supply them with information, and so forth. There still exist vast piles of correspondence, asking for and sending news of documents, of the contents of archives and copies of manuscripts. Prescott was very active at all of this, despite the terrible handicap of being almost completely blind. For we have now reached the age of the document and it is no longer possible to go on writing as the eighteenth-century intellectuals had done, with no first-hand information and without recourse to 'irrefutable documents', as Muñoz would have said. So it was that one so renowned as Prescott, without ever visiting Mexico, was able to describe sites and cities and lay the groundwork for that use of bibliographies that must always be part of all serious archaeology.

Eventually, in December 1843, there appeared Prescott's *History of the Conquest of Mexico*, which achieved extraordinary success and still has its readers. By 1852 it was going into its twenty-second edition. It is amusing to observe how, in England especially, people who are well-read in other fields but without special knowledge of matters American, cry 'Prescott!' at the mention of Mexico, having heard of no one but him. As its title indicates, most of the book lies outside our field of interest but Book I 'Introduction – View of the Aztec Civilization' and an appendix to Volume III 'Origins of Mexican Civilization' (which one would have hoped to find at the beginning), are in the nature of a summing-up of previous historical knowledge and, most importantly, they tell us what Prescott and his generation were thinking on the subject of ancient Mexico. The appendix, though it came out after the appearance of the first publication by John Lloyd Stephens, actually pre-dated it, which is why Prescott did not make use of what Stephens had to say, though by making some changes in what he himself had written he could have done.

In contrast, therefore, to his documentary materials Prescott's archaeological sources were poor; they seem to have been reduced to Humboldt, Dupaix, the volumes published by Kingsborough, Alzate and not much else. He believed ruins to be rare in the territory once ruled by the ancient Mexica Empire, but very often met with in Oaxaca, Chiapas and Yucatán (1852, III:404). He comes to the conclusion that, although having some similarities with other places, 'the civilization of Anáhuac . . . may be regarded in its essential features, as a peculiar and indigenous civilization' (III:418). He treats the subject of the Aztecs almost exclusively from the ethnohistorical angle, though much mention is made of codices and manuscripts which are themselves, of course, ethnographies.

He is still an aesthetic disciple of J. J. Winckelmann. What he most admired were two torsos that could pass for Greek (III:405, note 77). But it is always 'barbaric art'. In the table below I have tried to establish a chronology and 'cultural stratigraphy' for Prescott which was, in fact, that to be followed by many nineteenth-century students.

1325–	↑	Settlement by Mexica Tepanecs.
1150–1200		Chichimecs arrive with, among others, Aztecs and Acolhuas.
1050–1100		End of the Toltecs, who migrate southwards.
650–700		Arrival of Toltecs at Tula from the North.
?–?		Mitla – Palenque – Maya.

This simple table shows how the ideas of Sahagún, Torquemada, Clavijero or Veytia persisted. It is interesting to compare it with the one drawn up for Orozco y Berra (above, page 111).

In 1844 a Spanish edition of Prescott appeared, with notes by Lucas Alamán, and soon after that another, with notes by Ramírez (1844–46), accompanied by a generous supplement with plates of artefacts, along with an explanatory text by Góndra, then Director of the Museo Mexicano. Translations into French and German came out in the same year.

It is instructive to contrast the notes on Prescott prepared by each of the two great Mexicans. Alamán, who obviously took little trouble over his, hardly does more than point out genealogical or biographical errors made by Prescott. This is because Alamán belonged to a purely Spanish school of thought and he cannot be even remotely considered a pre-archaeologist. As his articles go to show, Alamán sees Mexican history as beginning with the Conquest, (although his famous *Historia* is concerned solely with the Independence and for that reason begins much later), which is an opinion he shares with Prescott and so many others. Alamán does not, in fact, think Mexican prehistory important.

Ramírez, on the other hand, uses a very different approach when he points to three general weaknesses in the work. One of these shows how Prescott is still an eighteenth-century European *philosophe*:

'Mr Prescott has taken up his pen to write the history of *barbarians*; a word that, alternating with *savages*, rampages through the whole length of the work, . . . as a result the Mexicans *howl*, and their armies generally speaking do not *fall back*, or *retire*, they *flee*. The force in the language itself insists that their indomitable courage should be labelled *rabid fury* . . .' (1945:II, Intro. XV).

It is interesting to reflect upon how much Prescott's use of language has impressed Lewis H. Morgan and his pupil Bandelier, both of whom were to criticize him so sharply.

Despite these strictures, Ramírez praised Prescott's work and took advantage of the occasion to note that 'students of our antiquities have never enjoyed the protection or support of national government . . .' (id.: notes, 29) and how

'the attention of the cultivated world was never caught by our antiquities until Humboldt studied them and Kingsborough published them, [men] to whom we owe esteem and veneration as the true restorers of the Mexican antiquities . . . an imperishable monument . . .' (id.).

After describing four carvings in the Museo, Ramírez concludes:

'. . . I have in the main devoted my sleepless nights to artefacts of my own country, finding in them fresh proof to confirm the truth of the historical sources . . .' (id.: 124).

In other words, Ramírez understands how archaeology can lend support to written history and believes that therein lies its value and its purpose. Every monument is a document to him. Although his aims were limited, in Ramírez we have another archaeologist in the spirit of León y Gama, whom he so admired.

'Ramírez and Orozco y Berra carry on the tradition of Clavijero and Eguiara, Mier and Bustamante in the interest they all take in the indigenous cultures without rejecting the Spanish heritage; to the enrichment of the synthesis derived from them both.' (De la Torre 1975:421).

So these nineteenth-century historians, whether Mexican or foreign, without being exactly archaeologists, were making use of archaeological data, obtained by others though occasionally by themselves, in this historical synthesis which is so important, and closing the circular movement begun in colonial times.

Orozco y Berra's history and Bancroft's magnum opus, *The Native Races of the Pacific States*, appeared in the same year, so neither was able to make use of the other's published work. The latter contains a bibliography of impressive proportions, and the many references to his contemporaries indicate the extent of the development of this field of study. Though few of the references can be called archaeological there are, even so, more pertaining to the science than in any previous publication. Lacking Prescott's talent, Bancroft produces what is 'necessarily to a great extent a compilation' (IV:3) of what had already been published on objects and sites; it finishes up by being a kind of archaeological guide which gives a good idea of everything known before 1880, the end-date of this chapter. Bancroft was not an archaeologist and visited hardly any of the ancient sites, yet he laid considerable emphasis on archaeology in his historical reconstruction. In some respects this was the first of those manuals of American archaeology which were to proliferate two or three decades later. He writes: 'I may claim . . . for this treatise a place among the most complete ever published on American antiquities as a whole' (IV:2).

Bancroft distinguishes between monumental archaeology (or, say, material remains) and written or traditional archaeology. The first 'is real and tangible, the relics are irrefutable' (IV:5) '. . . The

88 Head of Quetzalcoatl. After Góndra. Height 32 cm

study of the ancient monuments is a source of accurate information and bears out the chronicles . . . it is supportive evidence' (7–8). He has this to say, on the other hand, of the Spanish authors:

'In their antiquarian researches a passage of scripture as commented by the Fathers brought infinitely stronger conviction to their minds than any sculptures, monument, hieroglyphic record . . .' (V:143).

Earlier in the same work he writes:

'There are probably few eminent archaeologists but may trace the first development of a taste for antiquarian pursuits to the curiosity excited at the sight of some mysterious relic' (id. IV:9).

He is concerned to produce a stratigraphy, but a geological one, on the lines of the European model of the ages found there, and there is not included in his work a general chronology for Mexico. He does not fully understand it because, although he refers to many traces of contact between the Nahuas and the Maya, he continues to regard them as two culturally differentiated groups.

Another result of this period's interest in publishing the documents of, and writing historical works on, ancient Mexico, integrating archaeology into them wherever possible, is the appearance of serial publications. These, hardly more than an outline sketch at the end of the eighteenth century (much like Alzate's *Gazeta*), now begin more and more frequently to include articles on archaeology or related subjects, and to be produced also by some of the scientific organizations pursuing similar aims. Some of them put in only a fleeting appearance but others, like that of the Sociedad Mexicana de Geografía y Estadística – founded under another name in 1833 – maintained a very high standard over the years and are still in circulation. The Society's journal first came out in 1839 but only later do articles of interest to our field of study begin to appear in it.

The Mexican scientific series owe their birth to those many which were beginning to emerge in England, Germany and the United States around this time, joining the ranks of the old-established ones that continued to appear. Although dealing chiefly with subjects in which they specialized, or with the East, they tended to come gradually into contact with Mexico. Similarly a substantial number of books was appearing which was largely the result of the rapidly increasing flow of data now reaching Europe. In Chapter Seven we shall revert to these serial publications.

The greater part of their data came in from those many Mexicans who, usually by accident, discovered a site or some object of note and published what they found. There was a positive flood of announcements of this kind between 1820 and 1880, which went some way towards enlarging our knowledge of ancient sites, and copious references were made to recent discoveries. There were so many of them that they covered practically the whole of Mexico. Reports were published for the first time of finds such as the Olmec head from Hueyapan, vessels from the west coast or the north, and much fresh information on areas already explored. None of this can be called a schematized body of knowledge but, however incomplete and scrappy it may be, it does indicate a considerable and growing interest in archaeological remains. What is more, though some of the work is very superficial, genuine studies were from time to time produced which are still valuable today.

At the same time travellers from other countries, on the look-out for anything of unusual interest, were not lacking; Mexico being once again open to foreigners, some of these were men of substance. They were of many nationalities, many professions: diplomats, politicians, businessmen, artists and, occasionally, antiquaries, geologists or those representing some other academic discipline. A very few, like Charnay, (see page 126, below) were archaeologists who excavated at several sites.

This wide occupational range meant that many who wrote accounts of their journeys mentioned archaeology only in passing. It was only very rarely that the treasure hunt in the country turned into a permanent interest, let alone a profession. Nevertheless, in many instances the finds were genuinely appreciated by those who made them. It was thanks to their own private enterprise that a sizeable number of foreigners, both Europeans and North Americans – all of whom travel more than Mexican nationals do – were to be found at the sites; they were not there under the aegis of institutions providing a set programme. This is perhaps why their opinions do not reflect archaeological thinking already prevalent elsewhere, and as a result their theorizing about mankind's past was hardly ever

89 Giant Olmec head from Hueyapan

influential. The works of, say, Worsaae, Thomsen or Boucher de Perthes were not read at this stage, apart from what little they wrote about animal fossil bones. Some corresponding finds were however made, such as the sacrum from Tequixquiac or that described by Hamy in assorted short publications, and where their antiquity is demonstrated by stratigraphy, but this branch of the study is usually a later development, and refers only to remote prehistory.

The important journeys which later writers were to put to such good use, were through the Maya zone.

In 1838 Frédéric de Waldeck's *Voyage pittoresque et archéologique dans la province d'Yucatán pendant les années 1834 et 1836* was published in Paris. This picturesque, somewhat frivolous character had spent two years in Palenque. Prescott wrote, without even knowing of many of his startling adventures, 'I had a soupçon that Waldeck was a good deal of a charlatan'. Nevertheless, his book had its part to play in the general flow of interest towards the Maya remains, along with his very beautiful drawings which were yet, archaeologically speaking, so highly inaccurate. His main work *Monuments Anciens du Méxique* did not come out till 1866, and its ideas are so absurd as to preclude any intelligent discussion of them.

These are years when visitors to the Maya zone proliferate, among them a German, Baron de Friedrichsthal (1841) and a North American, B. M. Norman (1843). Copán reappears in the archaeological annals with the visit of Juan Galindo, commissioned in 1834 by the government to report on the ruins. His mission was therefore an official one, as were those to Palenque. I have already made mention in Chapter One of Galindo, that strange Englishman with a Spanish name, who became Guatemalan colonel and governor of the Petén. Not satisfied with having drawn up his 1834 report, he went on to publish a number of articles both in London and Paris. The twenty-five drawings he made have to be presumed lost. During one of his investigations he discovered a tomb (1945:220), which is I think the first ever described that had not previously been robbed, as those found by Dupaix had been.

Whilst on the subject of the Petén I will, even at the risk of a slight deviation from chronological order, here mention a less important researcher who, though he comes after Stephens, is nearer to Galindo and his predecessors. This is Modesto Mendez, Magistrate of the Petén. With a few others, he visited Tikal, stayed six days and later drew up a report (4 March 1848), first published in Germany (Ritters, 1853). This is the first we know for certain refers to that great city which he explores and describes, though not in much detail. He searches among the ruins for 'curious' objects but fails to find any. His (very mediocre) draughtsman produced a number of drawings (Mendez, 1930). He later visited Ixkun and drew some of the stelae there. Mendez refers to the wooden lintels found at this city, not previously mentioned, though Stephens had spoken of those at Uxmal. An ignorant and chauvinistic man, Mendez was incapable of holding any historical ideas of his own (1930:92).

With only a short interval between them, two pairs of visitors arrived at Palenque. What one of these teams achieved was to prove of little consequence, whilst the other would leave its mark upon the age.

The first was the expedition of Patrick Walker and John Caddy, which started out from Belize. For an odd variety of reasons, they thought it important that they should reach Palenque before Stephens, whom Walker at least had seen when he, Stephens, had passed through Belize.

Be that as it may, they rushed ahead and did, in fact, arrive first at Palenque, and although they were poorly equipped they described certain of the buildings in some detail and prepared maps and drawings. They stated more precisely the views we have spoken of before, in particular that there must have been two kinds of Maya culture. The first, and more ancient, having been highly advanced and responsible for the writing of the inscriptions; the second, the one which the Spaniards encountered on their arrival, much decayed. According to Walker and Caddy, those responsible for the first must have crossed the seas, probably as colonizers from a country in Asia, so that they 'might in ancient times have had frequent communications with the mother country'. These communications eventually broke down but the written characters remained Asiatic in form. Their bibliographical baggage was highly exiguous and, as the book to come out of it was only published recently (Prendergast, 1967), this expedition, packed with incident as it was, had little influence.

The second expedition, on the other hand, composed of John

113

90 John Lloyd Stephens
(1805–1852)

Lloyd Stephens, a North American and Frederick Catherwood, an Englishman, was epoch-making.

Even before he had left the United States, Stephens was much more interested in the ruins than in the diplomatic mission entrusted to him by his government, although with his usual sense of duty he neither shirked nor entirely neglected this. It was not his fault that he found no government to which his credentials could be presented, the Republic of Central America having in the interim ceased to exist.

Renouncing his mission as an impossibility, he set himelf whole-heartedly to the study of Maya antiquities, and these were to be the only reason for his second trip. That this was so is clearly shown by the growing number of pages he devotes to them in each succeeding volume: in the first, only about 15 per cent, rising to 30 per cent in the second volume of the first book. In the later volumes on Yucatán about half their content relates to archaeology or to Maya history. And that this is not even more I believe to be because Stephens was a man of his time, and may well have thought to make his work more agreeable to read by scattering it freely with personal anecdotes about himself or his companions, along with comments on the life and customs of the people he met with on his travels. In addition to the interest of the central theme itself, the simple pleasant style is congenial; his account is sympathetic, clear and orderly, and he can call upon real skill when describing in a few lines a landscape, a person, an accident, a heavy shower of rain, good lodgings or bad, even meals. So outstanding are the descriptions of the sites, the objects of his labour, the charm of his tale of travel and adventure, 3,6–8,26 enhanced by Catherwood's splendid drawings, that the four volumes were, and go on being, best-sellers among books on American archaeology.

But Stephens had other aims besides making his book easy to read. He argued that the Indian customs of his time reflected something of the ancient culture, that they were themselves ethnographic remains (1843, I:247).

Not content with visiting and recording sites, Stephens carried out small-scale excavations off his own bat. Sometimes he found vessels or human bones which he illustrated and described in exemplary manner. He discusses Maya thatching and vaulting techniques and shows considerable interest in Juan Pio Pérez, who makes him a present of a study on their chronology. They become great friends. During all this Stephens is collecting linguistic data, though of a rather simplistic sort; this multiplicity of interests makes of him a pre-anthropologist able to turn his hand to a variety of areas.

In spite of everything, Stephens could not quite free himself from the viewpoint of his day and his bibliography, especially where Spanish publications are concerned, is severely limited. But then, ignorance of what had been written in Spanish was rife even among the Yucatecos (*Registro Yucateco*, I:371–375, 1845). The author of the *Registro* (Justo Sierra O'Reilly?) thinks that, even among those living in the peninsula, few took any interest.

A paragraph of Robertson's, previously cited (page 70), that Stephens had read, makes us understand his astonishment on behold-
8 ing Copán, where he arrived 'with the hope, rather than the expection, of finding wonders' (1841, 1–9).

'The sight of this unexpected monument put at rest at once and forever, in our minds, all uncertainty in regard to the character of American antiquities, and gave us the assurance that the objects we were in search of were interesting, not only as the remains of an unknown people, but as works of art proving, like newly discovered historical records, that the people who once occupied the continent of America were not savages' (1941, I:102).*

The monument-document idea is clearly to be discerned and, if we take all ancient remains to be monuments, this is the true stuff of archaeology.

None the less, Stephens does not fail to observe that not all the Maya monuments can be dated in the same period. He repeats this several times: he can distinguish two styles, at Chichen at least, though he falls short of demarcating two stylistic periods. The summary of ancient history with which he ends his book (1843, 2:453 et seq.) convinces him that it all began with the Toltecs, whose advent he places in the seventh century, which would not make the

---

* This brings to mind François de Belleforest (1572:275–8) who wondered why the Aztecs should be taken for savages 'by men who can admit of no civilization beyond the frontiers of their own countries'.

Maya ruins particularly ancient. Despite his mistaken chronology, Stephens is getting away from the fairy tales surrounding the ruins, flights of fancy which will not take the weight of evidence, notably that the old culture originated on another continent.

Stephens's very logical view of the builders of the Maya cities leads him to over-condense the periods; he is a forerunner in the tendency to take the ruins for more recent than they are, a tendency which persisted at least into the time of George C. Vaillant. He puts forward various reasons for this belief, born of his observations at the ruins (the existence of wooden lintels and the good state of preservation of some of the buildings, which he believes centuries in a destructive climate would prohibit; comparison of the Tablet of the Sun at Palenque and the face of the star on the Mexica Stone of the Sun). It is an assertion which will be repeated later by Charnay (Catalogue, p. 9, 1883). At Copán his first idea – of fixing the date of a ruin by measuring the depth of earth and the height of the trees growing upon it – he soon gave up, realizing how unreliable it would be (1841, I:159). After a lapse of forty years Nadaillac (1882:323), following Charnay, was to give clear reasons why this should be so. Stephens also refers to historical arguments taken from chronicles and other documents which indicate that certain of the cities were occupied at the Conquest, and that some of the buildings then in use by the Indians were later taken over and used by the Spaniards in Mérida and Izamal.

Although he underlined the stylistic differences between the various cities and knew that their inhabitants spoke different languages, Stephens insisted on the cultural unity of the Maya. He points out that the hieroglyphs are the same everywhere, which seems obvious now, but nobody had said so since the seventeenth century. Humboldt leads him into error (1816, I: Plate XVI) owing to a page of the Dresden Codex mistakenly published by him as Aztec, and which he finds to be the same as an inscription from Palenque (1841, 2:454). He insists, perfectly properly, on the vital importance of deciphering the hieroglyphs (1841, 2:457).* It would be equally important to study the accumulation of papers in monastery libraries, since they might reveal the history of some of the cities. We must remember again how little had been published when he was writing.

Stephens came to some important conclusions and, without being aware that he was doing so, reverted to the old opinion of Landa and others concerning the builders of the monuments. The Phoenicians, Jews, Chinese and the rest take their leave again, though unfortunately only for a time, and abandon the stage to the Maya as builders:

'It is the spectacle of a people skilled in architecture, sculpture, and drawing, and beyond doubt, other more perishable arts, and possessing the cultivation and refinement attendant upon these, not derived from the Old World, but originating and growing up here without

---

* Don Juan Pío Pérez made a heroic attempt in 1842 to decode the calendar. But without Landa, without the stone inscriptions it was hopeless and his errors were fundamental. He was, however, the first to break the ground of this colossal task, which has so much later been crowned with success.

models or masters, having a distinct, separate, independent existence; like the plants and fruits of the soil, indigenous' (1841, 2:442).

He declares repeatedly that, unlike his rivals, he seldom theorizes but that, when he does, it is always upon a firm foundation of facts, though this cannot be taken to mean that he always comes to the correct conclusion. When Stephens is mistaken it is usually because he has used faulty data. He is aware of often being a pioneer in what he is doing. 'It is impossible to describe the interest with which I explored these ruins. The ground was entirely new; there were no guidebooks or guides; the whole was virgin soil', he says at Copán, and repeats in various places that he was the first to reach many sites. The wish to get to a site before anybody else was highly characteristic of that period.

His negotiations to buy ruins in order to transport their sculptures to New York were less happy, while his idea of taking away souvenirs for himself was disastrous. The wooden lintels from Uxmal and the panels from Kabah, unique of their kind, perished in the fire which gutted the 'Panorama' in New York. This 'Panorama' was to have been the nucleus of an American National Museum. Friar Estanislao Carrillo, and amateur archaeologist who had gone exploring at various sites (Uxmal with Catherwood and Cabot), gave Stephens a few pieces. These may have been among the consignment which, because they were delayed in reaching New York, were spared the fire and Spinden was able to recover a half century later.

Stephens's book was hugely successful, receiving rapturous reviews. That delightful woman, the Marquesa Calderón de la Barca, writes to Prescott:

'I received Stephens . . . the Travels are very amusing, and dashed off in a most free and easy style. I hear they are criticized as being very incorrect by those who know the country. One thing is evident . . . that he could not speak Spanish, which must have caused him many difficulties, but he might have got someone to spell it for him' (von Hagen, 1947:200).

The criticism is unfair, except where Stephens's awkward Spanish is concerned. For it is really remarkable how often Stephens is quoted in the *Registro Yucateco*, a journal that appears to have been the means whereby the intelligentsia of the peninsula kept in touch, and the praise which it showers on him. Editions soon began to come out in Spanish (the first in Campeche in 1848), and they are still coming out. His books were the first major contribution available to the public (since much of the Spanish work remained unpublished) that added to the fund of knowledge of the ancient Maya, and which considered the remains and the sculpture as works of high art and not simply as exotic curiosities. He did well to criticize those who clung to the old way of thinking, be they his predecessors or contemporaries such as del Río, Dupaix, Robertson, Waldeck, or Kingsborough, thereby exploding so many myths they had taken for truth. If he is not the discoverer of the Maya world, which had been known to Landa and Ciudad Real long before his time, it was he who brought it to the knowledge of the many, he who led us away

8

91 Yaxchilán. Lintel G. After Maudslay

from theological and *a priori* explanations. Science was coming into its own.

There were to be many who followed the footsteps of Stephens into the Maya zone, who travelled, described ruins, collected objects and disseminated their opinions, but few had much to contribute during the forty years before the appearance of Maudslay. So I shall only mention a few of them, and the changes that took place in the archaeological thinking of the day.

Within the Commission Scientifique du Méxique, already mentioned, the best-known archaeologist was Désiré Charnay, whose first journey to Mexico was made in 1853–9, before the Commission even existed. Although he did some work in Central Mexico, at Tula in particular, he did not have anything very new to say about Yucatán. His bibliography was extensive because a lot of important material was being published around that time. However, his book is an 'adventure and travel yarn', and he goes on thinking, like Humboldt and Stephens, that the Toltecs were precursors of the relatively recent Maya civilization (1855:lx); he presupposes a number of different races and that the Nahuas had come from Asia. He trots out various rather poor examples of parallel development in support of this. About this time an important new technological device, the camera, was introduced. Antiquaries took to clambering up hill and down dale encumbered with highly complicated equipment and brittle glass plates. Every photograph taken then – and some of them were marvellous – called for an act of heroism.

Charnay's opinions on the worth of the ancient art are very thin stuff:

'after all, we ought not to deceive ourselves about the beauty and real merit of the American relics. They are archaeological objects, nothing more . . . they call forth surprise, rather than admiration, everything is so badly done' (1885:348).

91 He has praise for only one piece of sculpture: the lintel of what Maudslay called house G at Yaxchilán.* 'We have here the most marvellous monument ever to be offered us by America, and we can be daring enough to present it as a work of art' (id.:392). This is the characteristic nineteenth-century attitude, from which few make good their escape.

And yet Charnay was ahead of his time in perceiving the cultural unity of Mesoamerica:

'. . . from north to south, on the high plateaux as in the hot lowlands, we are always within the bounds of the same civilization and the same religion, which offer us the same ceremonies, the same symbols and the same gods' (1904:291).

When it comes to chronology, he belongs to the 'short count' school, as he insists continually on the modernity of the ruins. After lengthy if somewhat unsound argumentation, he comes to speak of the Maya in these terms:

'So then we have here the remains of a civilization, whose oldest monuments would date from the end of the eleventh century:

* Lintel 24 at building 23 at that site in the Morley Enumeration.

Comalcalco . . .; the most recent from the middle of the seventeenth: Tayasal. This civilization thus covered a period of six centuries. It is, therefore, relatively recent and has nothing to do with the geological ages of the Abbé Brasseur, any more than it has with the fossil horse of the archaeologists from the Peabody who explored at Copán' (1904:308).

92 Ruins of a Toltec palace. Drawing by Charnay

His conclusions may be based on false premises, but for the first time the Maya and the Mexica of Central Mexico are seen as a unity, and their joint territories as a super-zone.

Part of an earlier (1863) work by Charnay included a long study by Napleon III's architect, Viollet-le-Duc. Although he never visited Mexico, the latter's contribution would be of some interest if he had not been so unfortunate as to come under the influence of Brasseur de Bourbourg, to whom I have already referred.

Auguste Le Plongeon was in Yucatán in the 1870s. Accompanied by his wife, he dug at Chichen where he discovered the famous 'chac-mool'. His books and theories are the wildest fantasies and quite useless, although in their day thought of as meriting a certain amount of attention (1886, 1895). Like Charnay, he produced fine photographs and maps.

Larrainzar, a lawyer, made a five-volume attempt to compile everything then known about monuments and sites. Though he did not quote the Bible as the Spanish chroniclers had done, he still fills his pages with comparisons with buildings all over the world, thus making himself as insufferable as Burgoa had been two hundred years before. Archaeology for him includes

'. . . the life and thought of the peoples of antiquity, their civil, religious and political institutions, the memory of events and human beings, works of art, habits, customs, private life in its many details; through it [archaeology] we come to a knowledge of the *progress of mankind* since the beginning of the world' (1875, II:VII).

Two volumes and the beginning of a third are given over to describing and analysing Palenque, comparing it with sites in other parts of the world (which oddly, he seems never to have visited). He refers later to many other Mexican ruins including those in the north and west, so that the work becomes a catalogue of what had been published to date.

He completes Volume III with brief descriptions of the entire continent. Volume IV deals with the origins of America, and V is mainly ethnographical. The whole opus serves little purpose today apart from giving us an idea of what was known, and what was being thought about what was known, around the mid-nineteenth century.

During this period Mexican archaeology forms part of the sphere of interest of those engaged in the study of other ancient civilizations such as that of Egypt; it begins to be known and practised in Europe and in the United States, supplementing the great volume of work undertaken by Mexicans. It is, and was to continue to be for very much longer, archaeology of the monumental kind, with exclusively historicist aims and an emphasis on the study of art styles, however little understanding of them might be shown. It is thus cut off from European nineteenth-century developments, as exemplified by the new stance adopted by Worsaae or Boucher de Perthes; the great evolutionist controversy does not affect it. Orozco y Berra, for example, believed in evolution as little as in Lamarck or Darwin (II:280), he pinned his faith on Adam and Eve and, like many another such, admitted only of trans-Pacific contacts, or with Atlantis (II:433–464; 487–488). Although it was becoming increasingly clear that Old World cultural sequences are worthless for Mexico, the absence of interests of this kind meant a failure to make connections with geology and a lack of any notion, however vague, of the existence of cultural periods previous to the construction of the first great cities. Before them, there was only a dark age represented by the finds of fossils of the antediluvian mammals that some associated with giants, but in any event without the accompaniment of man as we understand the term.

Their chronology, however, has no depth and only goes back a couple of thousand years, and that unsupported by stratigraphy of any kind. It attempts, on the basis of incorrect information, to establish an approximate order in which the great cities were founded and developed. Whether the Maya came first, or the Toltecs, or whether it was neither of these, was immaterial – nobody was giving a thought to the world of pre-urbanized man. The Formative is not even guessed at.

The origins of this urban world which the historians describe and whose ruins the travellers journey to see were not a problem. It never occurred to Prescott, for example, to wonder how the transition from rural villages to an urban society had come about. Apparently Humboldt had realized that some sort of explanation was called for, which is why he imported earlier and more highly advanced peoples, which disposed of the need to look for a local cultural development.

Hence perhaps the frequent insistence, from the colonial period onward, on creating fictitious earlier peoples who, whether they had died out or had returned whence they came, left evidence of their achievements and taught the local folk the rudiments of architecture and the other arts. Certainly wall painting was entirely unknown as – in my opinion owing to the lack of serious exploration – no frescoes had yet been found, although a large number are known today.

On the other hand, as Willey and Sabloff have pointed out (1974:43,64), the vast differences between the Mexican remains and the archaeological scene in Europe or the United States could hardly fail to influence the development of their study, and the main fields of interest to which it gave rise. The extraordinary richness of the architectural remains of Mesoamerica, the presence of Indian scripts and, in addition, the powerful general influence of European humanism necessarily directed research to make these remains, so visible and so exceptional, its prime concern. This trend is still active, as it is also I believe in Egyptian and Mesopotamian studies.

Right up to the close of this period archaeology in Mexico was neither scientific nor academic. It was not taught at universities and those few feeble groups that took an interest in it were still in their cradles. Lacking an excavational methodology and a more or less clearly defined objective for the pieces of information acquired, lacking discipline above everything else, it could be no more than a succession of individuals, sometimes outstanding ones, obliged to work in the dark, though they did occasionally stumble upon the truth when they based their speculations upon their archaeological discoveries. But the emphasis was still on the artefacts, not on problem-solving or on finding answers to the questions of history.

But, in spite of the gaps in it, and in spite of its backwardness when compared with developments in Europe at that time, Mexican archaeology did make some progress during this stage. We have seen the keen interest in amassing collections of papers and even objects to make the writing of history possible. Travelling served the same purpose. Antiquities were looked at more critically, as historical documents which could be made to yield descriptive material. Towards the end, photography was being used to make pictorial records more accurate. Efforts that we might call 'functional' were being made to determine the uses to which buildings might have been put, and to slot these into a living total culture. Similarly, there were attempts to formulate developmental sequences in art styles. Almost none of this was, strictly speaking, new but the pace of the work was hotting up, and foundations were being laid which will only carry visible weight in the ensuing stage.

Chapter Six

Museums and the Protection of Antiquities

ALTHOUGH A MUSEUM may be devoted to archaeology wholly or in part, its history may not at first sight seem to have a great deal to do with archaeological investigations in the usual sense of the term. But when we examine the matter more closely we see that there are really very close links between them. The foundation and growth of the Museo in Mexico City reflects many of the ideals and needs of the science evolving around it, which helps to explain how, in ways sometimes peculiar to Mexico itself, its archaeology developed.

The Museo is a place not only where objects are housed and displayed to the public, but where they can be studied. Under certain conditions and in certain cases, these museum studies can be every bit as important as field exploration. It also often happens that museums are a magnet for researchers, and that they thus come to share with universities and institutions the need to make research findings widely available, since not to do so is to make the advance of knowledge practically impossible.

The museum existed as a concept at least as long ago as the famous library at Alexandria which went by the name of Museum and was burned to ashes on one of the darkest days of human history. Over the ages the meaning of the word has changed a good deal, as at the beginning it had meant the dwelling of the Muses, patronesses of the arts and sciences. Even in the eighteenth century Boturini was to go on calling his collection of documents and a few assorted antique objects his 'Museo'.

Before the end of the seventeenth century there was as far as I am aware, not a single Mexican example of a collector of objects that would merit the term archaeological today, and indeed they seem to have been few and far between for a considerable time after that. As I said before, I exclude from this category treasure-hunters after gold and other valuables. But from 1520 on there begin to come to Europe things which are thought of not only as curiosities from foreign parts, but also sometimes as rare objects of great artistic merit. Of course many of these were not in fact old at that time, simply outside the European canon. A famous example is Moctezuma's gift to Cortés; part of what is left of this is now in Vienna and, until less than an century ago, was housed in the Castle of Ambras in the care of a branch of the House of Habsburg. Various notables such as Pedro Mártir and Las Casas have left glowing accounts of the gift. Dürer, one of the finest artists of his time, outstripped them all in enthusiasm when he confided to his diary:

'I have never in all my life seen things that so gladdened my heart as these did. Because amongst them I saw astounding works of art and I marvelled at the subtle skill of the men of those distant lands. The truth is that I cannot say enough about the things that lay there before me' (Thausing, 1888).

Other objects taken to Italy were scrupulously preserved in the royal or papal collections, or even by private individuals. In the rarefied atmosphere of Florence, the first dignitary to take an interest was Giulio de' Medici, later Pope Clement VII. Duke Cosimo I acquired a number of pieces, among them the well-known mask inlaid with turquoise mosaic, now in the Pigorini Museum in Rome. His successors to the dukedom of Florence continued to collect these curiosities.

In France, the last of the Valois kings housed such objects in the Palais des Cabinets as it came to be called. They were part of the *singularités* mentioned by the Franciscan André Thevet, of whom it was said that he was the 'first French Americanist' (Keen, 1971:149). Shortly afterwards, a number of codices reached England, and many objects were presented to various Kuntskammer of Germany by Emperor Ferdinand I. Rudolf II did the same for Prague, and Albert V for Bavaria.

Many examples must have remained in Spain, which explains why the viceroy of Peru, Francisco de Toledo, had the idea of suggesting to Philip II in 1572 that it might be appropriate to found in the Palacio Real a 'museum of curiosities and native Indian crafts' (*Relaciones de Indias-Peru*, I:L). In 1667 one of the attachés at the French embassy in Madrid described the objects preserved in the Palacio del Buen Retiro as follows:

'. . . a treasure-house of all that was most precious ever produced in the Indies. I mean the hangings of cloth made from the bark of trees, the costumes of Moctezuma and of the Incas of Peru, the strangely-wrought cases, the stone mirrors, the bed curtains made of feathers . . . one would have to spend a whole day there to be able to claim to have seen it all closely' (id., note).

I understand that these treasures were destroyed by fire so that, apart from what was housed in the Armería Real, there was little left in Madrid until, towards the end of the eighteenth century, new supplies began to come in, such as the material from Palenque.

Of course these collections made no kind of archaeological sense; they were the results of the wish to amass curiosities considered as works of art. But, thanks to that wish, we can now study them from a different point of view, as they begin to be exhibited in the museums of Europe. The history of some of these objects is highly curious. (See, for example, Heikamp and Anders, 1970 and 1972.)

Generally speaking, they aroused little interest between the end of the sixteenth century and the Age of Reason. London's British Museum was followed by Berlin (where Humboldt placed what he had brought back from his voyages) and elsewhere in a great revival of the collecting spirit. Objects began to be sought after, whether they came directly from Mexico, or from Europeans who later donated, or sold, them to museums.

Objects excavated at the Isla de Sacrificios off the coast of Veracruz went to the British Museum, though some have also found their way to France, where they have been housed in the Musée de Sèvres since 1842 (Reyniers 1966). There are in addition pieces from other sites such as Teotihuacán, and a vessel from Cholula, the gift of Lucas Alamán. In 1844 Evan Nepean excavated again at the Isla de Sacrificios, and donated more finds to the British Museum. Many museums considerably expanded their collections during the nineteenth century. After the Mexican War of 1846–48, Poinsett and Keating presented a large collection of ancient Mexican ceramics to the American Philosophical Society at Philadelphia (Prescott, 1852:143 note). In 1850 the Paris Louvre opened a gallery for the display of American antiquities, mainly from Mexico and Peru. Longperier published a catalogue of them the following year. There were 657 Mexican artefacts, not including 20 displayed elsewhere. The Louvre was, therefore, the first museum in Europe to publish a catalogue of its treasures (Longperier, 1851). There were at least two other collections in Paris, and the British Museum possessed other important pieces, among them those drawn by Aglio (Kingsborough, IV). In 1878 Mexican antiquities formed an important part of the Trocadéro Museum collections in Paris. This list could be extended, but I have said enough to show that these objects were being appreciated, and beginning to be studied, not simply as isolated curiosities but as elements in an integral culture.

In addition individuals in Mexico like, say, Sigüenza or Boturini, whom I have had occasion to refer to earlier in a different context, had been accumulating mainly documents from as early as the seventeenth century, or possibly even before that. The drastically reduced remains of these collections have ended up in museums or libraries in various parts of the world. Among these papers are native codices and a mass of post-Conquest documents which remain of enduring interest to the student of prehispanic Mexico.

The official urge to collect begins in Mexico with natural history, shortly to be followed by antiquities. The first initiatives came in fact from Spain where the number of museums and botanical gardens had been growing since the eighteenth century. At first sight, there is little connection between the two fields, but it is a strange fact that, even today, the antiquities of peoples outside the classical world, China or India, go on being exhibited in museums of natural history as though they had been produced by animals.

In order to distinguish between the histories, sometimes running parallel and sometimes widely divergent, of these three categories of object – natural history, antiquities and documents – which the Museo Mexicano was to collect, I shall begin with natural history, as these were the first to be shown.

It was from 1787 on that Charles III commissioned a group of naturalists to study and make a collection of the plants, animals and minerals of New Spain, in an attempt to complete the famous work of Doctor Francisco Hernández who had gone there in 1570, during the reign of Philip II, and had produced a number of splendid volumes on what he had seen. The commission's plan was to travel around the country, collect as many samples as possible, gather them all together in the Mexican capital and from there ship them off to Spain. For reasons that are not altogether clear the viceroy, the Count de Galvez, had with the royal approval organized a botanical section in Mexico City, with Vicente Cervantes and José Longinos Martínez in charge. Now, Longinos was an outstanding botanist and a first-rate taxidermist but also a thoroughly bad character who had quarrelled with every other member of the expedition, for which reason he decided to operate independently. The fact of the matter is that Longinos, having gone all over the country from Baja California to Guatemala, had accumulated vast numbers of plants and animals as well as a few minerals. On 25 August 1790, the celebrations surrounding Charles IV's accession to the throne included the opening in Mexico City of its first museum, with all the appropriate pomp and ceremony. It was devoted exclusively to natural history and was situated in a house which then belonged to the state at No. 89, Calle de Plateros, now Madero. It did not last long because, during the Wars of Independence, its organization collapsed. Such of the objects as could be preserved, desiccated animals and the minerals, went to premises lent by the University for the purpose.

As the botanical section had come to be so important, a real botanical garden was created in one of the patios of what was then the viceregal palace. Possibly thanks to the influence of Buffon, each plant was tagged with its species and variety, its medicinal or industrial use and its name in Latin, in Spanish and in the Indian language spoken in the part of Mexico where it had been collected.

H. G. Ward, who came to Mexico in 1827, fills out the history of the botanical garden a little. He tells us that, during the Wars of Independence, the viceroy saw himself obliged to house soldiers there for the defence of the palace and for his own protection, and so part of the garden became a barracks. Not long afterwards the vicereine had many of the plants dug out to make room for the cultivation of certain Spanish vegetables of which she was particularly fond. The disasters occasioned by the soldiery and the vicereine notwithstanding, the garden in 1823 still contained nearly three hundred species of plants, many of them unknown to Europe, as we learn from William Bullock, an English traveller who went into raptures about the place. He says:

'this beautiful establishment occupies one of the courts of the viceregal palace; and, though situated in the centre of a large and populous city, every vegetable production seems in perfect health, and vigorous. It affords to the stanger a most delightful retreat from the midday sun, and to the botanist, or admirer of the works of nature, a treat not to be met with elsewhere in New Spain, or perhaps in the world' (1824:123).

Then the traveller goes on to describe the plants and birds to be found there, even giving us a long list of them, all with their Latin names. It was a really valuable institution which was for many years to be the most important part of the Museo Mexicano, far more important than the antiquities or any other department. This seems to have been the first genuine step forward, and it was to retain this lead for a long time.

In Chapter Three I told the story of Boturini and the importance of his collection of documents on ancient Mexico. Subsequently, when the ideas of the Enlightenment had gained a hold, Viceroy Bucareli ordered that all that was left of the Boturini papers be sent to the University library, which had just been redecorated as a sumptuous drawing-room, and of which Boturini himself said that it was the 'store-house of the most exquisite documents of Mexican antiquity, the most appropriate place in which to receive intelligence of it'. Unfortunately, the papers did not stay there, but passed to the viceregal secretariat with the object of having them sent to Europe at the behest of Charles IV. They did get as far as Veracruz, but political events forced their return to the secretariat, which resulted in their dispersal. It has even been said that there was a public sale, at which Humboldt bought a number of documents, now in Berlin. The whole story is highly confused as so many people – too many to name here – had a hand in it. Years later, in 1822, they were taken to the Secretaría de Relaciones Exteriores and then, shortly after the museum was founded, deposited there. Since then the pitiful remnants of this wonderful collection have been stored in the Museo de Antropología.

As regards our main interest, the antiquities, their collection begins, as mentioned in the preceding chapter, with the famous monoliths found during reconstruction work in the Plaza Mayor in 1790. Certainly only one of them, the Coatlicue statue, reached the University, where the first museum was to be established. The Stone of Tizoc, on the other hand, only reached the Museo in 1824 (Ramírez, 1864:52), and the Stone of the Sun not until 1885, when it was dug out of one of the towers of the cathedral, in which it had been embedded.

56
95,96
60

In June 1808 Viceroy Iturrigaray had nominated a Junta de Antigüedades. One of its members, Ciriaco González Carbajal, studied the collections and drew up a list of them to send to Spain. I don't know what became of this list, though it would be highly interesting to see it, but its existence does show that even then the University had at least the germ of a collection (albeit not housed in a museum, nor even in a room set aside for it). For the first time, Clavijero's eloquent voice is heard clamouring for a museum where they could be properly looked after.

The Junta de Antigüedades suspended operations in 1813 and the collections formed by Dupaix during his travels (see pages 93–100, above) were now taken to be complete. Naturally enough, at that time few had energy to spare for these matters, and everything was left in abeyance, or ultimately called off.

Finally, in 1822, Iturbide, as Emperor, ordered that a safe place be established at the University to house both the collections from the old museum in Calle de Plateros, namely the natural history one, and the one comprising prehispanic artefacts. The Junta de Antigüedades was reinstated and, by agreement with José Manuel de Herrera, then Secretario de Ralaciones, charged Ignacio de Cubas with forming a museum and making a report on the Boturini papers. At the end of the same year Sebastian Camacho informed Congress of the founding of the Museo Nacional.

In 1823, however, we find Lucas Alamán issuing further instructions to Cubas to 'collect and put in order the papers and antiquities which previously were in the Secretariat and at the University, and also to trace the whereabouts of some that have been lost, so that they may be stored in a museum' (Castillo Ledón, 1924:9). The intention is there, pressure is building up, but still nothing is done.

At the end of the same year, Alamán himself, with Miguel Bustamante, a botanist, tried unsuccessfully to publish the drawings of the Dupaix expedition, left by Castañeda (see page 98). At the beginning of 1825, says Alamán, the government was still not thinking of founding the museum, and that it must bide its time. Strangely, however, on 18 March of that same year, he obtained from President Guadalupe Victoria a directive addressed to the Rector of the University, which resulted in the museum coming into being, formally and officially. The agreement reads:

'His Excellency the President of the Republic has been pleased to resolve that with the antiquities brought from the Isla de Sacrificios, and others already here in this our capital, a national museum be founded, and that to this end one of the rooms of the University be set aside, the supreme government taking upon itself the responsibility for the cost of shelving, locks, custody of the museum, etc. With this object, His Excellency wishes Your Worship to designate the room to be set aside for this purpose at once useful and an addition to our national glory, and to advise this Ministry accordingly, so that it may commission staff and proceed with their assistance' (Castillo Ledón, 1924:59).

93 Tenochtitlán. The cathedral. The Stone of the Sun is embedded in the base of the nearer tower. After Gualdi

76,77

This was the true Founder's Day of the Museo Nacional.

In all this Alamán was unquestionably the leading and central figure, and he played a major role, not only at this stage but in the succeeding years. In 1822 Bustamante had been premature in calling him 'Father of the Museo Mexicano'. The name it went by was the Museo Nacional Mexicano, and it soon brought out its first by-laws. These dealt in the first instance with what the museum was to house: all kinds of Mexican monuments dating from before, or contemporaneous with, the Spanish invasion; those of ancient peoples of other continents and of the other nations of America; prints, paintings, medals, carvings, inscriptions, etc. serving to illustrate the history of Mexico. It was also to have scientific equipment and models of useful inventions – which gives us another insight into how the museum was regarded at that time – and the fullest possible collections of the three kingdoms of nature, along with her rarest and most curious creations. The museum was to be open to the public only on Tuesdays, Thursdays and Saturdays between the hours of 10 a.m. and 2 p.m., a special permit having first to be obtained, which points to the orderly manner in which it was run.

At that time – and I shall from now on be dealing solely with the archaeological collections – the museum possessed, apart from the Coatlicue statue and the minor pieces studied by León y Gama, the objects from the Isla de Sacrificios, and others donated by various private collectors such as Bustamante, Cubas (who prepared a catalogue) and the Dominican Fathers, as well as half the objects

56,57

94 Objects in the Museo Nacional at the middle of the nineteenth century

95 The Stone of Tizoc from Tenochtitlán. National Museum of Anthropology, Mexico City

collected during the Dupaix expeditions. Father Isidro Ignacio de Icaza was appointed Director.*

More than forty years were to pass before the Museo acquired premises it could call its own, despite the gradual arrival of more pieces, some of them important. Various buildings were allocated but it never succeeded in gaining possession of them. One after the other, decrees were issued, but nothing happened. A succession of Directors wore themselves out pressing for action, but they got nothing done either. The collections remained where they had been from the start, in two wretched rooms at the University, badly housed and neglected. The larger pieces were outside in the patio. This is how many nineteenth-century visitors saw them, and some of them left accounts that were duly critical: Bullock (1824), Ward (1827), an article in the *Sol de México* of 4 November 1827, Beaufoy (1828), Latrobe (1834), Orbigny (1836), Calderón de la Barca (1843), Brantz Mayer (1844) and Mühlenpfordt (1844). A recital of these vicissitudes would not be entirely without interest, but it does not

* Baradère (1834, appendices: 36–40) refers to drawings by W. Franck representing some six hundred objects. I can find no trace either of him or of them. Eighty are from the Philosophical Society of Philadelphia, forty from the collection of the Conde De Peñasco and the rest relate to those in the Museo de Mexico, those still in the possession of the draughtsman Luciano Castañeda, and those of some English residents in Mexico, such as Rich, Exeter and Marshall. These objects are briefly described in a report to the Geographical Society in Paris. Its author distinguishes between three periods and two schools in the developmennt of this culture, Palenque being the oldest and Central Mexico the second oldest.

96 The patio of the Museo Nacional in the nineteenth century. The Stone of Tizoc is set up in the centre. National Museum of Anthropology, Mexico City

belong here. In 1827, Icaza e Isidro Góndra, who was to become its third Director, produced the Museo's only publication to see the light of day between the date of its foundation and 1852. Today it is no more than a bibliographical curiosity.

In 1855 we find Orozco y Berra writing:

'It contains truncated rumps of collections of objects of natural history and antiquities, even if in this latter section there are the most exquisite things, worthy of the highest praise. Among the most important are the several large tablets bearing hieroglyphs belonging to the emigration of the Mexica, manuscripts on maguey paper written in the symbolic writing of the Aztecs, weapons, tools, ritual objects, idols, jewels, ornaments, etc. As the establishment is considered to be no more than a curiosity, and accorded no importance, it goes unremarked in the capital city. In 1854 the Museo had a thorough and scientific overhaul, thanks to the personal efforts and intelligence of its present conservator, Don José Fernando Ramírez' (1855, V:778).

Leaving aside major events such as the war with the United States, the museum opened and closed in response to changes in the political climate at the University. In 1833 Gómez Farías orders it to be closed, Santa Anna reopens it the following year, but it is *in extremis*; Comanfort closes it in 1857, Zuloaga reopens it in 1858; Juárez suppresses it in 1861, but it breathes again in 1863; Maximilian extinguishes it in 1865. All these deaths and reincarnations made progress impossible. But it is just possible that the suppressions of the University may even have favoured the Museo, as in 1857 we have the Rector writing:

'I am advised finally to hand over the [University] buildings and everything they contain to the Director of the Museo in terms so strong that I can no longer defer doing so . . .' (*Plaza*, II:457).

Perhaps as a result of the suppression of the University in 1865 Maximilian himself, who took a considerable interest in Indian antiquities, decreed that the Museo should be an independent body with premises of its own. It was granted the beautiful house in the Calle de Moneda, part of the Palacio Nacional, which it was to occupy until 1964. Article 1 of the Decree reads: 'A public museum of Natural History, Archaeology and History is hereby established in the Palacio Nacional and will come under Our immediate protection' (Castillo Ledón 1924:69). The Museo was founded with the aim of ensuring 'that our country be raised to the stature she deserves'. Six months later it was inaugurated with great pomp, though it would seem that it was far from ready, as even in 1879 they were writing 'it is being put in order' and as late as 1882, 'because of shortage of space and problems of arrangement, the archaeological collections were in store and not on display' (Mendoza y Sánchez, 1882)

In Guatemala meanwhile the Sociedad Económica de Amigos had, back in 1831, been proposing to set up a museum. In the event it was not until 1866 that such a museum was opened, under the directorship of Juan Gavarrete, who had written a report on Santa Lucía Cotzumalhuapa. It did not prove a great success, and closed its doors in 1881. Nor did the Museo Nacional, which opened seventeen years later, appear to have fared much better, as in 1935 the problem of the museum was being considered anew.

The story of the Museo de Mexico after 1880 is part of the general history of Mexican archaeology; up until 1940 it was an increasingly active study centre. Suffice it to say that in 1877 it began the publication of its all-important *Anales*, and that from then on the Museo developed rapidly. Professors were nominated; the collec-

97 Model of the enclosure of the great temple at Tenochtitlán. National Museum of Anthropology, Mexico City

tions catalogued; the whole divided into the three sections stipulated in Article 1 of the Decree: natural history, archaeology and history. In 1909 a separate museum for the natural history department was set up, whereupon the one in the Calle de Moneda came to be called the Museo Nacional de Arqueología, Historia y Etnografía, a name it was to retain till 1939, when in their turn the history collections were hived off to a museum of their own. From then on its importance as a study centre diminished slightly, as at this point the Instituto Nacional de Antropología e Historia was founded, and it came to be called simply the Museo Nacional de Antropología, which name gives the clearest possible picture of its character and contents, as it is concerned with every branch of anthropology. On 17 September 1964 President López Mateos inaugurated its new and splendid premises, which renewed its importance and enormously extended its influence. The galleries devoted to archaeology are the best known and the most visited, and at the time of writing a total reorganization of all its material is about to be completed, particularly of the study collections, which are open to many researchers.

Meanwhile a number of provincial museums, devoting themselves wholly or in part to archaeology, had been formed. These included the Yucatán museum in the city of Mérida, founded in 1870 by the bishop-historian Crescencio Carillo y Ancona, the Morelia museum, founded by Nicolas León in 1886 and which two years later began to publish a series of *Anales* which are still continuing, and the museum at Oaxaca, which came into being in 1903. The Institutes of Anthropology of Guatemala and of Honduras were founded in 1946 and 1952 respectively.

With the coming of Independence officialdom began to see the urgent necessity of conserving and in some way protecting the ruins and monuments. But it took a long time to realize this aim. Larrainzar writes (1875, I:140):

'Our governments were content, belatedly and with reluctance, and almost by accident, to include in certain of the legal dispositions laid down with some other objective in mind, the prohibition on pain of confiscation of the export of monuments and Mexican antiquities . . .'

Apart from many other government decrees which were never enforced, the Sociedad de Geografía y Estadística proposed on 24 September 1859 that the government should claim as State property the archaeological monuments of Mexico. In 1862 the Sociedad presented another plan, the legal aspects of which are based on the old Leyes de Indias where State property is concerned.

Following the same precedent, the law of 11 May 1897 declares all archaeological monuments to be State property, thus exempting them from the scope of trade, a state of affairs which had in theory been in force since 1575. To keep the ruins under surveillance, an Inspector y Conservador de Monumentos Arqueológicos de la República was appointed in October, 1875.

Owing possibly to the success of Stephens, the Government of Honduras in 1845 passed its first declaration of intent to protect Copán, and in 1874 the boundaries of the archaeological zone were

delineated. By a decree of 1889 an antiquarian society was set up to preserve the beautiful old city and it was intended to establish a museum there. Nothing has, however, actually been done to date. There have been a number of more recently passed laws for the protection of monuments and objects, and prohibiting their export without official permission. The same happened in Guatemala as long ago as 1893, though a new protective law was passed in 1945. All this indicates a very long-standing concern to protect the antiquities of both countries, but until recent times the laws remained a virtual dead letter. Much the same could be said of Mexico.

98 Head of Coyolxauhqui, the Moon Goddess. National Museum of Anthropology, Mexico City

141

Chapter Seven

Positivism (1880–1910)

DURING THE THREE decades which this chapter covers many fundamental changes took place in Mexican archaeology, though most contributions to it continued to come from research in libraries, while fieldwork, although more of it was done than formerly, remained of minor importance. Prior to this published archaeological studies had been few and far between, and almost without exception were the work of Mexicans such as the explorers of Palenque, men like Dupaix, Alzate, León y Gama, Ramírez, to name but a few. Contributions of another kind came from the great travellers, led by Stephens, or from those who, like Prescott, Orozco y Berra, Bancroft, were more historians than archaeologists. These distinctions will blur a little during the period I am now about to deal with, the regrettable divorce between archaeology and history being still in the future. On the whole, we are about to see a reaction against grand theories based on flimsy evidence, and their replacement by a more modest hypothesis having its roots struck firmly in proven fact.

The above-named authors tended to overpraise Indian civilization; the Morgan school on the other hand considered the American cultures barbaric, an idea which is a legacy from the anti-indigenists of the Age of Reason. Around 1880 heated argument broke out between them and the holders of the contrary view, so brilliantly set out by Prescott. Although his thinking slightly pre-dates the years now under review, the ideas formulated by Morgan did not reach Mexico until later, which is why it seems appropriate to deal with them here.

As from the 1840s there began in the United States, under the principal leadership of Lewis Cass and Albert Gallatin, a revisionist and anti-Romantic movement stemming from Robertson's important *History of America* (1777), and holding the Indians incapable of ever having reached a high cultural level. Its tenets are racist, anti-Prescott and, later, anti-Bancroft, and those who shared these views wished to apply to Mesoamerica the conclusions they had come to as a result of their work on the North American Indians. Among their number were some whose work was valuable in their own particular field, but one at least – Robert A. Wilson – was an ignorant fanatic (1859). Lewis H. Morgan was to be the leading figure. A lawyer from Rochester, N.Y., Morgan began in the 1840s a major study of the social organization of the Iroquois, publishing his first important book in 1850, though the best known of his books,

Ancient Society, did not appear until 1877. The body of his work shows a profound knowledge of those North American tribes and a conceptualization of the cultural stages through which mankind had passed; this idea was to have very wide repercussions indeed, as it seized powerfully upon the mind of Marx.

So far as we are concerned here, the school's main error lay in believing that Mesoamerica had remained at almost the same cultural level as the Iroquois and others like them. In 1857 Morgan began, less happily, to concern himself with the Aztecs. Moctezuma and his Empire were the principal victims. In the eyes of Morgan and his disciples Moctezuma was a

14,31

'petty Indian chief and the great city of Mexico a collection of hovels in an everglade, the ruins of the country being accounted for by supposing them the relics of an ancient Phoenician civilization, which had been stamped out by the inroads of barbarians, whose equally barbarous descendants, the Spaniards were in turn to overcome . . .' (Winsor, 1887, I:174).

'. . . the fabric of Aztec romance is the most deadly encumbrance upon American Ethnology' wrote Morgan (1876:225). All the pomp and imperial trappings, according to him, were Spanish inventions which had come back into fashion thanks to the marvellous style and firm story-line shown in the work of Prescott. This line of reasoning is clearly a regression to the ideas of Pauw; it is also, of course, ethnological in essence, which is why I am content to treat it so summarily.

But Morgan had one follower who was interested in archaeology, if only in order to prove the theories of his master; this was Adolf Bandelier, who came to Mexico first in 1881. To begin with, Bandelier's ideas were somewhat different from Morgan's, but the latter's influence gradually led him, first to change his mind, and finally to capitulate entirely and align himself squarely alongside his mentor. Though the ideas he drew from that source may have been mistaken, his archaeological facts were not. In fact, in his most important book (1884), which tells of his voyage to Mexico and discusses the sites he visited, he gives frankly archaeological and factual information without much in the way of generalized hypothesizing, which puts him among those who after 1880 are going to change theory for knowledge. But his preconceptions set him apart from many of the more scientific authors of his day; although many did not accept his influence, it was nevertheless very long-lasting, persisting down into important and very much more recent studies such those produced by Vaillant.

Amongst Mexicans the battle lines of the argument were drawn, not so much according to the social and political organization of the Mexica, but rather according to whether one's thinking emphasized the horrors or the benefits of the Spanish Conquest, seen in the longest term. An obvious example of such an approach is Alfredo Chavero (1841–1906), mediocre man of letters whose first archaeological work was on the Aztec calendar and appeared in 1875. More than a decade later he produced his *Historia Antigua y de la Conquista* (1887), which clearly owed its inspiration to Orozco y

Berra whom he took as his mentor, though he remained his inferior. In this period, his book is the only ancient history in the tradition begun by Clavijero. It was enormously successful in spite of all the faults we can now detect in it. It did not entirely lack a political angle, given that in general terms the liberals were indigenists and the conservatives hispanists. Thus, Chavero, a liberal, was by definition opposed to the ideas of Morgan and Bandelier. He does not seem to have got on particularly well with the latter, as opposed to his relations with García Icazbalceta, a conservative.

An ethnologist who likewise could not accept the Morgan position was the Englishman, Sir Edward Tylor, whose *Anáhuac* came out in 1861. Archaeologically speaking, Tylor was *the* diffusionist of his time, with ideas that oddly foreshadow those of Wittfogel, author of *Oriental Despotism*. On his visit to Mexico he inspected ancient monuments and commented enthusiastically on sites such as Teotihuacán. Some passages of his remind one of the wonder felt by Stephens (1861:142–47). Other authors, not all of them English, reject Morgan's theories, but strangely enough no one in the United States with the sole exception of Baldwin (1872) took this line until 1920, when Paul Radin attacked the position adopted by Bandelier. Three years later Alfred Kroeber, in his classic text, also discarded Morgan's ideas.

It was no accident but because the time was ripe, that as from 1880 there appeared on the scene in quick succession the five most important researchers of their time, men who were to put their stamp upon Mexican archaeology for many a year to come. Their findings, taken together, go to prove that only after the minutest study of all the evidence can one hope to arrive at accurate conclusions without getting lost in the maze of earlier fantasizing. This is where archaeological science begins. One might apply to these scholars Alfonso Caso's words in praise of Seler (1949:26):

'This comparative method, minutely detailed and full, which consists in breaking down a problem into its smallest constituent parts before attempting a solution, is what essentially characterizes Seler's attitude, when it comes down to a question in archaeology'.

The important studies which began in 1880 and continued to appear till 1910 are very varied, but what holds them together, apart from their more strictly archaeological tone, is what we might call their scientific positivism, a realism that rejects general theorizing. Archaeology means essentially the study of objects. They abandon old barren arguments about Indian superiority or inferiority, whether the roots of their culture lay within the American continent or outside it, and others involving passing judgment on the Spanish Conquest and subsequent colonization. What was needed was understanding without pre-judgment, not a vain discussion of this theory or that, but the study of hard facts. This new style did not prevent a few from going on wasting paper and ink on the leavings of the old ideas; obviously the changed way of looking at the subject did not come about overnight, but made itself felt only very gradually. The new overtakes the old, which is not to say that the old has disappeared and been replaced. But these men tried, with the

99 Charnay in the jungle. A
typical rendering of the period

limited means at their disposal, to give fresh impetus to archaeology,
and with it ancient history and ethnology. They did not do much by
way of archaeological fieldwork, and for it they used techniques that
had not advaneed very far; but what little they did do, added to their
documentary research, made the outlook for genuine understanding
look brighter.

Largely because of their differing origins, the leading researchers
at that time were either professional men or, like Alfred Maudslay,
independents of a very English kind. They were also very variously
trained: Troncoso, in medicine, Förstemann in linguistics; Seler in
natural science and philology; Holmes in geography. Only later
were they to focus their interests on ancient history. But all were to
contribute masterly work.

A theme of fundamental importance which is still being enthusiastically studied is the deciphering of the Maya script. Although the

100 Maudslay at work in a
Maya palace

stelae with hieroglyphic inscriptions had been known and identified
as writing since the Conquest, little progress had been made with
deciphering them. During this time the documents and what we
now call the Maya codices were, with the exception of the Dresden,
unknown until the nineteenth century. I have already mentioned
how Brasseur and others rescued a few of them from the discard pile,
and have described the meeting at Peto between Juan Pío Pérez and
Stephens (see page 122). A few glyphs, including the one for month,
were identified by León de Rosny.

But the great genius in the study of the codices was, without any
doubt, the librarian of the Royal Public Library at Dresden, Ernst
Förstemann. Förstemann did not become interested in the Maya
script till he was fifty-eight but, like Seler, he was fortunate enough
to live to a ripe old age, and in the twenty-six years that still
remained to him he succeeded in making remarkable strides in the
decipherment of the glyphs. As Eric Thompson wrote: 'In 14 years
this brilliant man had wrested the secret of the Maya calendar from
codex and stela; he stands shoulders above any other student of Maya
hieroglyphs' (1950:30). Although to begin with he concentrated on
the famous document in the library where he worked – hence called
the Dresden Codex – he later extended the range of his activities to
include the other codices as well as the stelae, and succeeded in

27

cracking the calendrical code. He deciphered many of the basic concepts for the first time, among them the initial series which begins with 4 ahau 8 cumku, the first date of the Long Count. For his work on the Dresden Codex Förstemann used the original, which he published in 1880, at the beginning of his brilliant career in this field. The fascinating story of the discovery of the meaning of the Maya script, calendar and mathematics has been told a number of times by specialists in this area (see for example Morley 1940 or Thompson 1950). The theme is such a vast one that there is no room to do more than touch on it here.

101 Maudslay with his wife and students

But the interpretation of the stone inscriptions could only be embarked on thanks to the work of another great scholar, Alfred Percival Maudslay (1850–1931) (whose illustrious name, incredibly, does not appear in the *Encyclopaedia Britannica*). Educated at Cambridge, it was not until 1881 that he paid his first visit to Guatemala, fired by a reading of Stephens. He kept up his visits until 1894, and the scientific result was the eight splendid volumes published by Goodman in the *Biología Centrali-Americana*. He had then no equal where the beautiful precision of his plates, the acccuracy of his plans, his detailed architectural observations, and his careful drawings of the hieroglyphic inscriptions (Tozzer, 1933:64) are concerned. He always worked independently, and though he had a brilliant mind he was without any trace of vanity.* Without his work much of the

* That this was so is exemplified by an incident related by Charnay (1883:379). When he learned that the 'tall fair young man' had reached Yaxchilán (which Maudslay called 'Menché' but he 'Château Lotillard') before him, Charnay was put out. Maudslay, however, set no store by being the first at a newly-found site; he was far more interested in exploring ruins than in discovering them.

progress made would have been impossible, work which has been, and goes on being, useful to many generations of Maya scholars in the field of the decipherment of that people's calendar and script, a theme begun by Landa centuries before.

As an appendix to Maudslay's great work an important article by J. T. Goodman appeared in 1897. Although written in a self-satisfied manner that Maudslay would surely never have approved, it does give an account of major discoveries such as that of the identification of the variations in the heads on the numerals. This body of work left the way open for the decipherment of the calendar itself, in both the codices and on the stone stelae.

It was then still necessary to correlate these dates with the European calendar for them to be of any use and to enable the two chronologies to be synchronized. The method discovered by Good-man, with a few subsequent minor modifications by Eric Thompson, is still the one in most common use. I shall revert to these matters in the next chapter when considering the advances made in this field after 1910.

The fame of the Maya ruins then attracted a good number of other explorers who were no longer the curious travellers of earlier times, but nearer to professional archaeologists. For example, Gordon (1898:12), on finding a mound in the Valley of Ulúa that had been built on, deduced that it was two separate constructions, i.e. from two different periods. This can be contrasted with the fantastic theories of Batres:

'They were built in the way common to all ancient peoples: they built a small base of the same shape and having the same number of units as the one they wished the finished construct to have; the first served as the nucleus of the second and larger, still others were placed on top afterwards, leaving a space between them of 80/90 cms until the desired height was reached' (1902:11).

Investigators in the Maya zone began at this time to sense the importance of material found *in situ* and the need to understand, not only what it is in itself, but the relationship it bears to the rest of its environment. However inadequate this fieldwork may appear to us, it is better than what was then being carried out in Central Mexico. Although most of it was the work of individuals, some was beginning to be done by teams attached to institutions. The best known was that of the Peabody Museum of Harvard University which began its archaeological series in 1888. Teobert Maler pub-lished almost all his fine work there, including his wealth of splendid photographs. The Peabody was also then beginning, with Gordon and Saville, the first large-scale Mesoamerican excavations, at Copán. In the preceding period Bastian (1876) and Habel (1878) had studied the important sculptures of Santa Lucía Cotzumalhuapan in Guatemala, now in the custody of the Dahlem Museum, Berlin.

Among workers in the central area the figure of Francisco del Paso stands head and shoulders above the other Mexican archaeologists of his time. His area of fieldwork was unfortunately very restricted as he confined his operations to the neighbourhood of Cempoala. They suffered in addition from regrettable weaknesses, both technical and theoretical, scarcely imaginable when compared with his magnificent work in other fields. The first of his works to show the vigour of his mind came out in 1883, the *Ensayo sobre los signos cronográficos de los mexicanos* [Essay on the chronographic signs of the Mexicans]. Heir to the noble tradition of Ramírez and Orozco y Berra, he produced relevant studies of the highest importance, such as his interpretation of the Codex Borbonicus (1899). He published, among many other things, the manuscripts of Sahagún, along with the codices that illustrate them, and the two series of *Papeles y Epistolario de la Nueva España* [Papers and letters from New Spain]. Despite all his fine talent and wide learning, he lacked the ability to organize, so that much of his work was left in truncated form and finished by other scholars after his death in 1916.

William Holmes, then curator of the Field Columbian Museum in Chicago, was much more of a field archaeologist. He visited Mexico in 1895 and made a fairly rapid circuit of the country, which was nevertheless to result in a book still useful today, with very accurate drawings of the Maya ruins, those at Teotihuacán and Oaxaca, and of a number of sculptures of varying provenance including Veracruz. Despite his underlying loyalty to the theories of Morgan, Holmes was quite exceptionally enthusiastic about ancient Indian art. His description of Monte Albán (1897:214–221) deserves to be read; it could have come from the pen of Stephens on seeing Copán. He has a clear idea of the importance of architectural studies in archaeology for the understanding of a culture. Other works of his deal with various aspects of archaeology, including the Tuxtla statuette, one of 102 the first publications on an object attributed to the Olmecs, they being then unknown. Though Holmes did no fieldwork, his wonderful drawings and panoramas, and his accurate discussion of architecture, ceramics and other objects make him essential reading even today. He belongs to the tradition that particularly admires Maya art, but he is also alive to the beauty of the Mexica (1897:301 *et seq.*). Like the other major figures of his time, he formulates no theories but sticks closely to the facts. He often makes us wish that he had taken us a little more into his confidence about what he is thinking, rather than tying us up in long flat descriptions of ruins and objects; he makes no attempt either at historical perspective or at chronological sequence.

Before dealing with the fifth great researcher of those years there are one or two others who deserve a mention. Between 1885 and 1910 Leopold Batres carried out a considerable number of explorations and even reconstructions of monuments, at Teotihuacán and Mitla in particular. He found important caches of offerings at the Escalerillas in Mexico City, better described by Tweedie (1901:210–13) than by Batres himself, he being self-taught and doing his explorations without the benefit of any technical skill and without making a serious study of the subject. We get more useful information from Charnay's modest digs at Teotihuacán than from all Batres did in the huge city. But for all that he deserves to go on record as a real Central Mexican pioneer, and it was thanks to him that the Mexican government found funds for the excavation and restoration of ancient monuments; not since the last days of the

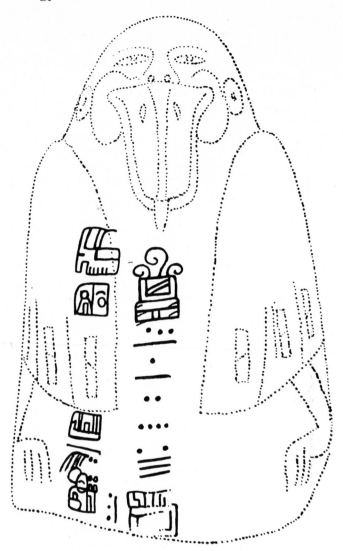

102 The Tuxtla statuette, with hieroglyphs. After Holmes. Actual height 15 cm

Bourbons in connection with Palenque and the expeditions of Dupaix had anything comparable happened. So it is to the enthusiasm of Batres that we largely owe the present practice of re-forging traditional links with the past through the study of Mexican ruins.

In the course of the years we are now considering, Marshall Howard Saville, 'an extremely good-looking man' (Tweedie 1901:380–400) examined sites in the Valley of Oaxaca, prepared important bibliographies for a number of others, such as Uxmal or Copán, and interested himself in objects of various kinds, in metals, turquoise or stone, even in wood. Hermann Strebel was working in Veracruz, William Niven in Guerrero, while Carl Lumholtz was covering the west coast. But this is by no means all who were engaged in such work, and the resulting publications were increasing; those I have mentioned are simply a few examples to give an idea of how much attention each area was receiving. The infrastructure was now being created, even if it was still a little shaky, which would lead to an understanding of Mesoamerica, not only ethnographically during the final phase of the indigenous cultures, but archaeologically, so that its concepts could be projected back into the remote past.

With the information already available it was possible for the concept of Mesoamerica, only awaiting clarification, to be extended and built upon by the most versatile researcher of the late nineteenth and the early twentieth century: Eduard Seler. His principal aim was to show Mesoamerica's essential unity, which is why he worked in many areas and in many branches of both archaeology and ethnography. Although he travelled widely throughout Mexico, gathering data and objects, he did almost no excavating and the vast bulk of his work was done at home in Germany. He has bequeathed to us masterly commentaries to codices such as the Tonalamatl of Aubin, the Borgia, the Vatican B and the Fejérváry Mayer, perfectly reproduced thanks to funds provided by that eminent Maecenas, the Duc de Loubat. Seler went deeply into the Indian calendar and religion, not in broad outline but in the minutest detail. His impressive monograph on Teotihuacán (1915) shows that he was aware of the importance of even the tiniest particular. Of course he belongs to the years before stratigraphy, which means that he could give us no real chronology, nor be aware of the various peoples who might have occupied the same site in succeeding periods. His instinct for methodical, meticulous analysis meant that this Berlin professor's work was to be the basis for many subsequent studies.

103 Eduard Seler (1849–1922)

His dislike of unfounded generalization led Seler to adopt a highly pragmatic and empirical stance – a much-needed corrective, as I have said, to the many baseless theories then current. This is evident from his first Americanist publication, a translated arrangement of Nadaillac (1883), then a basic text. Seler believed that parts of that book were insufficiently anchored to sound research; he preferred not to translate these sections, substituting for them studies of his own.

In his work on the codices, his greatest mistake was probably to lay too much emphasis on their religious meaning. That is to say, he did not see that many of them contain historical material of a nature which makes them much more interesting to us. Zelia Nuttall was already studying them from this angle, and was in 1902 to publish the codex that bears her name. This event is not only notable for the quality of the document itself, but because the commentator has succeeded in reconstructing various of the biographies, showing that the document is less religious than historical. The difference is vital: the ritual or mythological codices were being read by Paso y Troncoso, Seler and others, while the historical ones were not yet understood. Yet despite all the progress Nuttall made she was unable to ascribe a single date in the European calendar, and thought that the document was Aztec. Ten years later J. Cooper-Clark published in England a very important study based on ideas not unlike Nuttall's, but with an attempt at dating. These dates, in the light of

104 Monte Albán. Stone of
8 Venado. Height 1.65 cm.
Venado was a great conqueror
of Mixtec origin. National
Museum of Anthropology,
Mexico City

later events, turned out to be incorrect, but they did represent an
attempt at a chronology. Cooper-Clark believed the stories to refer
to Zapotec lords since the principal figure, 8 Deer-Tiger's claw, is
found on a carving from Monte Albán. As we shall see in the next
chapter, thirty years would have to elapse before these subjects were
better understood.

But to Nuttall, the first woman to make an important contribution to this field of study, falls the honour of having been the
pioneer, even if she did have a number of ideas that have not stood
the test of time.

That these documents were, despite their importance, very little
known, is clearly shown in the memoirs of an interesting student of
the Maya codices, Paul Schellhas, a Berlin judge by profession. He
tells how, in 1885 'I was surprised and fascinated to see that in the
New World a hieroglyphic writing system existed, quite unknown

105 Mexican building designed for the 1892 Exhibition in Madrid

to me and scarcely more known to archaeologists and ethnologists in Germany, France and in America' (1936:129). In the course of his researches Schellhas identified the Maya gods in the codices, and designated them by letters of the alphabet (1897).

To return to Seler, the sheer magnitude of his oeuvre enables him to devote the main part of it to objects and sites, other parts to the commentaries on the codices or stone inscriptions. But Seler was not alone in his day in taking up this particular work; we owe a great number of studies to other writers of the period, as can be seen in Bernal (1962:143–168), whose list, although most certainly not exhaustive, is none the less impressive. This was a highly productive period, during which also a great deal of pictographic material was published – a side-effect of the work of Seler, Troncoso and of innumerable others such as Peñafiel, who apart from the Codex Fernández Leal and the Zacatepec produced three enormous folio volumes *Monumentos de Arte Antiguo Mexicano* in 1890.

Peñafiel also attempted to bring order out of the chaos of the huge collections of the Museo Nacional, researching at the same time into the origins and provenance of those many objects for which documentation was lacking. In pursuit of this objective he worked at many sites; wherever there were similarities between his finds and objects in the Museo he attributed origins. The method is a sound one so far as it goes but Peñafiel never went on from there to differentiate the periods by style. What is more, he held – in direct opposition to Seler – that the Maya and Mexica cultures were completely independent of one another. He even went so far as to say that the Mexica civilization bears no resemblance whatever to the Maya and is, indeed, as far from it as is Egyptian civilization. Years later Morley, one of the most brilliant researchers of our century, was still thinking along similar lines.

Many other codices were published by the Junta Colombiana, formed on the occasion of a major exhibition held in Madrid to celebrate the fourth centenary of the discovery of America. This Columbian Exhibition in Madrid, and others such as that held the same year in Chicago, and the Paris one of 1889 for which Peñafiel planned a building 'in the purest Aztec style' (which would probably have horrifed Moctezuma), had at least one section devoted to American antiquities, which goes to prove the wider popular appeal they were beginning to have. Mexico lent Madrid an enormous quantity of original pieces, as well as a number of copies and models (Paso y Troncoso, 1897).

The great majority of the studies we have mentioned were individual productions, but some of them show the beginnings of a new way of treating archaeology; namely, by enlisting the help of scientific bodies that produced reviews or publications in series, devoted more and more exclusively to the anthropological aspect. With the notable exception of the *Boletin de la Sociedad Mexicana de Geografía y Estadística*, which sometimes carried articles on archaeological subjects, it is not until around 1880 that Mexico sees the foundation of the other journals or annals of a more or less permanent nature and given over to the studies that concern us. The most important of these was certainly the *Anales del Museo Nacional* of which I have already spoken and which, after many years and some changes, still appears today as the *Anales del Instituto Nacional de Antropología e Historia*. Granted that its somewhat random pages contain a fair amount of chaff, much space is nevertheless given over to an endless stream of old documents and a constant flow of modern work, both original and translated, which compel us to think of these *Anales*, now celebrating their hundredth birthday, as one of Mexico's true glories. Towards the end of the century, too, the Sociedad Antonio Alzate, which later became the Academia Nacional de Ciencias, began publication.

The *American Anthropologist*, which first came out in the United States in 1888, and is still being published, has devoted many a page to Mexican archaeology. Also in that year the Peabody Museum of Harvard University began its archaeological series, in which some of the most important work of this time was recorded.

Important too are the publications – alas, since discontinued where our field is concerned – of the Field Columbian Museum of Chicago and, above all, those of the still extremely active Smithsonian Institution in Washington; the first report of its Bureau of American Ethnology came out in 1881. It carried at that time important work by Holmes, Cyrus Thomas and others. The series of *Bulletins* followed later. These, along with other, younger publications, are discussed below (page 187).

The Archaeological Institute of America with its American series also deserves a mention (it published Bandelier's *Archaeological Tour*), as does the Museum of the University of Pennsylvania which, from 1904, has been interested in the Mesoamerican field and has continued to be one of the major North American institutions to take up Mexican archaeology.

Many European publications came into the picture around this time, such as the *Zeitschrift für Ethnologie und Urgeschichte* and the *Journal of the Royal Anthropological Institute of Great Britain and Ireland*, begun in 1869 and 1870 respectively, but which contain only occasional contributions to our field.

The old Société Américaine de France was the initial organizer of the international Congresses of Americanists, the first of which took place on 30 September 1875 in the old palace of the Dukes of Lorraine, at Nancy, and which have steadily gained in importance since. Perhaps better than anything else could do, the papers read there at the time give us an idea of the contemporary approach to archaeology: those on the origins of American culture still hark back to the Phoenicians, Buddhism, Fu-Sang, Atlantis and such fancies. How differently this central subject was handled at another congress seventy-five years later is clearly to be seen in the papers concerned with the connections between America and the Pacific read in New York before the XXIX Congress of Americanists in 1949. The only one referring to Mexico (which did not send a representative to the first Congress) is a study of León de Rosny's on the Maya numerals. In 1891 the Congress met in America for the first time (Mexico 1897).

Another invaluable contribution by the French Americanists was the *Journal de la Société des Américanistes* founded in 1895 and still going strong. An extraordinary wealth of first-class work is contained in its pages. Hamy, Diguet, de Jonghe, W. Lehmann and Seler were among its contributors during the period under review. All this is an indication of the beginnings of the professionalization of archaeology which was, from now on, to make it possible for trained personnel to count on educational centres, institutes and all the other support mechanisms of science.

But it is not so easy a matter to arrive at a decision about just what researchers in this century thought about their own work. With a few rare exceptions, field excavators were hardly more than glorified antiquaries; they were not interested in objects for their commercial value nor, on the other hand, seeking to fill museum show-cases or mount public displays of them, but to find support for their own theories. Thus, for example, Paso y Troncoso's explorations on his second trip to Veracruz, and the work done by Gerste, Villado and Río de la Loza at Casas Grandes, in the Huasteca area and at Comalcalco respectively, were undertaken with the object of getting together a collection of material for the Madrid exhibition of 1892 and, as they put it, 'to prove the unquestionable importance of the American Egypt'. There can be no question of the praiseworthiness of the motive, but it was scarcely scientific. Other digs, such as those led by Edward Thompson at Chichen Itzá, were the work of amateurs.

Even where excavation technology remained so primitive, the use to which the finds were finally put was not always secondary. For example, in two books very closely linked with artefacts, *Die Ausgrabungen am Orte des Haupttempels in Mexico* (1901) and *Die Teotihuacán Kultur des Hochlandes von Mexiko*, Seler achieves a true interpretation of the culture, essentially on the basis of archaeological objects, helped along by documentary evidence.

Such men were none the less genuine functionalist archaeologists, however crude their methodology and, in this respect at least, they had a better idea of where they were going than some of us today, so great is our danger of losing our historical and cultural perspective in the clash of contending typologies.

It is only in the latter years of this period that a vague notion of stratigraphy begins to emerge, even though the germ of the idea behind it can be traced back here and there to the middle of the nineteenth century. Monuments and objects that could be called 'interesting' were the only ones sought after. But perhaps this is rather too much of a generalization: there is a great gulf fixed between the immense pains taken by a Maudslay when he copies down or takes an impression of a Maya stela and the amazing carelessness of a Batres slicing into the Pyramid of the Sun at Teotihuacán, or of a Saville destroying the splendid façade of a Zapotec tomb in order to cart away the urns that ornamented it.

29

Perhaps the best commentary on this period, and a piece of advice still sound today, appears in an article by Walter Lehmann (1907). Translated, it reads:

'Despite this wide range of sources of data, despite the enormous mass of documents already collected, we find so little diminution in the degree of error, so much uncertainty, so many prejudices, that we must take warning from all this to be cautious and modest in our assertions. We cannot repeat often enough that the study of prehistoric and historic Mexico is still in swaddling bands and that, before going any further with it, we have first to unlearn a number of built-in fallacies, and to realize that what is left is totally inadequate to provide us with anything resembling a coherent picture of how things were in ancient Mexico. This will remain a dream until we have carried out systematic excavations throughout the country. The whole of it is a rich archaeological site. In days gone by archaeologists thought it sufficient to collect potsherds and clay figurines without concerning themselves in the very least with their exact provenance. Only much later did travellers begin to take careful note of exactly where each find had come from, which made it possible for us to classify them according to locality. Seler, for example, in the course of his many long journeys, defined a number of clearly distinguished local types which are not without importance for the tracing out of trade routes' (1909:2–3).

If Lehmann's article gives a fair idea of the state of research in 1910, it is interesting to observe how many of his observations, certainly fresh and brilliant in their day, seem out of date now. To take only one example: in the passage quoted, he points to two stages in the collection of materials; one that we might call 'national', in which the word Mexico is enough, and one we might call 'regional', in which the name of the region or people suffices. But he does not even mention a third, to which we could give the name 'stratigraphic'; in that event we would want to be told not only the site where the object was found but also its precise locality and what others, if any, were found along with it.

The way Lehmann divides his book up is in itself interesting; for all the archaeological material he selects for study fits perfectly into a few paragraphs in his ethnographical section, and everything is taken to be more or less contemporary with everything else. In fact, to treat this material historically would have been quite impossible at that time, which is why it is all aggregated in this fashion, or divided at best into the two great periods then known, the Toltec and the

Aztec. But it is, on the other hand, genuinely functionalist and how he handles material objects shows that he had a sound idea of cultural interpretation. As in every German, particularly one of his day, the geographer shows through (1909:2).

Lehmann's slight work, advanced though it is, was not however the earliest of its kind to be written in this style. The honour of having provided the first compendium of known information concerning America belongs to John Baldwin (1872). His archaeological data, necessarily limited, are taken from authors ranging from Humboldt to Charnay, with Stephens's contributions in the lead. He is only interested in cities, one might say only in architecture, and with the exception of the occasional mention of Mexica monoliths, codices and documents, no other objects are mentioned and he only discusses a few sites. He makes a considerable effort – which does not, alas, meet with success – to establish a chronology of the ruins based mainly on Brasseur. In the historical section of the book, still following in the abbé's footsteps while trying to prune away the grossest of his errors, he does not achieve a great deal; ethnographically speaking, he is violently opposed to Morgan and his school; in him what Morley was to call 'the Maya empires old and new' can be seen in preliminary outline. He ridicules suggestions of Phoenician origins and similar roots, and thinks that the story began in America, though possibly in the southern continent, and that it has close connections with the Mound Builders who were so very much in fashion just then. The importance of Baldwin is that in spite of all his many errors he does manage to introduce into his work a note of sobriety and cool reason.

As Pollock has noted (1940:187) both Baldwin and Short (1880) 'contributed excellent ideas in pointing out unknown areas, different periods at the same site, and the position of architecture in the reconstruction of history'.

In 1883 they were to be followed by Nadaillac, who also attempted a recapitulation of existing knowledge in *l'Amérique Préhistorique*. It is a very different piece of work from Baldwin's and an even clearer pointer to other similar productions to appear shortly after 1910. His central position reflects the caution that was the keynote of his time:

'I know of nothing so fatal to genuine science as that wild theorizing, the guesses lauded by the crowd only to be proved false the following day by the facts: "When one knows as little as we do", Mr Virchow has said recently, "one cannot let one's theories stray too far afield" ' (1883:VII).

Nadaillac devotes much of his work to descriptions of archaeological sites and occasionally takes time off to admire their beauty. But he remains a believer in remote influences.

A book by another Frenchman, Lucien Biart, which came out shortly afterwards (1885) is candidly ethnological, and its author himself describes it as a kind of resumé of Orozco y Berra. Of neat archaeology there is no sign. But if, as Cyrus Thomas thinks, 'Archaeology in its widest sense and by derivation includes the investigation of the origin, language, beliefs, customs, arts, everything, in a word, that can be learned of the ancient life of a people' (1903:1), then Biart's book is a part of that group of handbooks which in one form or another was expanding steadily at this time.

Cyrus Thomas, however, from whose second edition I have taken the observation cited above, falls squarely into the archaeological camp, and I believe his book reflects accurately the 'establishment' thinking of his day. When they reorganize the data, these writers are not trying to introduce new ideas – even should they have them – but to give wider circulation to what is already known.

Although it actually appeared in 1912, Beuchat's *Manuel d'archéologie Américaine* gives a good picture of the period. It tackles the whole continent and is full of articles on subjects which today would hardly find a place in a manual of archaeology, such as a history of the discovery of America and a long 'life' of Columbus. In the 250 pages it devotes to Mesoamerica we find an ordered layout of historical and archaeological information; precise, shorn of the fantastical, and in candid reaction to the overblown style of Brasseur. It has an extensive and well-chosen bibliography, even if this is almost devoid of archaeological titles. The book is of little use today, not so much because of the factual errors it contains, but because it is still without a chronology of any kind.

Although Beuchat is already thinking in the down-to-earth manner that was now widely adopted, the book's ethnography is still in the style of Bandelier, following the Robertson-Morgan trail. It still adheres to the tradition, a little out of date by this time, of concentrating exclusively on Maya and Aztecs while practically ignoring all the rest of Mexico. This is a residue, I repeat, of an already obsolete form. All the same, it is a good summary of the knowledge available to its time, at least as far as European intellectuals are concerned.

I think that all these 'broadcasters' are important: they encouraged people and institutions to get on with the more significant investigations that will be carried out in the succeeding period. Their activities reached out beyond the specialists to a wide lay public, which was showing a keener interest than ever in making the acquaintance of archaeology, a new trend for which we have already seen some shreds of evidence, such as the greater variety and number of publications. Another pointer to the trend is the appearance of fake objects on the antiquities market, showing that there was a lively interest, with eager buyers.

It must have been ideas of this kind that moved the Mexican government to finance the large-scale explorations that then got under way at Teotihuacán. About this time it also gave the public an example of everyone's duty to protect ancient monuments, by passing stronger laws.

Those who are today called physical anthropologists made up a group already concerned exclusively with the study of bones, chiefly skulls; from these they inferred a series of human types which enabled them to reconstruct, with a lapse into fantasy here and there, the migratory movements of the ancient American peoples. Cyrus Thomas gives us one interesting example, in that he distinguishes between Atlantic and Pacific types and deduces from this the existence of flows of migration along both coasts. Hamy's theory is another example: he postulates a whole history of conquest on the basis of long-headed and short-headed types. So it was that, on these very shaky foundations, they built historical castles in the air which would have seemed to fit in better with the preceding period, so old-fashioned were they beginning to appear. Lehmann (1909:127) did well to criticize.

Although the finds as such were being made many years before this period opens, the discoveries of fossil bones, animal as well as human, were now beginning to take on a new importance. That of Peñón man (del Castillo y Bárcena, 1885) seems to be the most relevant but there were many more, as we can see from the relatively voluminous literature devoted to the subject during these years. Its importance to archaeology stems from the fact that it demonstrates the antiquity of man in America and, therefore, of man in Mexico, despite all the criticisms that Hrdlicka was to make of it. This problem is only partly archaeological, and can be read up in Aveleyra (1950). In any event, the appearance in America of very early man does at least rule out the ancestors from Europe or Asia which had been so fashionable earlier on. Even so, much shorter time-spans were envisaged than nowadays. The new ideas coming to the surface did away with all the earlier theories of population movements, and the myths about ancient Mexican migrations became, as Lehmann said (1909:48), of no more than local historical interest. Civilization had to be thought of as having begun 'thousands of years ago' (Lehmann, 1909:127).

To sum up, I believe that the achievements of this period lay, not so much in the collection of a mass of data on every area of Mesoamerica, in coming to an understanding of previously obscure areas of ancient life, or in the publication of many and important documents, but in the fierce struggle to rid the subject of so much of the unfounded theory that had taken root in it, and which was making any approach to a genuine understanding of the facts so difficult. We are dealing with a Positivistic world, and Comte would have been proud of the way these new archaeologists only believed the evidence of their own eyes. In addition, as León Portilla did well to point out, 'they laid down as an iron rule that one must always keep the written evidence in constant relation with the material findings in archaeology' (1971, I:47).

Chapter Eight

Potsherds Victorious (1910–1950)

THE FIRST TEN years of the period covered by this chapter found Mexico in the grip of armed revolution, while for several of them the outside world was caught up in the First World War. These two turbulent events might suggest that archaeology made no progress but, in spite of everything, significant advances took place during that decade, work did get done, work that was important enough for its repercussions to be felt to this day.

First in point of time comes the founding of the Escuela Internacional.

As early as 1904 the then Rector of Columbia University began to rough out a plan for a study centre in which the universities of France, Germany, the United States, as well as the Mexican Government, would all be represented. On 20 April 1909 Justo Sierra, then Secretary of State for Education, approved the project. The intention was that students, whose studies were already far advanced, should be trained to do research and to publish their findings. On 14 September 1910 Seler, Capitan, Gordon, Boas and Dixon, as foreigners, and Ezequiel Chávez for Mexico signed the by-laws of the Escuela Internacional de Arqueología y Etnología (International School of Archaeology and Ethnology). It was inaugurated on 20 January 1911. Seler was its first Director. Boas, Tozzer, Engerrand and Gamio followed him in a sequence of annual appointments. Despite its name the Escuela did not give classes, as it had been decided

'that the school should not devote itself to popularization of these subjects [archaeology and ethnology], but to the training of productive investigators and to the advancement of our knowledge. Accordingly, it was decided that the fellows of the School should be men who had completed their preliminary studies and who were able to devote themselves to field researches' (Tozzer, 1915:384).

Its closure in 1920 brought to an end 'one of the most positive and courageous attempts to channel anthropological studies in a strictly scientific direction . . .' (Comas, 1950:104).

Beginning in 1906, courses were given at the Museo, until the faculty of archaeology passed to the University where a complete syllabus was never taught, but a series of isolated classes was held within the history department. Hermann Beyer held the Chair of Archaeology between 1919 and 1924; a follower of Seler at several removes, he was not only an excellent teacher, but one lucky enough to have among his few pupils Alfonso Caso (Caso, 1961). The latter rose rapidly to become a Professor of Archaeology, probably the best Mexico has ever had. He gradually expanded the syllabus, initiating in 1931 an anthropology subdepartment within the Facultad de Filosofía y Letras. There were only two courses offered in archaeology: Mexica archaeology and Maya archaeology. In 1937 a Department of Anthropology was formed at the Escuela Nacional de Ciencias Biológicas (National School of Biological Science), to be enhanced the following year by a greatly amplified syllabus. This department and the courses at the University merged in 1939 to become the Escuela Nacional de Antropología (National School of Anthropology), which is still in existence. It now became possible for the first time in Mexico to take a university degree in archaeology, which brought to an end the very long period indeed, when only a few researchers were able to do their training abroad, while the others were necessarily self-taught, as I have shown in my earlier chapters.

Possibly the most important effect of the opening of the Escuela Internacional was that Mexicans now began for the first time to use stratigraphic methods in their excavations. What we could call the stratigraphic revolution brought about extensive change, not only in the methodology used at the digs but also, and obviously, in the results to emerge from them. This is to some extent the key to what was being done in the field during the entire period. It continues to be the essential bedrock on which to build sequential division by time, and it was thanks to it that the archaeologists of those days put all their energies into the search for a chronology which, though it might not be finally and scientifically irrefutable, was still an essential requirement if progress was to be made.

The idea of stratigraphy in itself was by no means new, and is of course derived from geology, which arrives at the ages of strata in the earth's crust by studying how they relate to other levels. Archaeology took advantage of this method to study human remains, or those objects that man had left behind, thereby establishing their sequential distribution through the different levels and, from this, inferring their relative ages. The method had been in use in the Old World from the middle of the nineteenth century on, but in Mexico the evolutionist idea of cultures and the interest in studying their slowly-changing nature had never struck root. We had to wait for Boas to begin it at the Escuela Internacional before we put it into practice.*

Regarding the Escuela Internacional Engerrand writes (1913:263):

'The method adopted in archaeological studies is the modern, or stratigraphic one, which is fairly remote from what I propose to call the traditionalist. In the first, excavations are undertaken and accompanied by a most careful scrutiny of whatever emerges from the

---

* Willey and Sabloff suggest the possibility that Engerrand, another future director of the Escuela, had brought the stratigraphic method to Mexico, as he had had geological training in Europe. He could have passed it on to Boas (1974:215).

successive layers, so that a fragment of sherd is accorded the same value as a fossil, as each is a fixed point in the chain of evidence and, from its stylistic characteristics, one can proceed to allot it a relative position in time.'

To date, potsherds provide the most reliable chronological evidence, and their changing styles the best way of ascribing dates to the layers in which they are found. So the archaeologist must learn everything he can about pottery: shape, decoration, slips, firing methods and the rest. It is no accident that potsherds have been chosen for dating by periods, and for marking the passage of slow intra-period development; being non-perishable, pottery is the material most frequently unearthed at any dig. The Indians evidently produced vast quantities of pottery. Once broken and thus useless, the pieces were tossed aside to form layers which tell us when they were discarded. This opened up a whole new field of study and led to the developments that are described in this chapter.

The stratigraphic method, as it was then thought of, only took account of the succession *in situ* of the three great cultural horizons which soon came to be recognized through their pottery, and this was not classified strictly according to types and strata, but according to which of these horizons it belonged to. Thus there was no way of knowing where, say, the 'Toltec' material was concerned, which types were the oldest and how long each had lasted. In other words, it was impossible to divide a long epoch into its various ceramic phases; what is more, only the decorated pieces were studied:

'Practically no attention has ever been paid to this phase of the subject . . . A fertile field is open to the student of ceramics in the study of the undecorated pottery' (Tozzer, 1921:46).

Building on the foundations laid in the previous period, and using the remarkable advances in the technology of excavation, archaeologists were at last able, between 1910 and 1950, to divide the long Indian past roughly into stages which, though they were not always clear in their cultural context, did at least make it possible to slot objects and ruins into a genuine sequence, and without recourse to immigrations from elsewhere, to establish relationships between one sequence and another. Thus the great periods of Mesoamerica's past began to take shape, though it was not until later that their underlying unity became evident and won general acceptance.

We cannot here refer in any sort of detail to the huge output of these forty years and I shall have to restrict myself to giving a few examples which I believe to be among the most relevant, and concentrating upon the Valley of Mexico, the Maya zone, the Valley of Oaxaca and the Olmec discoveries in Veracruz.

The first studies undertaken by stratigraphic archaeology took place in the Valley of Mexico. Let us remember that till then the accepted view had been that only two cultures had existed there: the Toltec (confused with the Teotihuacán) and the Aztec. This supposition made any understanding of the past out of the question. It is true that Holmes (1885) had found pottery that was neither Toltec nor Aztec, whilst Paso y Troncoso (1893, 1:24, 384–389) had even before 1892 begun to group together by type objects he called Olmec. In

106 (*opposite*) Classification of archaic heads. After Gamio/Tozzer

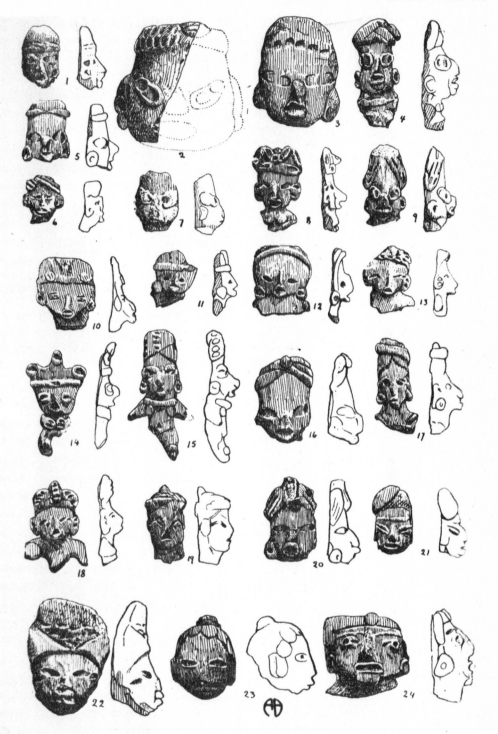

addition, Nuttall had, from 1907 on, taken bones, sherds and figurines from the lava deposits at Coyoacán. Gamio (from 1909) and Seler, each working individually, had made similar finds in the Atzcapotzalco area. All this material was dissimilar in type from the better-known finds from Teotihuacán and later cultures. In the confusion then reigning the name of 'Cerro culture' was applied to it, because it was thought that this culture had only flourished along the hillsides without extending down into the Central Valley, a misapprehension under which Seler was to labour for some time. But much later, in the course of journeys elsewhere in the Valley to places like Ticomán and Zacatenco – sites which Vaillant was to make famous only years later – sherds and little pottery heads in identical style were to appear. These first findings, superficial though they were, proved that the 'Cerro culture' had also existed in the Valley, indicating that this was therefore a misnomer. It was then re-named 'the Archaic'. However, it was still not possible to assign it a fixed chronological position relative to the other two periods. In view of this, Boas got together a great collection of sherds which he entrusted to Gamio for dating. Gamio thereupon began the exploration of a deep shaft at Culhuacán (which he could not complete) and,

147 most importantly, the study of a mound at San Miguel Amantla, 'the first and the only excavation carried out by the scientific method in the Valley of Mexico' (Gamio, 1928, II:109). There he found the sequence Archaic-Teotihuacán-Aztec but, as he himself admits, he was unable as yet to extend it to the entire Valley, and still less to areas beyond it.

The importance of the influential teachings of the Escuela Internacional and of the introduction into Mexico of stratigraphic methodology is exemplified in the person of Manuel Gamio, researcher and later director of the Escuela. Before the Escuela came into being he had published a work (1909) on finds made in the ancient Tepanec lands in the Valley of Mexico. It did not yet occur to him to classify them in chronological order, describe their ceramic types and so forth, but only to lump them into lots under headings such as 'heads', 'spindle whorls', and the like. Obviously this is what had always been done up till then. The Tepanec typology was Seler's

147 work. But later, when the excavations at San Miguel Amantla came to be discussed, the system had changed materially because of the existence of a stratigraphy. Archaeology that we can begin to call modern had arrived. We have to bear in mind that in 1909, Gamio was still very young, which is apparent even in his style, but there is a lapse of barely two years between then and his second dig. Thanks to the teachings of the Escuela, his development was remarkable.

Gamio is far and away the most important Mexican archaeologist of this period. He was later to abandon the subject almost entirely and devote himself to social anthropology. He was lucky enough to study at Columbia under Franz Boas; he knew how to put this apprenticeship to best account, and turned himself into the first properly trained archaeologist to emerge from Mexico. In 1917 he founded the Dirección de Antropología, and it was he who directed it.

It was not long afterwards that Alfred Tozzer, the noted Harvard teacher, began his excavations at Santiago Ahuitzotla, in a mound

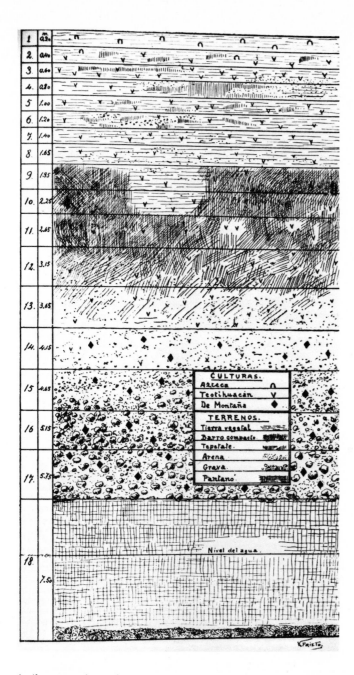

107 Stratigraphy at San Miguel Amantla. The first to be made in Mexico

similar to, and not far away from, the one at Amantla that Gamio had researched. Tozzer describes his dig into the site's modest architecture and the stratigraphic pits he sunk there, but makes no reference to the pottery sequence he found in them, although he gives careful consideration to the sequential order of the buildings. He identifies nine periods and gives a schematized list of the levels in which he found clay heads and decorated sherds. In 1913–14 he opened up the mound called Coyotlatelco; the pottery found there

108 Ceramic sherds from
Coyotlatelco. After Tozzer

and the period in question are still known by this name, and
correspond with the last years of Teotihuacán (Tozzer, 1921).

Another notable figure, Franz Boas 'Father of American anthropology', a German who became an American citizen, was also
engaged on this problem which, then still in its earliest stages, was to
come in time to change our whole concept of ancient Mexico.
Although his Mexican studies were severely limited and even his
presence in the country only very occasional, the thinking of Franz
Boas had far-reaching if indirect effects on the way archaeological
work was regarded in Mexico. Boas was of the opinion that the
importance of fieldwork and the study of its findings could be no
more than descriptive, given that the time was not yet ripe for explanatory cultural theories, in view of the many gaps that remained
in the data coverage. This is clearly a hangover from the Positivism
of the century before. The new stratigraphic school was to yield its
most significant results, above all for the Maya zone, in the first

decades of the twentieth century and, for Mesoamerica as a whole, after Vaillant's activities in this field. Still, we must not exaggerate: in much of this work, and in certain aspects of most of it, although the emphasis was on fieldwork and accurate dating, we shall find at least attempts at historical reconstructions, even though they might be limited to local history and not spill over into generalizations about the rest of the world.

But to go back to the matter of the Archaic in the Valley of Mexico. In the mid-nineteenth century Tarayre was writing, 'they have just found the ruins of a city buried under the lava flow' (1867:401), and by the turn of the century investigators such as Bárcena, Herrera and Villado were beginning to mention the discovery of human bones and pottery vessels when digging in the slopes of the Pedregal, that huge area of volcanic lava that covered part of the Valley. This proved that under the lava and, therefore, before the eruption that brought the Pedregal itself into existence, this area had been inhabited. In 1917 Gamio arranged to explore below the lava in the area of Copilco, and had tunnels dug for the purpose. The finds were sensational: the remains of buildings, burials, stone tools and an abundance of pottery which was clearly similar in style to that from the lowest levels at San Miguel Amantla and other sites at Atzcapotzalco were unearthed, indicating that they must belong to the Archaic. As this style appeared at Copilco free from later admixtures it was possible that it came from the earliest period (of those then known at least), which was not that met with at Teotihuacán. It was believed to be the oldest in the country (Gamio, 1928:116). Gamio insisted that it was the work of the Otomís, a mistaken notion that was to persist for quite a time, as the documentary evidence took these to have been the most ancient of the local peoples.

The body of thinking that came out in support of the Otomí theory would not be worth a mention, were it not for the fact that it does show the extent of the failure to grasp a concept basic to the study of ancient Mexican history. And that is, that the written sources only go back into the relatively recent past and that archaeology, and it alone is capable of reaching much further back in time. This faith in the possibility of explaining all the past in terms of the written word accounts for the brevity of the time spans that were then accepted even for finds known to be from the Archaic.

A few years later, while digging at Cuicuilco, Byron Cummings exposed a large portion of a circular pyramid, the most ancient building known up till then, and also associated with the Archaic world.

A. L. Kroeber went deeply into the problem of the relationship between the Archaic and Teotihuacán in the course of his work on the pottery from inside the Pyramid of the Sun. Comparing the vessels from the Pyramid with the Copilco wares, he decided that the latter were the older. Further, when he went round the Sierra de Guadalupe sites (Zacatenco, Ticomán, El Arbolillo) he noted that their material was intermediate between that from below the Pedregal lava and that of the particular period in the life of the Pyramid which came later to be known as Teotihuacán I. Although still very tentatively, Kroeber came to the conclusion that the Archaic ought to be divided into four, not two, levels on a seriation basis, which is a typological procedure. The first phase would be from the Pedregal type sites, Copilco in the main; the second, Zacatenco and El Arbolillo; the third, Ticomán and possibly Cuicuilco; and the fourth and last, Teotihuacán I. This chronology has held up at least in part until today, which goes to prove the essential soundness of Kroeber's reasoning and the discoveries made before he began work in 1925, discoveries which shed the first glimmerings of light on the subject.

H. J. Spinden mentions sites outside the Valley of Mexico where Archaic finds have been made: Cerro Zapote in El Salvador, Finca Arévalo in Guatemala, and Copán in northwest Honduras – always at levels below Maya material; at Uaxactun Archaic figurines appeared below floors on which the very oldest Maya monuments stand. This Archaic presence is also met with in the Valley of Ulúa and in Pánuco:

'To sum up: for the entire Mexican and Central American field the cultural sequence established by stratigraphy is: first Archaic; second Maya; third Toltec and fourth Aztec. The priority of Maya over Toltec does not come out clearly in the superimposed series in the Valley of Mexico because the Maya development took place in the humid overlands' (1932, 227).

This whole process of the discovery and understanding of the Archaic culture reached a peak before 1940 with George Vaillant's work in the Valleys of Mexico and Morelos. Between 1927 and 1934 he was digging at Zacatenco, Ticomán, Gualupita and El Arbolillo, which provided supporting evidence of an antecedent culture to Teotihuacán; this he went on to divide into various phases, which are broadly speaking those still used today. On the other hand, Vaillant's theories about the time spans covered by these various phases has been shown to be mistaken, as he gave them dates that were always much too recent. His error proceeded in part from the confusion that was then often made between the Teotihuacán culture and the Toltec which, if they are run into one, necessarily make them cover too brief a span. Much of this erroneous dating can also be attributed to the very vague written evidence that has come down to us. This compression of the passage of time meant that the Archaic, which ended with the beginnings of Teotihuacán, was given dates that were too recent. So in Vaillant's schema (1938:554) the most ancient phase, El Arbolillo I, is shown as beginning at the time of Christ. Despite these errors Vaillant, in the body of his work taken as a whole, succeeded in advancing the state of knowledge, particularly of the culture still called Archaic, to a truly remarkable extent. This is thanks to his very meticulous techniques of excavation and study of the recovered material, and to a very clear general understanding of the archaeologist's work.

From this same period dates a big advance in the understanding of the immediately post-Archaic. The large-scale excavations directed at Teotihuacán by Gamio were begun in 1917. They were to last five years and make for a clearer view of the second great stage of the history of the ancient world as it was then understood. They break the bounds of archaeology to become the first major anthropological

study carried out in Mexico, though considerations of space limit me here to considering it only in its archaeological aspects.

Gamio and his associates differed from Joyce (1914) and Spinden (1913) in that they believed the ruins at Teotihuacán to be far older than the oldest Maya cities. It is interesting that for many years Mayanists thought precisely the opposite, namely that the Maya ante-dated the Teotihuacános. The arguments put forward by both sides can no longer be upheld, and the simultaneous development of both areas is generally accepted.

Gamio excavated and almost completely reconstructed the Ciudadela, or Temple of Quetzalcoatl at Teotihuacán; it was the beginning of a practice which in the following years was to become widespread throughout Mexico. But, apart from that, he carried out a series of stratigraphic studies. His is an unusual form of stratigraphical system in that it implies that the layers are divided into modules of equal thickness; also he only expresses the quantity of decorated potsherds found as a proportion of the undecoratted, without paying much attention to the latter. The principal object of the exercise was to fix the periods of 'maximum habitability' of the great city, and he decided that there had been two of these. He came likewise to the even stranger conclusion that the Aztec pottery was contemporaneous with the Teotihuacán, only there was less of it (1922, I:266). At the same time the interesting question of Teotihuacán's roots in the Archaic began to crop up.

In order to arrive at a date for Teotihuacán this team adopted the method of measuring the depth of the strata and comparing it with accumulations in Colonial churches, the ages of which were accurately known. This did not give convincing results (id:267).

It must have been obvious that the Teotihuacán culture had spread, not only into the rest of the Valley, but as far afield as the Maya zone, an assumption for which the manifest relationship between Tula and Chichen was taken as proof. Reygadas Vertiz, however, asserted that this belief was mistaken, as he took the Tula columns to be Aztec and therefore later than the Teotihuacán/Toltec period (id:268). Beyer (id:282) points to the impossibility of considering the Teotihuacán remains as similar to those at Chichen and, for him, either one site or the other is Toltec, but not both. He would like to see the vague term 'Toltec' done away with, and continues to think that Chichen and thence Tula are more Aztec than anything else as regards their style.

All of this goes to show the muddle the chronology was in and the urgent need to get it into order. Clearly it was quite impossible under these conditions to understand the sequence of events or to make any sense of the past. Here is what Spinden has to say on the subject:

'In the list of roughly contemporaneous works I include the Toltec reliefs at Chichen Itzá, the Zapotec sculptured slabs at Monte Albán, the Olmec stelae at Cerro de las Mesas, the Totonac panels of the newly discovered ball courts at Tajín, the sculptured boulder at Maltrata, and the Temple with plumed serpent reliefs at Xochicalco, together with . . . Pipil sculpture . . .' (1933:243).

I think that those who now so sharply criticize archaeology for being 'chronological' or historicist have not given sufficient thought to these matters. For as long as it was possible to group together only contemporaneous elements into cultures, their more hypothetical aspects had to remain undiscussed.

Vaillant, over and above his work at the Archaic sites, was also concerned with Teotihuacán; Noguera was another who made a contribution (1932–36:3–81) with a dig which began in 1933. As a result of all this the greater antiquity of the Archaic over Teotihuacán was established, and the periods pertaining to this city fell more into place, along with its relations with, say, the West Coast (id: 77–78). Since the appearance of Gamio's great work, its relations with Veracruz, the Maya zone and other areas were already known. With occasional gaps, excavation was to be continuous at Teotihuacán through the years.

This and much other work show Mesoamerica (though not yet so-called) as having frontiers much like those now generally assigned to it, and that in the Archaic lay the roots of all the later cultures. This is what Spinden had thought. But even, as late as the 1930s no one was yet talking either about the Olmec or about the mother culture and related problems.

To resume our discussion of the cultural sequence in the Valley of Mexico, let us look at the central problem of the Toltecs, the identification of their capital and the time span covered by their culture, as distinct from that of Teotihuacán. As I have already said, for a long time previous to this, confusion had surrounded the Toltecs, and it had been thought that Teotihuacán might be the Tula of the documentary sources.

As from 1931, Vaillant (1935), looking for similarities between the Archaic and Teotihuacán, had found at San Francisco Mazapan near Teotihuacán a hitherto unknown ceramic type to which he gave the name Mazapan; it was earlier than Aztec but later than Teotihuacán. Acting on the advice of this outstanding North American researcher, the Swedish archaeologist Sigvald Linné decided to excavate at Teotihuacán, chiefly at Xolálpan, where he made some remarkable discoveries, such as an immense 'apartment house' which it would be inappropriate to describe here, interesting though it is. He also found Teotihuacán objects underlying the Mazapan pottery the character and positions of which

'. . . reveal as clearly as possible not only that here the Teotihuacán culture came to an abrupt end [i.e. at this place], but also that the new occupants were unacquainted with the ruins. Judging from the artifacts, points of contact of the two civilizations must have been exceedingly slight' (Linné, 1934:215).

Nobody thought then that Mazapan was one of the most accurate time markers of the Toltec period. Not, that is, until in 1940 Jorge Acosta had finished his first season's digging at Tula. His main findings, still somewhat tentative, were that the ware called Mazapan was basic at Tula, that it appeared before the Aztec and that it made up the Toltec cultural complex which reached its peak in central Mexico between the collapse of Teotihuacán and the rise of the Aztecs (1940:194). For the first time a clear demarcation line had been drawn between the two cities, with Tula emerging as obviously the later. Wigberto Jiménez Moreno (1941) was able to show by his brilliant ethnohistorical studies that the Tula we know was the Tula of the historical sources, and the Toltec capital. In the same year, 1941, the Mesa Redonda de la Sociedad Mexicana de Antropología met to study the problem of Tula and the Toltecs in the light of these new findings.

Many and contradictory were the points of view expressed at the meeting, but the consensus was in favour of that held by Jiménez Moreno, Caso, Vaillant and Acosta among others, and it was accepted that there had been a Toltec period with a capital at Tula between Teotihuacán and the Chichimeca. This meant incidentally that an earlier date had to be assigned to the rise of Teotihuacán, and thus also to the whole of the Archaic. Later exploration of Tula added daily to the stack of evidence showing that it had in fact been the Toltec capital, that it had very strong stylistic links with Chichen Itzá and that it is later than Teotihuacán. This revindicated the opinion expressed seventy years previously by Orozco y Berra, which had then been universally rejected. 'The Toltecs' he wrote, 'did not put up buildings of this [Teotihuacán] kind, and we know that they were already built when they got to Tollan' (188, II:354).

Archaeological knowledge of the immediately post-Tula period took a great leap forward with the exploration of the pyramid at Tenayuca which began in 1925 and continued for several years. An in-depth study was made of the site's architecture in particular, and of the various later, superimposed structures. The archaeologists who excavated there came to the conclusion that the pyramid 'was built by one of the tribes called Chichimeca who occupied the site after the collapse of Teotihuacán' (Tula) (Marquina, 1935:101).

From very ancient times, but particularly from the rise of Teotihuacán, the four areas that surround the Valley of Mexico (Toluca, Morelos, Puebla and the Teotlalpan) were all historically linked to it. That is why I think this is a suitable place, although it does take us outside the Valley of Mexico, to say a word about some of the important work done in these outlying areas. Nothing was known of the Toluca area until José García Payón had carried out his two digs, the one at Calixtlahuaca begun in 1930 and the other at the marvellous monolithic temple at Malinalco begun in 1936. The findings of the first have not yet been fully published, which is why this work has had little influence on archaeological thinking. A part-publication of Malinalco came out in 1946. Quite apart from its beauty, it is one of the few buildings known to date that unquestionably derives from the zenith of the Mexica culture.

51,70 The most important ancient city in Morelos is certainly Xochicalco, which had already been studied by Alzate in the eighteenth century, as mentioned in the previous chapter. The site attracted the attention of many researchers throughout the nineteenth century and interest in it is still lively. In 1910 Batres explored and reconstructed the main structure, which facilitated a number of interpretations of the famous low reliefs that decorate it. But it was not until 1934 that Noguera and his team began their stratigraphic and architectonic studies that were to continue for many seasons. Excavation at the site continues at the time of writing, which of course takes it well outside our period. Digging at other Morelos sites began in 1921; in Teopanzolco a Mexica temple was unearthed. El Tepozteco, studied by Seler from 1895, the Cerro de la Cantera (Guzmán, 1934), which we know today as Chalcatzingo and which was to become so interesting with the discovery of the Olmec, and Vaillant's Gualupita explorations, already mentioned in connection with the Archaic, all added greatly to our store of knowledge of the area.

Among the most important investigations in the Puebla Valley were those carried out at Cholula over many years by means of endless tunnels, which showed the superimposed layers that go to make up the great pyramid and hence the whole chronology of the site; and those at Tizatlán, which revealed a very late temple with paintings of exceptional interest in that they made it possible to trace the probable origins of the codices of the Borgia group. There were also a number of digs on a lesser scale, though still of great interest, undertaken by Noguera at various sites such as Tepeaca, Tehuacán, and elsewhere.

In the Teotlalpan region the sensational discoveries in and around Tula which transformed our appraisal of Mexican prehistory have already been mentioned. Up until 1950 so many sites were beginning to be known in the Central Plateau region that it would be impossible to mention them all here, but the cultural sequence for the area was well established and some of the periods could now be broken down into shorter phases. The bare bones of the subject were known and named, though they still lacked the flesh that would qualify them for a place in history.

Let us turn now to the other major zone with which we have to deal: the Maya. Apart from those sites I mentioned in the preceding chapter, Copán in particular, and the careful work done at Holmul in the years 1910–11 (Merwin and Vaillant, 1932), the Carnegie Institution, Washington DC was from 1914 and for many years thereafter to be the most important excavator in the area. The fieldwork was directed by a series of outstanding archaeologists, of whom Sylvanus G. Morley was the first upon the scene. It was in 1914 that he embarked upon his extraordinary journeyings throughout the region which were to span some ten years. In this decade, not only did he discover a number of stelae and inscribed stones which he was to publish in part in 1938, but he also produced sketch plans for an ambitious project of which shortly afterwards Alfred V. Kidder was to take charge. The most important excavations were carried out in the early thirties of our century at Uaxactún and Chichen Itzá. According to what was then current thinking, the Maya culture – the Classic as we now call it – reached a peak at two main centres: the more ancient in the Petén lowlands and called the Old Empire, and the more recent in the Yucatán Peninsula and called the New Empire. They did well to select for study Uaxactún and Chichen as the most truly representative centres of the two eras. In addition, Morley had already shown that Uaxactún possessed the earliest inscribed date then known,* the one on the famous stela 9 discovered by him on 6 May 1916. Beginning in 1923, first under the direction of Frans Blom, and then until 1931 under O. Ricketson, the excavation of the city went on. Shortly afterwards, in 1937, the excavations were reported in the deservedly famous series put out by the Carnegie Institution, which organized and funded many other Maya projects.

The second important site to be explored and partly rebuilt by the Carnegie under Morley's direction was Chichen Itzá. The work was begun in 1924 and had a number of objectives which Kidder sums up in his usual capable fashion:

'The Chichen Itzá project has differed from most archeological undertakings in the New World in that from its inception Dr Morley has striven for three definite objectives over and above the usual single one of recovering specimens and information. These may be stated as follows: to conduct the work in a manner calculated to create a feeling of confidence by the Mexican government and people in the good faith of foreign scientific agencies; to handle the site in such a way as to make it a permanent record of the artistic achievement of the Maya; and to develop Chichen Itzá as a focal point for correlated researches' (1930:96).

The author follows this up with detailed explanations of how these aims were achieved and the problems met with along the way. It is a

---

* The oldest known today is stela 29 at Tikal.

110 Chichen Itzá. The Castillo before restoration

great pity that these high ideals are not now pursued, and that even in Mexico itself some see as unacceptable even accurate reconstructions that give a wide public the chance to appreciate something of their country's ancient art.

To forget these ideals 'would pave the way for destruction by weather and vegetation which would very shortly reduce the city to a meaningless jumble of stone' (id: 98). Kidder shows foresight when he adds his view of the role of the archaeologist:

111 Chichen Itzá. The Castillo after restoration

'Emphasis in archeology is gradually shifting, however, from things to what things mean; and archeological finds are fortunately coming more and more to be considered as historical documents' (id: 91).

Among various explorations on the Guatemalan Plateau I ought to mention that at Kaminaljuyú, also under the aegis of the Carnegie Institution, directed by Kidder and with invaluable support from such as Shook, Jennings and Wauchope. This work made it possible for the first time to get the cultural stages in order, as well as to tackle other problems of the Maya area. A number of connections with other areas, Teotihuacán in particular, were also substantiated.

Kidder had for some fifteen years worked with great success in the southwestern United States where he developed various new techniques, particularly in stratigraphy. All of this was good preparation for Maya studies, as was also the idea – which many take to be startlingly modern – that archaeological work should be supported by contributions from a number of other related fields. Towards the end of the period the work of the Carnegie (Taylor, 1948) was coming in for sharp criticism, not all of it justified. In my opinion Kidder and his group gave a great boost to Maya studies and,

112 Mosaic disk recovered from the Castillo at Chichen Itzá. National Museum of Anthropology, Mexico City. Diam 24.5 cm

beyond them, to the rest of Mexico. This is shown, for example, by the fact that Vaillant was a pupil of Kidder's.

From 1910 onwards Maya studies, reverting to an earlier tradition, concentrate largely on the deciphering of the hieroglyphs and the understanding and translation of the almanac. This is what Morley was working on for many years. With the explorations at Uaxactún and Chichen Mexican archaeology moves out into other areas of research such as architecture; but let us not forget that it was Morley's epigraphic studies that sparked this off. In 1937 we find Kidder again summing up the Carnegie's work, adding that all the Mayanist researches were 'inaugurated more than twenty years ago by Dr S. G. Morley as a purely epigraphic study' (1937:1–2). He then goes on to list these activities: racial, medical, ethnographic, linguistic studies, to say nothing of research into the ecology, geology, climate, geography, flora and fauna. Whilst they all have their connections with archaeology, I shall confine myself to the historical aspects here because 'the gap between the present and the prehistoric Maya must be bridged by study of the documentary history' (id. 6).

But the fieldwork of the Carnegie Institution did not stop there: it carried on until 1956 (Pollock, 1956), or outside the limits set for this chapter. Its last archaeological publications dealt with Mayapan, that late city which is nevertheless so important to an understanding of the history of Yucatán. In the early stages the Institute was by far the most important contributor to Maya archaeology, which is not to detract from the work done in the area by a number of other scientific bodies and museums, both Mexican and foreign.

By, say, the end of the Second World War, then, remarkable advances had been made in the spread of knowledge, thanks to a now established technology of excavation and reconstruction applied to large urban complexes which was capable of yielding considerable quantities of information, not on the basis of a reading of the inscriptions alone, but also on the stratigraphy of both buildings and pottery. What has now come into being is a fully professional archaeology, though obviously one that still displays certain features then in fashion. It did not set itself to study each and every problem, only those that were newly emerging. These are still worth working on, even today, though further new ideas have since extended the frontiers of possible investigation. But if we can now stand and gaze with pleasure at Chichen, Uxmal or Copán, we owe this not only to the work being done at that time, but also to the series of underlying assumptions which went on influencing Mexican archaeology until very recently, as can be seen in the later explorations at Palenque or Tikal. Even if only in broad outline, the progress of the Maya across time and space could be visualized for the first time, how their culture worked, and something of its orgins. Only thus is it possible to understand the appearance of a work like *The Ancient Maya* (Morley, 1946).

From now on various Mexican archaeologists adopted the stratigraphic techniques of the South-West and the later Mayan experience for excavations in areas of their own, and this to remarkable effect. Around 1950, at the close of this period, they had arrived at a very different perspective on the past. We shall have to

113 Tikal. Temple 1

look at these developments more closely, particularly for Oaxaca and the Olmec area.

What the Carnegie did for the Maya zone, the explorations at Monte Albán and elsewhere, directed by Alfonso Caso, did for the Valley of Oaxaca. Until almost the end of the 'twenties nothing coherent had been done in this area. It is true that descriptions of some important sites such as Mitla had existed for many years, also that a number of objects had found their way into private collections, but this did not add up to a historical sequence. No distinction had even been made as yet between the Zapotec and Mixtec styles, to say nothing of all the other peoples of the area whose distinctive styles were not even known. Despite a few explorations such as those of Saville, barely even partly published, the Oaxacan past tended to become more and more legendary, though with pretensions to history in the work of such local writers as Martínez Gracida, or Gay (1881) before him. As Caso writes:

23

'Even where the literature on Oaxacan archaeology is not scarce we realize, when we have done with it, that its authors are usually repeating what others have said before them. Few add anything from research of their own, or from any other source of fresh information. What has been written on Mitla is a typical example' (1928:7).

He goes on to add that there exists in Oaxaca an ideographic script that may also be phonetic, in codices as well as on engraved slabs, and which has certain similarities with, as well as differing in some important respects from, scripts from other parts of Mexico. In the first of his books Caso recommended that as full a study as possible should be made of these stone inscriptions. This was the start of his *Estelas Zapotecas* (1928), which marks the beginning of the acquisition of basic knowledge of the region's archaeology. He soon became aware of his inability to date each slab, or even to say which of them was contemporary with which. Despite this fundamental disadvantage he did succeed in drawing up an impressive catalogue of glyphs and even in reading parts of some of them.

78

The logical result of this work was to demonstrate the essential need for stratigraphic exploration and a sound knowledge of the monuments at any given site. Monte Albán being an obvious target for such an investigation, December 1930 saw the beginning there of the eighteen seasons of fieldwork that were to be the 'open Sesame' to the archaeology of the Valley of Oaxaca. It is interesting that, in Oaxaca as in the Maya area, modern archaeology begins with epigraphy. Of course this is to some extent true throughout Mesoamerica, owing to the importance of documents and inscriptions, which have given to the archaeology of this area a complexion very different from that of other regions which have never had a written script.

Work at Monte Albán, which came in time to spread to other sites, not only in the Valley but also out into the Mixtec area, provided us with the first time-sequence for the area and also paved the way for a number of other highly illuminating studies.

But many years were to pass before the deepest mystery to emerge from Monte Albán was revealed. Work here had from the beginning pointed to an advanced culture. It could not have been the first to have settled in these valleys; but who were its predecessors, and where had they come from? Very recent research has shown that the dawn of local history is not to be found at Monte Albán but in other parts of the Valley of Oaxaca. On the other hand, the other periods as then defined by Caso have stood the tests of both time and increasing knowledge of the area and, except in some matters of detail, are still considered sound. It is a matter for regret that an account of these impressive results cannot be included here, but they did not appear till after our closing date of 1950.

The same thing was to happen at Veracruz. It seems barely credible today that, except for a few isolated mentions (Melgar, 1869, 1871), studies of small finds (Saville, 1902, 1929), or travels such as those of Blom and La Farge (1925) or Weyerstall (1937), what we now call the Olmec culture was totally unknown. It was in fact only in 1938 that the Smithsonian Institution and the National Geographic Society began work in the area, under the enthusiastic leadership of Matthew Stirling. In a few years they achieved the most sensational results by means of the exploration, albeit incomplete, of Tres Zapotes and La Venta. The extraordinary monoliths found in these cities and at other places in the area (to which Stirling was soon to add further equally marvellous finds from Cerro de las Mesas, a site which is not really Olmec though the finds to which I am referring *are*) caused a great stir in archaeological circles and threw up a whole series of problems of the highest importance for an understanding of the past.

Perhaps the first of these problems was: to what date are we to assign this culture? Is it part of the horizon then still being called the Archaic? Is it a forerunner of the Maya and other cultures and thus the mother-culture of Mesoamerica as a whole? Or are we dealing with a late local culture corresponding with the 'historic' Olmec of the written sources? Each of these obviously related questions elicited a different answer.

The somewhat sceptical position taken up by Eric Thompson, the greatest of the Mayanists (1941), and many others with regard to the antiquity of the Olmecs was based mainly on his refusal to accept the very early dates ascribed to the stone inscriptions, as on stela C at Tres Zapotes, and to the possibility that they might even antedate the Maya calendar. In effect, another of the basic changes in archaeological dating was the discovery that the Maya calendar is not strictly speaking Maya at all, but was in use before the first inscriptions at Uaxactún were set up. The Maya, therefore, did no more than elaborate upon it, refine it and make improvements upon it. The initial date inscribed on stela C was much disputed but there is now little doubt about it. Stirling's theory, formulated even before the discovery of the other half of the stela, is the correct one (1940). This proved not only that he had been justified in thinking of the date as very early – in fact it strikes us now as being if anything too recent – but that the whole Olmec culture is earlier than the Maya. This was anathema at the time because, as we have already seen, almost all the endeavours of the Carnegie and other institutions, North American in particular, had been directed towards Maya research, the consensus of opinion then being not only that the Maya culture was the oldest, but that all the other Mesoamerican cultures had stemmed from it.

At the celebrated meeting held under the aegis of the Sociedad Mexicana de Antropología in 1942 to discuss the Olmec problem, archaeologists headed by Caso, Covarrubias and Noguera, along with Stirling, all maintained that the Olmecs belonged within the Archaic horizon. Caso claimed that the Olmec 'is beyond doubt the parent of such other cultures as the Maya, the Teotihuacán and that of El Tajín' (1942:46). Covarrubias held that 'whereas other cultural complexes share "Olmec" traits, this style contains no vestiges or elements taken over from other cultures, unless it be from those known as Archaic' (1943:48). Vaillant was one of the few North Americans to back up these theories and he did so because, in the course of his fine work on the Central Plateau with which we are already familiar, he had come across Archaic figurines displaying undoubted kinship with Olmec types. Eric Thompson, on the other hand, thought that the Olmec was a late culture within what we have now come to call the Post-Classic.

And yet the name Olmec, first used by Beyer (1927) to designate this particular art style, has prevailed until today, incorrect though it may be. It is a source of confusion because it is lifted from historical sources which apply the term Olmec to very much later peoples. In 1942 Jiménez Moreno cleared the matter up by showing that the name Olmec properly refers to the inhabitants of the natural rubber-growing areas, but even so we have to distinguish clearly between the relatively recent bearers of the name and the archaeological Olmecs, which is why he proposed that these be called the 'La Venta people' to make confusion less confounded. But the name given at baptism was not to be shaken off, and is the one still used today.

At the Mesa Redonda de Tuxtla in 1942 the Olmecs were given a provisional starting date around 300 B.C. But somewhat later work at San Lorenzo, carried out with the aid of radiocarbon analysis – the use of which was spreading throughout the area – showed that 1200 BC was a more realistic date. This fitted in perfectly with what was being discovered all over Mesoamerica. It is a part of the general process that has already been discussed. Nineteenth-century scholars had often proposed fabulously early dates for the prehispanic peoples, and it produced in this century a vigorous counter-reaction which in its turn condensed them too drastically. But after 1950 this difficulty was to be overcome by the use of dating techniques that are not essentially archaeological.

Many problems concerning the Olmec culture still remain unresolved, but its existence and its importance are now beyond question. Work at a number of sites outside the limited areas I have already mentioned aided serious discussion of Mesoamerican archaeology as a whole. Research focussed mainly on architecture, sculpture and pottery, without as a rule paying much attention to those sidelines that we might call ethnological. In spite of this the results were remarkable, and by 1950 there was an immense amount of material awaiting study.

The north and the whole central area of the Republic of Mexico, which lie outside the frontiers of Mesoamerica, were a good deal neglected, owing in large part to the very peculiar nature of the archaeology of those regions. A few permanent centres excepted, the area contains no clearly defined sites to be explored. Researchers had therefore to investigate caves, woods and valleys for the scarcely visible traces of the wandering peoples who had once lived there, while primitive settlers had been few. This problem is to some extent common to everyone engaged in the study of prehistoric man who did not, of course, leave the kind of traces that are clearly visible to all at well-defined sites.

But despite these difficulties, investigations *did* continue and interesting studies *did* emerge from these areas and from Baja California; among those taking part were Amsden, Brand, Carey, Kidder, Noguera, Gamio, Sayles, Mason and Margain. Work was also done at such permanent settlement sites as Casas Grandes, Chalchihuites (begun by Gamio long before), La Quemada and El

Teúl. The whole zone was, however, still without a chronology and, more important still, without any kind of cultural analysis that might tie up its relationship with agricultural, sedentary Mesoamerica.

Ekholm, Stresser Pean and Meade were the main contributors where the Huastec area is concerned, and it is thanks to their work that its geographical boundaries were drawn and a chronology roughed out for it. The Totonac area had been fairly well explored previously, but it gave up more of its secrets thanks to Krickeberg and to the work done at Zempoala, Tajín, Isla de Sacrificios, Remojadas and so forth, undertaken in the main by García Payón, Melgarejo and Medellín.

The west coast of Mexico grows clearer too, and here we are indebted to Ekholm, Isabel Kelly, José Corona Núñez at Sinaloa, Nayarit, Jalisco and Colima, and to the Museo Nacional in the Lake Pátzcuaro area and in Chupícuaro. But even before this, Noguera and Caso had worked at other Michoacán sites. Almost nothing had however been done in Guerrero except a series of surveys and fairly superficial explorations.

In the domain of library studies the main preoccupation continued to be the vital one of correlating the codices both with the historical documents and with the cultural sequences being turned up by the spades of the fieldworkers. For in order to understand bygone cultures it is vitally essential to use every means at our disposal. Disentanglement of the Indian cultures through their codices, stone inscriptions and the calendrical information set out in their documents and stelae, may one day make it possible for us to dig deeply enough into history to dredge up biographical details of individual personages, which is not within the competence of the field archaeologist.

The year 1938 saw the appearance of an article by Vaillant, one of the first to try seriously to tie-in the material finds of archaeology with the historical sources; in other words, to write history using archaeology not on its own as one must where written sources are absent, but bringing into play the vast stores of these. This particular attempt has since been superseded, but it did point the way.

Alfonso Caso's great and unhappily still unpublished work on the Mixtec codices falls outside the scope of this book, but a lot of ground had been gained in historical and calendrical enquiries into the Mixtec written records since the days of Nuttall and Cooper-Clark. Caso himself delivered before the Sociedad Mexicana de Antropología (1942) a memorable lecture containing much that was fresh. Published years later as *El Mapa de Teozacualco* (1949) it was the first to assign dates from our calendar to events in Mixtec history and 'opened up wide vistas in precolonial history' (Jiménez Moreno, 1952:75). Many other pieces of writing on the codices and ancient documents appeared in these years, among them Robert Barlow's many articles written between 1943 and 1950. 'His work so dominates these years that they might well be called "the Barlow period" ' (Jiménez Moreno, 1952:76).

I have already referred to the work done on the Maya calendar in the preceding periods, as well as in the one we are concerned with in this chapter, but this marvellous detective story has had to reconstruct, step by step, not one death but many; because Mesoamerica had, not one but many calendars which, though they do have their interrelationships, sometimes close ones, retain their differences.

They all share similar origins and are branches of a common stock, though the Maya went on to achieve a prodigious development unmatched by any of the others. So advanced were they, that it seems advisable to distinguish the Maya from all the rest. In other words to divide them into those who used the Long Count* and knew the use of the zero and those who did not, having not made that remarkable intellectual leap. Of course we can at least suspect the existence of intermediate states, though we cannot here concern ourselves with them.

The history of Western awareness of the Mexica calendar begins at the Conquest but it was not until 19 May 1938 when Alfonso Caso delivered before the Sociedad de Antropología a remarkable lecture on the correlation between the Aztec and the European calendars, that the last doubts were cleared away. As Muñoz would have said, he based his arguments on 'irrefutable' documents. This brilliant piece of deduction, by revealing the true dates when the year began and ended, cleared up many basic confusions.

But there remained yet another difficulty, which Caso had already examined with extensive help from Jiménez Moreno and Kirchhoff: the Aztec system was not the same as the one used by other peoples such as the Mixtecs or the Texcocans. It was in 1940 that Jiménez Moreno, after a study of the Yanhuitlán codex, explained that the Mixtecs did not begin their year in the same month, so that the same year would be named differently for them and for the Aztecs.

Kirchhoff took this knowledge further, proving that this rule applies not only to the Mixtecs but to many of the other peoples; with this for base, he went on to draw up invaluable tables of correlation which give us the correct chronology for a further eight groups. This work went a long way towards clearing up confusions in the chronicles, and it is of the greatest importance in enabling us to assign dates to historical events that affected various peoples in the Mexican heartland.

Caso has at various times written articles on the Zapotec, Tarascan, Otomí, Matlazinca, Totonac and Huastec calendars. Strangely enough, the detectives are baffled precisely when faced with the best of them all, that Zapotec calendar which Caso could not reconstruct, not because he did not try hard enough, but because there is not enough material available to make it possible. Time has not only effaced most of the clues; there is only a bone here and there to suggest that there might once have been a corpse.

So by 1950 there could be no question that not only the Mixtec codices but those of certain other Mesoamerican peoples as well, contained various items of historical information that could be pieced together. Genealogies of a number of personages began gradually to be unravelled. Thus it came about that the dates given in these documents, interpreted according to the particular calendar of

* The Maya system of a day-by-day count from a starting date of 3113 BC.

which they form a part, allow us to establish chronologies which are not only valid in themselves and much more precise than anything to be learned from the reading of a pottery sequence, but which can be precisely related to the phases and horizons shown up in field archaeology.

Around 1920, for reasons that have little to do with archaeological research and more to do with changing aesthetic norms in Europe, ancient art forms come to be assigned a value and importance hitherto unknown. This is something that Europeans as well as Mexican painters such as Rivera experienced. The English sculptor Henry Moore himself admits that he took inspiration from a number of Mexican pieces, particularly the 'chac-mool' at Chichen and the Xochipilli at the British Museum. His admiration, which was widely shared, brings to mind Dürer's of four centuries before, and we ought to remember too that by 1889 Paul Gauguin 'was copying Aztec sculpture at the Paris Exhibition of that year' (Keen, 1971:510).

Ancient art forms began to be seriously studied in 1910 or thereabouts, with Spinden's formidable monograph on Maya art coming out in 1913. Although it was still not possible to arrange them in chronological order, he leaned heavily on the evolution of stylistic traits, while introducing, along with the forms of the undated monuments, dates from associated stelae or even of the more recent ones taken from the Yucatán codices. Despite these shortcomings, inevitable at that time, Spinden's book was a landmark that stood unchallenged for years and showed what could be done with archaeological material in a way quite exceptional for its time; it reminds one of Seler, whose scientific output was still prolific. Years later Marquina was to study prehispanic architecture, a theme he brought up to date in his book published in 1951, while a series of writers, notably Joyce, Lehmann, Proskouriakoff and Kelemen, either studied particular aspects of it, or tried to give an overall evaluation of the artistic productions of ancient Mexico.

Within the same category of ideas must be put work such as that of Toscano (1944), who handled the theme with great good sense and maturity of judgment. Eulalia Guzmán (1946) was important too, so was Justino Fernández, though the bulk of his output falls into a later period. Others who deserve a mention are Miguel Covarrubias, already cited in connection with the Olmecs, and George Kubler from 1943 onwards. Although the movement's main thrust came after 1950 it had begun before then, and showed how great an interest a wide public was taking in Mexican archaeology.

Another fast-developing kind of basic research that now comes into its own is ceramic studies, where Anna Shepard begins to distinguish herself in 1936, and whose most important pre-1950 book appeared in 1948.

The study of the pre-sedentary, earliest prehistoric cultures had not advanced very far until the discoveries of 1945 (De Terra *et al*: 1949) in the old swamp at Tepexpan, which made it possible to prove that in Mexico man had existed alongside 'antediluvian' animals. An obsidian point was found associated with a fossil elephant and two years later the same geological layer produced the remains of a man. This find has been spectacularly borne out by the mammoth, associated with human remains, dug up at Santa Isabel Ixtapan. Even in cases where the dates were still in dispute, the finds have proved to be of fundamental importance and, when tied in with various palaeolithic objects found in several places in Mexico, allowed something to be glimpsed which is slightly more than just a theory. It is an assemblage of morsels of information which reveals that early horizon which we know must have been there, even though there is no way of demonstrating it archaeologically. In this connection *Los Orígenes Americanos* by Pablo Martínez del Río and *Prehistoria de México* by Luis Aveleyra (1950) supply valuable information.

When it comes to books or manuals which tried via one approach or another to give an overview of the state of knowledge in the discipline as a whole, two influential publications came out between 1914 and 1917, describing the changes that were taking place, not so much in what was regarded as acquired knowledge, but in how archaeology itself was viewed, how it was becoming more modern. The first, by an English archaeologist, Thomas Joyce, is largely given over to ethnographic and historical material, though it has a sound archaeological base, and is in this respect very much the superior of any of its predecessors. Even though it deals with pre-stratigraphic archaeology, this is a high-quality work and some of its ideas held together for a long time. A number of them have, though, been successfully challenged, such as the existence of a civilization among the Maya before there was any development in Central Mexico in the Toltec era (Teotihuacán to us). The chronology to support this contention cannot be accepted, as Joyce dates the Maya stelae around 500 years earlier than he should have done. It is odd that he did not make use of Goodman's synchronology, which had been available since 1905. He gives us interesting data in support of his theories about Mesoamerica having been a unity since remotest antiquity and not just in the sixteenth century, much as Kirchhoff was to do, but much later.

In his *Ancient Civilization of Mexico and Central America* (1917) Spinden gives, for the first time in a manual, a time sequence based on archaeological findings. He shows the unity of Mesoamerican cultures, at least in their beginnings. This small, insignificant-looking book has probably done the subject greater service than many a library.

Later arrivals that covered a smaller geographical area in far greater depth are two very interesting attempts to turn archaeology into history. Both are examples of *haute vulgarisation*. I refer to *Aztecs of Mexico* by Vaillant (1941) and *The Ancient Maya* by Morley (1946). It is clear from the date of publication that it was too late for Vaillant to alter his vision of a Teotihuacán without the Toltecs, however freely he may have accepted the conclusions of the Mesa Redonda De Tula, as we have already remarked. We ought to remember that Vaillant is perhaps the last archaeologist of standing to follow the Morgan-Bandelier guidelines discussed in the previous chapter, even though he, Vaillant, does make extensive concessions to the opposite point of view. His untimely death prevented him from correcting this in later editions, as I think he would have wanted to. This was in

114 Drawing of prehispanic birds erroneously interpreted as elephant trunks. After Spinden

fact done, but much later, by another hand. His book is a fine one which skilfully combines the documentary sources and the archaeological findings.

Morley achieved the same success with his study of the Maya, one of the first histories of this people to be written with a sound grounding in archaeology. Despite the no longer acceptable division of Maya history into Old and New Empires, the book still makes worth-while reading. Both scholars made an enormous contribution by arousing interest in the field among a wide public. It was no accident that till then the Maya and the Aztecs were the only peoples to have monographs devoted to them, other regions not having been studied before the archaeological discovery of Oaxaca and the Olmecs.

From the point of view of the organization of archaeology, we have already seen how Batres and the Junta Colombiana had succeeded in persuading the government of Porfirio Díaz to finance archaeological investigations, but it was not really until Gamio founded the Dirección de Antropología in 1917 that an official organization devoted to these studies became established in Mexico. In 1925 came the creation of the Departamento de Monumentos Prehispánicos which, in terms of the law passed on 3 February 1939, joined with other services to become the Instituto Nacional de Antropología e Historia. This was one of the crowning efforts of its founder and first director, Alfonso Caso.

The Instituto took over the sole direction not only of exploration and Mexican studies, but also of museums, the national as well as the many provincial ones that were now being created. The example caught the imagination of many of the Mexican states which now set themselves to organize regional institutes of their own, which have done a great deal, particularly since 1930, to encourage the spread of knowledge. We have a shining example of this at Jalapa in the State of Veracruz. Many new archaeological museums were opened, over and above those already functioning at places such as Guadalajara, Campeche, Tuxtla Gutiérrez, Tepic and Toluca. But above all, museums were no longer content to display their objects with no mention of provenance, or only a very vague one. They had begun to look at their displays as documents, not as collections of curiosities.

All this post-1930 activity is due primarily to Caso, who took the lead and brought into being not only the Instituto but also the Escuela de Antropología. The fact that he had a genius for organizing institutes and study centres made him a driving force for beneficial change, though of course the credit does not belong solely to one man, but also to the many others he led towards genuine professional maturity, a maturity hitherto unknown in Mexico, however much it might already have been in evidence elsewhere.

Independently, though closely linked with the earlier development, Caso established on 28 October 1937 the Sociedad Mexicana de Antropología whose Mesas Redondas – two of which I have mentioned – have not only widened the scope of knowledge of the areas studied in each case, but have come to conclusions of the greatest importance.

Some of the publications that appeared prior to 1910 have already been referred to in the preceding chapter. Many more were started up subsequently; both their nature and their degree of importance have fluctuated during the period of their existence. The first in point of time was launched by Beyer and called *Mexico Antiguo*. This, the organ of the Sociedad Alemana Mexicanista (German Mexicanist Society), has published a great deal of important material and is still going strong. In 1920 Gamio began publication of *Revista Ethnos*, not to be confused with the journal of the same name put out by the Ethnographic Museum of Sweden from 1936 onwards, which has also given space to Mexican archaeological material.

In 1927 Caso and Toussaint brought out the first issue of the *Revista Mexicana de Estudios Históricos*, which became in 1937 the *Revista Mexicana de Estudios Antropológicos*. This published much of the most important work produced in this period, and it is at the top of its class for this kind of publication in Mexico.

The American Archaeological Society began publication of *American Antiquity* in 1935; this has also given space in its columns to many valuable contributions, though without of course giving special preference to Mexico.

Various other periodicals appeared more or less regularly, among them: *Acta Americana, Acta Antropológica, Tlalocan*, the *Anales* of the Instituto de Investigaciones Estéticas of UNAM (from 1937) and *Tlatelolco a través de los tiempos*, which is an appendix to the *Memorias* of the Academia Mexicana de Historia, as well as *Cuadernos Americanos* and others which often carry articles having important bearing upon our subject.

A number of scientific institutions published entire issues devoted to Mexican archaeology. In addition to the already mentioned Carnegie Institution of Washington, to which we owe a very high proportion of all the knowledge we possess of the Maya region, the Peabody Museum at Harvard University, the Smithsonian Institution, the Universities of California (particularly with their Ibero-American series begun in 1932), Chicago and Tulane, the Museum of the University of Pennsylvania, the American Museum of Natural History, the Museum of the American Indian, the Institute of Andean Research and the Museum of the South-West have all either operated in Mexico or, at least, published (often magnificently) studies in Mexican archaeology. In Guatemala, too, the Sociedad de Geografía e Historia has from 1929 on published a great deal of material in its *Anales*. Journals have also come out of Honduras and El Salvador, while the European series have (except for an interruption caused by the Second World War) kept up their publication of important articles on Mexico.

In the Valley of Teotihuacán Gamio had begun a series of important moves to get archaeology accepted as a branch of anthropology in the North American manner. But despite these, and despite the fact that, from 1939 onwards, the Instituto, the Escuela and the Museo all added 'de antropología' to their name, very little attention was paid in this period to anthropological problems, either in a general way or as they pertained to areas outside the Indian world. The idea that archaeology might have a contribution to make to these wider fields did not occur to those concerned.

As Willey and Sabloff have fully explained, in Mexico this period applied itself especially to establishing a chronology, that is, to the ordering of the cultures and periods in correct sequence. How right they were to do so has, I think, been amply demonstrated in this chapter. In Mexico it was not until about 1950 that other problems began to compete with chronology, which is nevertheless still not abandoned. Stratigraphy came to be the dominant technique for the establishment of this sequence of cultures and periods based on typologies, and so essential for the making out of the shape of each culture in its progress through time and space. All this made for a considerable improvement in excavation techniques, which had to become more precise and careful if they were to produce sound results. Descriptions of the finds were no longer enough: the typologies were becoming the pages of a history. Context, function and attempts to explain the past in terms of cultural change had yet to emerge as recurrent themes, although the groundwork for them was already done.

It is difficult to sum up the work of these forty years, simply because there was such a huge amount of it; archaeology, while still very young, was striding briskly into adulthood. There is no question but that this was the most important of the stages to date. Though all the data might not yet be available, there was enough good material to make a solid base for future constructions. For the valleys of the Central Plateau, the Valley of Oaxaca and the Petén a sound chronology had been established at least as far as the succession of periods was concerned. In Yucatán, the Guatemala highlands, Veracruz, the Huastec regions, Tabasco and (to a lesser extent) the West Coast, excavation had revealed important cultures, though a sure and certain sequence for them was still lacking. So many places were being dredged up out of total obscurity. Yet there were still many unexplored areas on the map and many gaps to be filled in, even for the best-known regions.

By 1943, studies – stratigraphic in the main – had enabled the frontiers of sixteenth-century Mesoamerica to be determined with a fair degree of accuracy. Archaeology could prove a number of local historical sequences, as well as the antiquity of the area as a whole.

The science differed from what it had been in 1900 in that it was now an organizational whole, containing within it not only an institute, but laboratories, museums and so forth, along with a growing corps of well-trained personnel. It was no longer necessary to stand around and wait for the rare self-taught genius. Work was beginning to be done by teams able to call upon specialists in the different branches, and research subjects which had been entirely ignored or else seen in terms of information from the written sources could be undertaken. Mexican archaeology was coming out of its exclusively descriptive phase and beginning to embark upon interpretations, even when these had to be tentative and subject to countless corrections. This is by no means to say that the collection of data had come to the end of its term; it had not, and possibly it never will. The fact that most of the probing had now assumed the form of as yet unanswered questions showed that problems previously ignored could at least be tackled; this constituted an enormous advance in itself.

That the potsherds emerged victorious is really a symbol of the victory of the field archaeologist over the digger in the archives who had been dominant before 1910.

Postscript

THE LAST CHAPTER, I have to admit, presented many problems. For I found it no easy matter to discuss archaeology without exceeding the limits of my brief and making sorties into the other anthropological sciences. Hence some of the chapter's evident short-comings. But in any case, to study archaeology on its own becomes a virtual impossibility from about 1950 on; it so reduces the scale of the subject as to make even the whys and wherefors of the research incomprehensible. But once it is accepted that Mexican archaeology must be treated as part of world anthropology, we have to tear down the whole existing framework, aware that this is a necessary process in the development of the science all over the globe. And such considerations take us a long way from our point of departure.

Moreover, my interpretation of events during the last quarter-century would not be an entirely balanced one, not only because many of these events have taken place too recently, but also because I myself have played a part in them. This makes it hard for me to see them in historical perspective. My judgment would be swayed by personal considerations, by feelings of like and dislike for persons still living, and this would cast doubts on the soundness of my opinions as to the value of their contributions to the developments in the field. I might well become bogged down in a mass of detail which a longer view would reveal as trivial; or, conversely, give insufficient attention to precisely those areas that would only later come to be seen as the most significant. For happenings, finds, excavations, studies that we regard as absorbing today may seem at some future date to have been not so important after all.

PHOTOGRAPHIC ACKNOWLEDGMENTS

Nearly all the illustrations in this book are of archive material or objects in the National Museum of Anthropology, Mexico City, photographed under the supervision of the author and reproduced by kind permission of the Museum. The following are reproduced by courtesy of: British Museum, London, 20, 64, 65; INAH, Mexico City, 29, 97; Museum of Anthropology, Florence, 31.

Bibliography

ABBREVIATIONS
UNAM: Universidad Nacional Autonoma de México
INAH: Instituto Nacional de Antropología e Historia

ACOSTA, JORGE R. 'Exploraciones en Tula, Hidalgo 1940'. *Revista Mexicana* de Estudios Antropológicos, IV. 1940: 172–94.

ACOSTA, JOSÉ DE *Historia natural y moral de las Indias.* Mexico 1940. (First published 1590.)

ALAMÁN, LUCAS *Historia de Mexico desde los primeros movimientos que preparon su Indépendencia,* 5 vols. Mexico 1849–52.

— *Disertaciones sobre la historia de la República Mexicana . . .,* 3 vols. Mexico 1844–49.

ALCINA FRANCH, JOSÉ *Expediciones acerca de los antiguos monumentos de Nueva España.* Madrid 1969.

ALZATE Y RAMÍREZ, JOSÉ ANTONIO 'Descripción de las antigüedades de Xochicalco'. Supplement to Gaceta de literatura, No. 31. Mexico 1791.

ANGLERIA, PEDRO MARTÍR DE *Décadas del Nuevo Mundo,* 2 vols. Mexico 1965.

Archives de la Commission Scientifique du Mexique, 3 vols. Paris 1865–67.

ARIAS MONTAÑO, BENITO 'Phaleg, sive de gentium sedibus primis, orbisque terrae situ'. In *Biblia Sacra* (1885 edn). Antwerp 1569–72.

ATKINSON, R. J. C. *Archaeology, History and Science.* Cardiff 1960.

AUBIN, J. M. A. *Mémoire sur la peinture didactique et l'écriture figurative des anciens mexicains.* Paris 1885. (First published 1849.)

AVELEYRA, LUIS *Prehistoria de México.* Mexico 1950.

AVENDAÑO, ANDRES *Relación de las dos entradas que hizo a la Conversión de los gentiles Itzaes y de Cehaches . . .* Manila 1696.

BALDWIN, JOHN D. *Ancient America, in notes on American Archaeology.* New York 1872.

BANCROFT, HUBERT HOWE *The Native Races of the Pacific States of North America,* 5 vols. San Francisco 1886.

BANDELIER, A. F. A. 'Report of an Archaeological Tour in Mexico in 1881'. *Papers of the Archaeological Institute of America,* American series 2. Boston 1884.

BARADÈRE H. 'Note sur la découverte de poteries antiques à diverses profondeurs'. In *Antiquités Mexicaines,* I, Part 1. Paris 1834.

BÁRCENA, MARIANO 'Descripción de un hueso labrado de llama fósil encontrado en los terrenos post terciarios de Tequixquiac'. *Anales del Museo Nacional de México*, Period I, Vol. II. 1882: 439–44.

BASTIAN, ADOLF 'Steinsculpturen von Sta Lucia Cotzumalhuapa'. *Zeitschrift für Ethnologie*, VIII. 1876: 322–26, 403–04.

BATRES, LEOPOLDO *Exploraciones de Monte Albán*. Mexico 1902.

— *Reparación y consolidación del edificio de las columnas en Mitla*. Mexico 1908.

BEAUFOY, MARK *Mexican illustrations founded upon facts*. London 1828.

BELLEFOREST, FRANÇOIS DE *Histoire Universelle du Monde*. Paris 1572.

BERISTAIN DE SOUZA, JOSÉ MARIANO *Biblioteca Hispano-Americana Septentrional*, 3 vols. Mexico 1816–19.

BERNAL, IGNACIO 'La arqueología mexicana de 1880 a la fecha'. *Cuadernos Americanos*, XI. Mexico 1952: 121–45.

— 'La arqueología mexicana del siglo veinte'. *Memoria del Congreso Científico Mexicano*, Vol. XI. Mexico 1953: 235–62.

— 'Humboldt y la arqueología Mexicana'. In *Ensayos sobre Humboldt*, *UNAM*. Mexico 1962: 121–32.

— 'Bibliografía de Arqueología y Etnografía. Mesoamerica y Norte de México (1514–1960)'. *INAH*. Mexico 1962.

BERNAL, RAFAEL *Mestizage y criollismo en la literatura de la Nueva España en el siglo XVI*. Ms. Freiburg 1972.

BERNASCONI, ANTONIO 'Informe sobre Palenque'. In CASTAÑEDA PAGANINI, *Las ruinas de Palenque*. Guatemala 1946: 37–41.

BEUCHAT, H. *Manuel d'archéologie Américaine*. Paris 1912.

BEYER, HERMANN Review of Blom and La Farge, 'Tribes and Temples'. *México Antiguo*, II. 1927: 305–13.

— 'Sobre antigüedades del pedregal de San Angel'. *Memorias y Revista de la Sociedad Científica Antonio Alzate*, 37, I, 1918: 1–16.

BEZERRA TANCO, LUIS *Felicidad de México en el principio y milagroso origen que tuvo el Santuario de la Virgen María de Guadalupe . . .* Mexico 1675.

BIART, LUCIEN *Les aztèques. Histoire, moeurs, coutumes*. Paris 1885. *Biblioteca Americana*. London 1789.

BIENVENIDA, LORENZO DE 'Carta al príncipe Don Felipe' (1548). In *Cartas de Indias*, I. Madrid 1877: 70–82.

BLOM, FRANZ and OLIVIER LA FARGE *Tribes and Temples. Middle American Research Institute Publication* I, 2 vols. 1925.

BOBAN, EUGÈNE *Documents pour servir à l'histoire du Mexique*, 2 vols, Atlas and Index. Paris 1891.

BORUNDA, IGNACIO *Clave general de los jeroglíficos americanos*. Rome 1898.

BOTERO, GIOVANNI *Relationi universali*. Venice 1596.

BOTURINI BENADUCCI, LORENZO *Idea de una nueva historia general de la América Septentrional*. Madrid 1746.

BRASSEUR DE BOURBOURG, C. E. *Histoire des nations civilisées du Mexique et d'Amérique Centrale durant les siècles antérieurs à Christophe Colomb*, 4 vols. Paris 1857–59.

— *Popol Vuh. Le livre sacré et les mythes de l'Antiquité américaine . . .* Paris 1861.

— *Relation de choses de Yucatán de Diego de Landa*. Paris 1864.

BUFFON, GEORGES LOUIS LECLERC, COMTE DE *Oeuvres complètes mises en ordre et précedées d'une notice historique . . .* Paris 1825–28.

BULLOCK, WILLIAM *Six Months' Residence and Travels in Mexico*.

London 1824.

— *A description of the Unique Exhibition called Ancient Mexico*. London 1824.

BURGOA, FANCISCO DE *Geográfica descripción*. Mexico 1934. (First published 1674.)

CALANCHA, ANTONIO DE LA *Crónica moralizada del orden de San Agustín en el Perú*. Barcelona 1638.

CALDERÓN, JOSÉ ANTONIO 'Informe sobre Palenque'. In CASTAÑEDA PAGANINI, *Las ruinas de Palenque*. Guatemala 1946: 22–29.

CALDERÓN DE LA BARCA, FRANCES ERSKINE *Life in Mexico*. London 1843. (London and New York 1913 and 1914, and many subsequent editions.)

CARBIA, ROMULO D. *Historia de la Leyenda negra hispanoamericana*. Madrid 1944.

CÁRDENAS, JUAN DE *Primera parte de los Problemas y Secretos maravillosos de las Indias*. Mexico 1591.

CARLETTI, FRANCISCO *Ragionamenti sopra le cose da lui veduti ne suei viaggi*. Florence 1701.

CASO, ALFONSO *Las estelas Zapotecas*. Mexico 1928.

— 'La correlación de los años aztecas y cristianos'. *Revista Mexicana de Estudios Antropológicos*, III, 1. 1939: 11–45.

— 'Definición y extensión del complejo olmeca'. In *Mayas y Olmecas, Segunda Reunión de Mesa Redonda de la Sociedad Mexicana de Antropología*. 1942: 43–46.

— 'El mapa de Teozacoalco'. *Cuadernos Americanos*, VIII, 5. 1949: 145–82.

— 'Influencia de Seler en las Ciencias Antropológicas'. *México Antiguo*, VII. 1949: 25–28.

— 'Homenaje a Hermann Beyer'. *México Antiguo*, IX. 1961: 23–32.

CASS, LEWIS Review of Baradère in 'Antiquités mexicaines'. *North American Review*, LI. 1840: 396–433.

CASTAÑEDA PAGANINI, RICARDO *Las ruinas de Palenque*. Guatemala 1946.

CASTILLO LEDÓN, LUIS *El Museo Nacional de Arqueología, Historia y Etnografía, 1825–1925*. Mexico 1924 (*sic*)

CATHERWOOD, FREDERICK *Views of Ancient Monuments in Central America, Chiapas and Yucatan*. London 1844.

CERVANTES DE SALAZAR, FRANCISCO *Crónica de la Nueva España*. Madrid 1914. (First published 1570).

CHARNAY, DESIRÉ *Cités et ruines américaines*. With a text by M. VIOLLET-LE-DUC. Paris 1863.

— *Catalogue de la collection archéologique provenant des fouilles et explorations de* . . . Paris 1883.

— *Les anciennes villes du Nouveau Monde*. Paris 1885.

— 'Les explorations de Teobert Maler'. *Journal de la Société des Américanistes de Paris*, new series I. 1904: 289–308.

CIUDAD REAL, ANTONIO DE *Relación breve y verdadera de algunas de las muchas cosas que sucedieron al Padré Fr. Alonso Ponce en las Provincias de Nueva España*, 2 vols. Madrid 1873.

CLARK, J. GRAHAME D. *Archaeology and Society*. London 1939. (Reissued London 1964.)

— *Aspects of Prehistory*. Berkeley and London 1970.

CLAVIJERO, FRANCISCO JAVIER *Historia Antigua de México*, 4 vols. Mexico 1945. (First published in Italian in Cesena 1780–81.)

Codex Nuttall. Facsimile of an ancient Mexican Codex belonging to Lord Zouche. With an introduction by ZELIA NUTTALL. Peabody Museum of American Anthropology and Ethnography. 2 parts. Cambridge, Mass. 1902.

Codex of Yanhuitlan. Facsimile edition with preliminary study by WIGBERTO JIMÉNEZ MORENO and SALVADOR MATEOS HIGUERA. Mexico 1940.

COLÓN, FERNANDO *Historia del Almirante*, 2 vols. Madrid 1932.

COMAS, JUAN 'Bosquejo histórico de la Antropología en México'. *Revista Mexicana de Estudios Antropológicos*, XI. 1950: 97–191.

COOPER-CLARK, J. *The Story of 'Eight Deer' in Codex Colombino*. London 1912.

COVARRUBIAS, MIGUEL 'Origen y desarrollo del estilo artístico "Olmeca" '. In *Mayas y Olmecas, Segunda Reunión de Mesa Redonda de la Sociedad Mexicana de Antropología*. 1942: 46–49.

CUBERO, SEBASTIAN PEDRO *Peregrinación del Mundo*. Madrid 1680.

DALY, CÉSAR 'Note pouvant servir a l'Exploration des Anciens Monuments du Mexique'. *Archives de la Commission Scientifique du Mexique*, I. Paris 1865: 146–61.

DANIEL, GLYN *The origins and growth of archaeology*. Harmondsworth 1967.

— *A hundred and fifty years of archaeology*. London 1975.

— *Cambridge and the back-looking curiosity*. Cambridge 1976.

DE LA TORRE, ERNESTO 'Dos historiadores de Durango'. *Historia Mexicana*, 95. 1975: 403–41.

DE TERRA, HELMUT, JAVIER ROMERO and T. D. STEWART 'Tepexpan man'. Viking Fund Publications in *Anthropology*, XI. 1949.

DEL CASTILLO, ANTONIO and MARIANO BARCENA *El Hombre del Peñón*. Mexico 1885.

DEL RÍO, ANTONIO *Description of the ruins of an ancient city discovered near Palenque* . . . London 1822.

— 'Descripción del terreno y población antiguamente descubierta en las inmediaciones del pueblo de Palenque . . .'. In CASTAÑEDA PAGANINI, *Las ruinas de Palenque*. Guatemala 1946: 48–68.

DÍAZ DEL CASTILLO, BERNAL *Historia verdadera de la conquista de la Nueva España*. Mexico 1939.

DÍAZ, JUAN 'Itinerario de la Armada del rey Católico a la Isla de Yucatan . . .'. In J. GARCÍA ICAZBALCETA (ed.), *Colección de documentos para la historia de México*, vol. I. Mexico 1858: 281–308. (First published in Italian in Venice 1522.)

DRUCKER, PHILIP 'The Cerro de las Mesas offerings of jade and other materials'. Smithsonian Institution, *Bureau of American Ethnology Bulletin* 157. Washington 1955: 25–68.

DUPAIX, CAPITAINE 'Relation des trois expeditions pour la recherche des antiquités du pays . . .'. In *Antiquités Mexicaines*, 2 vols. Paris 1834.

DURÁN, DIEGO *Historia de las Indias de Nueva España e islas de Tierra Firme*, 3 vols. Mexico 1867–80.

DYMOND, D. P. *Archaeology and History. A plea for reconciliation*. London 1974.

EGUIARA Y EGUREN, JUAN JOSÉ *Prólogos a la biblioteca mexicana.* Prepared by Agustin Millares Carlo. Mexico 1944.

ENGERRAND, JORGE 'Discurso inaugural a la exposición de la Escuela Internacional de Arqueología y Etnología Americanas'. *Boletín del Museo Nacional de México*, Period II, Vol. I. 1913: 263–65.

FEYJÓO Y MONTENEGRO, BENITO JERONIMO 'Solución del gran problema histórico sobre la población de la América y Revoluciones del Orbe Terraqueo'. In *Dos Discursos de Feijóo sobre América*, Biblioteca Enciclopédica popular. Mexico 1945.

FERNÁNDEZ DE OVIEDO and GONZALO VALDES *Historia general y natural de las Indias, islas y territorios del Mar Océano.* Madrid 1851.

FINNEGAN, JACK *Light from the ancient past.* Princeton 1959.

FLORENCIA, FRANCISCO DE *La estrella del Norte de México.* Mexico 1688.

FRIEDRICHSTHAL, EMMANUEL DE *Carta a Justo Sierra.* El Museo Yucateco, Campeche 1841.

FUENTES Y GUZMÁN, FRANCISCO ANTONIO DE *Recordación Florida . . . del reino de Guatemala,* 3 vols. Guatemala 1932.

GAGE, THOMAS *A new survey of the West Indies.* (2nd edn) London 1655.

GALINDO, JUAN 'Informe de la Comisión Científica formada para el reconocimiento de las antigüedades de Copán (1834)'. *Anales de la Sociedad de Geografía e Historia de Guatemala*, XX. 1945: 217–28.

GALINDO Y VILLA, JESUS *El Museo Nacional de Arqueología, Historia y Etnografía. Breve reseña.* Mexico 1922.

GALLATIN, ALBERT 'Notes on the semicivilized nations of Mexico, Yucatan and Central America'. *Transactions of the American Ethnological Society*, I. New York 1845.

GALVAO, ANTONIO *The Discoveries of the World, from their first original unto the year of our Lord, 1555.* London 1862. (First published in Portuguese 1555.)

GAMIO, MANUEL 'Restos de la cultura tepaneca'. *Anales del Museo Nacional de México*, Period III, Vol. I. 1909: 235–53.

— 'Arqueología de Atzcapotzalco, D. F.' *Annals of XVIII International Congress of Americanists.* London 1913: 180–87.

— 'Investigaciones arqeológicos en México, 1914–1915'. *Annals of XIX International Congress of Americanists.* Washington 1917: 125–33.

— 'Las excavaciones del Pedregal de San Angel y la cultura arcaica del Valle de México'. *Annals of the XX International Congress of Americanists*, II. Rio de Janeiro 1928: 127–43.

GAMIO, MANUEL (ed.) *La Población del Valle de Teotihuacán.* Mexico 1922.

GARCÍA DE PALACIO, DIEGO *Carta al rey de España, 1576.* In PACHECO, ARDEÑAS and TORRES DE MENDOZA, *Colección de documentos ineditos . . .,* Vol. VI. Madrid 1866.

GARCÍA, GREGORIO *Origen de los Indios del Nuevo Mundo e Indias Occidentales.* Valencia 1607. (Second edition, annotated by Fernandez Barcia, Madrid 1729.)

GARCÍA ICAZBALCETA, JOAQUIN *Colección de documentos para la historia de México*, 2 vols. Mexico 1858–66.

— *Don Fray Juan de Zumarraga.* Mexico 1881.

GARCÍA PAYON, JOSÉ *Zona arquéologica de Tecaxic-Calixtlahuaca*. Mexico 1936.

— 'Los monumentos arqueológicos de Malinalco'. *Revista Mexicana de Estudios Antropológicos*, VIII. 1946: 5–64.

GEMELLI CARRERI, JUAN FRANCISCO *Viaje a lá Nueva España*. Mexico 1927. (First published in Italian 1708.)

GENEBRAND, GILBERT *Chronografía*. First of two parts. Paris 1567.

GERBI, ANTONIO *La disputa del Nuevo Mundo*. Mexico 1960.

GÓNDRA, ISIDRO R. 'Explicación de las láminas . . . de Prescott . . .'. In PRESCOTT 1844, Vol. 3 1846.

GOODMAN, J. T. 'The archaic maya inscriptions'. In *Biologia Centrali-Americana*, Appendix. London 1897.

GORDON, GEORGE BYRON 'Researches in the Uloa Valley, Honduras'. *Memoirs of the Peabody Museum of American Archaeology and Ethnology*, Vol. I, No. 4. Cambridge, Mass. 1898.

GRIJALVA, JUAN DE 'Itinerario de la armada del Rey Católico a la isla Yucatán'. In J. GARCÍA ICAZBALCETA (ed.), *Colección de documentos para la historia de Mexico, I*. *México* 1858.

GROTIUS, HUGO *De origine Gentium Americanarum dissertationes et alteram . . .* Paris 1642.

GUZMÁN, EULALIA 'Los relieves de las rocas del cerro de La Cantera, Jonacatepec'. *Anales del Museo Nacional de México*, Period V, I. 1934: 237–51.

— 'Caracteres fundamentales del arte'. In *México Prehispánico*. Mexico 1946.

HABEL, S. 'The sculptures of Santa Lucia Cotzumalhuapa in Guatemala . . .'. *Smithsonian Contributions to Knowledge*, Vol. 22, 3. 1878.

HAGEN, VICTOR WOLFGANG VON *Maya explorer. John Lloyd Stephens and the lost cities of Central America and Yucatán*. Norman 1947.

HAMY, E. T. Introduction to AUBIN, *Mémoires sur la peinture didactique et l'écriture figurative des anciens mexicains*. Paris 1885.

HAWKES, JACQUETTA 'The proper study of mankind'. *Antiquity*, XLII. 1968: 256.

HEIKAMP, DETLEF and F. ANDERS 'Mexikanische Altertümer aus süddeutschen Kunstkammern'. Pantheon, XXVIII. 1970.

— Mexico and the Medici. Florence 1972.

HEIZER, ROBERT F. *Man's discovery of his past*. Palo Alto, Cal. 1969.

HERRERA, ANTONIO DE *Historia general de los hechos de los castellanos en las islas y tierra firme del mar océano*. Madrid 1601–15.

HOLMES, WILLIAM H. 'Evidences of the antiquity of man on the site of the city of Mexico'. *Transactions of the Anthropological Society of Washington*, Vol. 3. 1885: 68–81.

—'Archaeological studies among the ancient cities of Mexico'. *Field Columbian Museum, Anthropological Series*, I. Chicago 1895–97.

HOOTON, E. A. *Apes, Men and Morons*. London 1938.

HUDDLESTON, LEE ELRIDGE *Origins of the American Indians. European concepts 1492–1729*. Austin 1943 and London 1967.

HUMBOLDT, ALEXANDRE DE *Essai politique sur le Royaume de la Nouvelle Espagne*. Paris 1811.

— *Vues des cordillères et monuments des peuples indigènes de l'Amérique*. Paris 1810.

— *Vues des cordillères . . .*, 2 vols. (Abridged edn) Paris 1816.
ICAZA, FRANCISCO A. DE '*Miscelanea historica*'. *Revista Mexicana de Estudios Históricos*, Appendix, II. 1928.
IMBELLONI, JOSÉ *La esfinge Indiana*. Buenos Aires 1926.
Isagoge Histórica apologética de las Indias Occidentales. Guatemala 1935.
ISRAEL, MENASSEH BEN . . . *Origen de los Americanos. Esto es esperanza de Israel*. Madrid 1881. (First published 1650.)
IXTLILXOCHITL, FERNANDO DE ALVA *Obras Históricas*, 2 vols. Mexico 1892.
JEFFERSON, THOMAS *Notes on the State of Virginia*. 1782. (8th edn, 1801).
JIMÉNEZ MORENO, WIGBERTO 'Tula y los toltecas según las fuentes históricas'. *Revista Mexicana de Estudios Antropológicos*, V. 1941: 79–83.
— 'El enigma de los olmecas'. *Cuadernos Americanos*, 5. 1942: 113–45.
— 'Los estudios de Historia Precolonial de México (1937–1950)'. *Anales del Instituto Nacional de Antropología e Historia*, 32. 1952: 71–83.
JOYCE, THOMAS A. *Mexican Archaeology. An introduction to the archaeology of the Mexican and Mayan civilizations of pre-Spanish America . . .* London 1914.
KEEN, BENJAMIN *The Aztec image in Western thought*. New Jersey 1971.
KIDDER, ALFRED V. Division of Historical Research, Carnegie Institution of Washington, *Year Book* 29 (1929–30). 1930.
— 'A program for Maya research'. Carnegie Institution of Washington, *Supplementary Publications*, 28. 1937.
— 'Excavations at Kaminaljuyu, Guatemala'. Carnegie Institution of Washington. *Publication* 561. 1946.
KINGSBOROUGH, LORD *Antiquities of Mexico*, 9 vols. London 1831–48.
KLINDT-JENSEN, OLE *A History of Scandinavian Archaeology*. London 1975.
KROEBER, A. L. 'Archaic Culture Horizons in the Valley of Mexico'. *University of California Publications in American Archaeology and Ethnology*, Vol. 17, No. 7. 1925: 373–408.
— *Anthropology*. New York 1924.
LAET, JOHANES DE *Notae ad dissertationem Hugonis Grotii de Origine Gentium Americanarum . . .* Amsterdam 1643.
— *Responsionem ad dissertationem secundam Hugonis Grotii . . .* Amsterdam 1644.
LAFAYE, JACQUES *Quetzalcoatl et Guadalupe*. Paris 1974.
LANDA, DIEGO DE *Relación de las cosas de Yucatán*. Mexico 1938.
LARRAINZAR, MANUEL *Estudios sobre la historia de América, sus ruinas y antigüedades*, 5 vols. Mexico 1875–78.
LAS CASAS, BARTOLOMÉ DE *Historia de las Indias. Fondo de Cultura Económica*, 3 vols. Mexico 1951.
— *Apologética Historia Sumaria*, 2 vols, Preface and Notes by EDMUNDO O'GORMAN. Mexico 1967.
LATROBE, CHARLES JOSEPH *The Rambler in Mexico: 1834*. London 1836.
LE PLONGEON, AUGUSTUS *Sacred Mysteries among the Mayas and the Quichés. 11,500 years ago . . .* New York 1886.

— *Queen Móo and the Egyptian Sphinx.* New York and London 1896.

LEHMANN, WALTER *Methods and Results in Mexican Research.* Paris 1909. (Translation of the paper published in *Archiv für Anthropologie*, VI. 1907: 113–68.)

LENOIR, ALEXANDRE 'Parallèle des anciens monuments mexicains avec ceux de l'Egypte, de l'Inde et du reste de l'ancien monde'. *Antiquités Mexicaines*, Vol. I, Part 2. Mexico 1832.

LEÓN Y GAMA, ANTONIO *Descripción histórica y cronológica de las dos piedras* . . . Mexico 1792. (Second edition, containing Part 2, Mexico 1832.)

LEÓN PINELO, ANTONIO *El Paraíso en el Nuevo Mundo, Comentario apologético, Historia Natural y Peregrina de las Indias Occidentales Islas de Tierra Firme del Mar Océano* . . . Mexico 1943. (Written about 1650.)

— 'De Teotihuacán a los Aztecas'. *UNAM.* Mexico 1971.

LEONARD, IRVING A. *Don Carlos de Sigüenza y Góngora.* Berkeley 1929.

LINNÉ, SIGVALD 'Archaeological researches at Teotihuacan, Mexico'. *Ethnological Museum of Sweden Publication* No. 1, new series. Stockholm 1934.

LIZANA, BERNARDO DE *Historia y conquista espiritual de Yucatán.* Mexico 1892. (First published 1633).

LONGPERIER, ADRIEN DE *Notice des monuments exposés dans la salle des antiquités américaines au Musée du Louvre.* Paris 1850.

LÓPEZ DE COGOLLUDO, DIEGO *Historia de Yucatán.* Madrid 1688.

LÓPEZ DE GÓMARA, FRANCISCO *Historia general de las Indias,* 2 vols. Madrid 1941. (First published 1552.)

LORENZANA, FRANCISCO ANTONIO DE *Historia de Nueva España.* Mexico 1770.

LUMNIUS, JOANNES FREDERICUS *De Extremo Dei Iudicio et Indorum Vocatione.* Venice 1567.

MANEIRO, JUAN LUIS *De vitis aliquot mexicanorum,* 3 vols. Bologna 1791–92.

MARAÑON, GREGORIO *Las ideas biológicas del Padre Feijóo.* Madrid 1934.

MÁRQUEZ, PEDRO JOSÉ *Due Antichi Monumenti di Architettura Messicana.* Rome 1804.

— 'Sobre lo bello en general y dos monumentos de arquitectura mexicana'. *UNAM.* Inst. de Investigaciones Estéticas. Mexico 1972.

MARQUINA, IGNACIO 'Estudio arquitectónico de la pirámide'. In *Tenayuca.* Mexico 1935: 77–102.

— 'Arquitectura Prehispánica'. *INAH.* Mexico 1951.

MARTÍNEZ, ENRICO *Reportorio de los tiempos, y historia natural desta Nueva España.* Mexico 1606 (author's imprint). Another edition, Mexico 1948 (imprint of Secretary of Public Education).

MARTÍNEZ DEL RÍO, PABLO *Los orígenes Americanos.* (3rd edn) Mexico 1952.

MAUDSLAY, ALFRED P. 'Archaeology'. In *Biologia Centrali-Americana,* 5 vols. London 1889–92.

MAUDSLAY, ANNE CARY and ALFRED PERCIVAL *A Glimpse at Guatemala, and some notes on the ancient monuments of Central*

America. London 1899.

MAYER, BRANTZ *Mexico as it was and as it is*. New York 1844.

— *Mexico, Aztec, Spanish and Republican . . .*, 2 vols. Hartford 1852.

MELGAR Y SERRANO, JOSÉ MARIA 'Estudio sobre la antigüedad y el origen de la cabeza colosal de tipo etiópico que existe en Hueyapan en el cantón de los Tuxtlas'. *Boletín de la Sociedad Mexicana de Geografía y Estadística*, Period 2, III. 1871: 104–09.

— 'Antigüedades mexicanas' *Boletín de la Sociedad Mexicana de Geografía y Estadística*, Period 2, I. 1869: 292–97.

MENDEZ, MODESTO 'Descubrimiento de las ruinas de Tikal'. *Anales de la Sociedad de Geografía e Historia*, VII, 1. Guatemala 1930: 88–94.

MENDIETA, GERONIMO DE *Historia eclesiástica indiana*. Mexico 1870.

MENDOZA, GUMERSINDO and JESUS SÁNCHEZ 'Catálogo de las colecciones historica y arqueológica del Museo Nacional de México'. *Anales del Museo Nacional de México*, Period I, Vol. II. 1882: 445–86.

MERWIN, RAYMOND E. and GEORGE C. VAILLANT 'The Ruins of Holmul, Guatemala'. *Memoirs of the Peabody Museum*, Vol. II, No. 2. Cambridge, Mass. 1932.

MIER, SERVANDO TERESA DE 'Sermón sobre la Virgen de Guadalupe pronunciado el 12 de diciembre de 1794'. In J. E. HERNÁNDEZ Y DAVALOS, *Colección de documentos para la historia de la guerra de la Independencia en México*, Vol. III. Mexico 1877–82.

MILLARES CARLO, AGUSTIN 'Noticia biográfica'. In EGUIARA Y EGUREN, *Prólogos a la biblioteca mexicana*. Mexico 1944.

MOLINA MONTES, AUGUSTO 'La restauración arquitectónica en edificios arqueológicos'. *INAH*, Colección Científica, 21. Mexico 1975.

MORGAN, LEWIS H. *Ancient Society*. New York and London 1877.

— 'Montezuma's dinner'. *North American Review*, CXXXII. 1876: 265–308.

— 'Houses and house-life of the American Aborigines'. *Geographical and Geological Survey of the Rocky Mountain Region. Contributions to North American Ethnology*, Vol. 4. 1877.

MORLEY, SYLVANUS GRISWOLD *The Inscriptions of Petén*. Carnegie Institution of Washington, 5 vols. 1938.

— 'Maya epigraphy'. In *The Maya and their neighbors*. New York and London 1940: 139–49.

— *The Ancient Maya*. Stanford and London 1946.

MOTOLINIA, TORIBIO DE 'Historia de los Indios de Nueva España. In J. GARCÍA ICAZBALCETA (ed.), *Colección de documentos para la historia de México*, Vol. I. Mexico 1858: 1–250.

MÜHLENPFORDT, EDWARD *Intento de una descripción exacta de la República de México*. Hanover 1844.

MUÑOZ, JUAN BAUTISTA 'Informe sobre Palenque'. In CASTAÑEDA PAGANINI, *Las ruinas de Palenque*. Guatemala 1946: 41–45.

— *Historia del Nuevo Mundo*. Madrid 1793.

NADAILLAC, MARQUIS DE *L'Amérique Préhistorique*. Paris 1883.

NAVARRO, BERNABÉ 'Cultura mexicana moderna en el siglo XVIII'. *UNAM*. Mexico 1964.

NOGUERA, EDUARDO 'Antecedentes y relaciones de la cultura Teotihuacana'. *México Antiguo*, III, Nos 5–8. 1931–36: 5–90.

— 'Veinticinco años de arqueología en México'. In *Homenaje al*

Doctor Alfonso Caso. Mexico 1951: 283–92.

NORMAN, B. M. *Rambles in Yucatan; or notes of travel through the Peninsula, including a visit to the . . . Ruins of Chichen, Kabah, Zayi and Uxmal.* (2nd edn) New York 1843.

'Noticia del descubrimiento de la pirámide de Tajín. *Gazeta de México*. 12 July 1785: 349–51.

O'GORMAN, EDMUNDO 'La Apologética Historia, su genesis y elaboración, su estructura y su sentido'. In LAS CASAS, *Apologética Historia Sumaria*, Vol. I. *UNAM*. Mexico 1967.

— *Cuatro historiadores de Indias*. Mexico 1972.

ORBIGNY, ALCIDE *Voyage pittoresque dans les deux Amériques*. Paris 1836.

ORDOÑEZ Y AGUIAR, RAMÓN 'Historia de la creación del cielo y de la tierra conforme al sistema de la gentilidad americana . . .'. In NICOLAS LEÓN, *Bibliografía Mexicana del Siglo XVIII*, Part 4. 1907: 1–272.

ORDOÑEZ DE CEVALLOS, PEDRO *Historia y viaje del mundo*. Madrid 1614.

OROZCO Y BERRA, MANUEL 'Noticias de la Ciudad de México'. In *Diccionario Universal de Historia y Geografía*, V. Mexico 1855: 778.

— *Historia antigua y de la conquista de México*. 4 vols and Atlas. Mexico 1880.

ORTEGA Y GASSET, J. 'El siglo XVIII educador'. In *Obras completas*. Madrid 1932: 624–26.

PALLOTTINO, MASSIMO *The Meaning of Archaeology*. London and Florence 1968.

PASO Y TRONCOSCO, FRANCISCO DEL *Catálogo de los objetos que presenta la república de México en la exposición Histórico-Americana de Madrid*, 2 vols. Madrid 1892.

PAUW, CORNELIUS DE *Recherches philosophiques sur les Américains*. Berlin 1768.

PENDERGAST, DAVID M. *Palenque. The Walker-Caddy expedition to the ancient Maya city, 1839–40*. Norman 1967.

PEÑAFIEL, ANTONIO *Explication de l'édifice mexicain à l'Exposition Internationale de Paris en 1889*. Mexico 1889.

— *Monumentos del arte mexicano antiguo; ornamentación, mitología, tributos y monumentos*. Berlin 1890.

PÉREZ, JUAN PÍO 'Antigua cronología Yucateca'. In *Registro Yucateco*, III. Mérida 1846: 281–89, 323–32.

PEYRERE, ISAAC DE LA *Men before Adam*. London 1656.

PIGGOTT, STUART *Approach to Archaeology*. Harmondsworth 1966.

PLANCARTE Y NAVARRETE, FRANCISCO *Tamoanchan*. Mexico 1911.

PLAZA Y JAEN, BERNARDO DE LA *Crónica de la Real y Pontificia Universidad de México*. Mexico 1931.

POLLOCK, H. E. D. 'Sources and methods in the study of Maya architecture'. In *The Maya and their neighbors*. New York and London 1940: 179–201.

— Carnegie Institution of Washington, Department of Archaeology. *Boletín Bibliográfico de Antropología Americana*, XVIII, 1. 1956: 91–96.

POLLOCK, H. E. D. *et al.* 'Mayapan, Yucatán', *Carnegie Institution of Washington Publication 619*. 1962.

PORCACCHI, THOMASO *L'isole piu famose del mondo descritte* . . . Venice 1590.

PRESCOTT, W. H. *History of the Conquest of Mexico*. London and New York 1843.

— Historia de la conquista de México, 3 vols. Translated by Joaquín Navarro with notes and a commentary by J. F. Ramírez and I. Góndra. Mexico 1844–46.

PURCHAS, SAMUEL *Purchas his Pilgrimes*, 5 vols. London 1625.

RADIN, PAUL 'The sources and authenticity of the history of the ancient Mexicans'. *University of California Publications in American Archaeology and Ethnology*, 17. 1920: 1–50.

RAMÍREZ, JOSÉ FERNANDO 'Notas y esclarecimientos a . . . Prescott'. In PRESCOTT, 1844, Vol. 2, 1845.

— 'Cuadro histórico-geográfico de la peregrinación de las tribus aztecas que poblaron el Valle de México. . . . In GARCÍA CUBAS, *Atlas Geográfico, Estadístico e Histórico de la República Mexicana*. Mexico 1853.

— 'Antigüedades mexicanas conservadas en el Museo Nacional'. In *México y sus alrededores*. Mexico 1864: 48–57.

— 'El Apóstol Santo Tomas en el Nuevo Mundo . . .'. In NICOLAS LEÓN, *Bibliografía Mexicana del Siglo XVIII*, Section 1, Part 3. Mexico 1906: 353–67.

— *Viaje a Yucatán*. Mérida 1926.

RASTELL, JOHN 'The Interlude of the four elements. An early moral play'. In *Early English poetry, ballads and popular literature of the Middle Ages*, Vol. 22. The Percy Society. London. (First published about 1520.)

REDMAN, CHARLES L. (ed.) *Research and theory in current archaeology*. New York and London 1973.

Registro Yucateco: Periódico literario redactado por una Sociedad de Amigos, 4 vols. Mérida 1845–46.

'Relación de Kansahcab', in *Colección de documentos inéditos relativos al descubrimiento, conquista y organización de las antiguas posesiones españolas de ultramar,* second series, II. Madrid 1898: 190.

'Relación de Mitla' in *Papeles de Nueva España*, second series, Vol. IV. Published by Francisco del Paso y Troncoso. Mexico 1905: 147–54.

Relaciónes Geográficas de Indias—Peru—published by Ministerio de Fomento, 2 vols. Madrid 1881.

REYNIERS, F. *Sèvres-Céramiques américaines*. Paris 1966.

RICKETSON, OLIVER G. 'Uaxactun, Guatemala, Group E—1926–31. Part I The Excavations'. *Carnegie Institution of Washington Publication* 477. 1937.

RITTERS, CARL 'Ueber neue Entdeckungen und Beobachtungen in Guatemala und Yucatan'. *Zeitschrift für Allgemeine Erdkunde*, I. Berlin 1853: 161–93.

ROBERTSON, WILLIAM P. *The History of America*. London 1777.

ROCHA, DIEGO ANDRES *Tratado único y singular del origen de los Indios*, 2 vols. Madrid 1891.

ROJAS, FERNANDO DE *La Celestina*, 2 vols. (Clásicos Castellanos edn) Madrid 1913. (First published 1499.)

ROJAS GARCIDUEÑAS, JOSÉ *Don Carlos de Sigüenza*. Mexico 1945.

ROMÁN, JERÓNIMO *Repúblicas del Mundo*, 2 vols. Madrid 1897. (First published in Medina del Campo 1575.)

SAHAGÚN, BERNARDINO DE *Historia general de las cosas de Nueva España*, 4 vols, Editorial Porrúa. Mexico 1956.

SÁNCHEZ DE AGUILAR, PEDRO 'Informe contra idolorum cultores del obispado de Yucatán'. *Anales del Museo Nacional de México*, Period I, Vol. VI. 1892: 13–122. (Written about 1635.)

SARRAILH, JEAN *L'Espagne éclairée de la seconde moitié du XVIIIème siècle*. Paris 1954.

SAVILLE, MARSHALL H. 'A votive adze of jadeite from Mexico'. *Records of the Past*, I. 1902: 14–16.

— 'Votive axes from Eastern Mexico'. *Indian Notes and Monographs*, VI. Museum of the American Indian, 1929: 266–99, 335–42.

SCHELHASS, PAUL *Die Göttergestalten der Maya Handschriften. Ein mythologisches Kulturbild aus dem alten Amerika*. Dresden 1897.

— 'Fifty years of Maya research'. *Maya Research*, III. 1936: 129–39.

SELER, EDUARD 'Die Ausgrabungen am Orte des Haupttempels in Mexiko'. *Mitteilungen des Anthropologischer Gesellschaft in Wien*, XXI. 1901: 113–37.

— 'Die Teotihuacan Kultur des Hochlandes von Mexiko'. *Gesammelte Abhandlungen*, V. 1915: 405–585.

SEPULVEDA, JUAN GINÉS DE *Sobre las justas de la guerra contra los indios*. Mexico 1941.

SHEPARD, ANNA O. 'Plumbate. A Mesoamerican trade ware'. *Carnegie Institution of Washington Publication* 573. 1948.

SHORT, JOHN T. *The North Americans of Antiquity*. (2nd edn) New York 1880.

SIGÜENZA Y GÓNGORA, CARLOS DE *Parayso Occidental . . .* Mexico 1683.

— *Obras*. Mexico 1928.

SIMÓN, PEDRO *Noticias historiales . . .*, 5 vols. Bogotá 1882–92. (First published 1627.)

SOLORZANO Y PEREYRA, JUAN *Política Indiana*. Madrid 1639.

SPINDEN, HERBERT J. 'A Study of Maya Art. Its Subject Matter and Historical Development'. *Memoirs of the Peabody Museum*, VI. Cambridge, Mass. 1913.

— 'Origin of civilization in Central America and Mexico'. In D. JENNESS (ed.), *The American aborigines their origin and antiquity*. Toronto 1933: 217–46.

STEPHENS, JOHN LLOYD *Incidents of Travel in Central America, Chiapas, and Yucatán*, 2 vols. New York and London 1841.

— *Incidents of Travel in Yucatán*, 2 vols. New York and London 1843.

STIRLING, MATTHEW W. 'An Initial Series from Tres Zapotes, Vera Cruz'. *National Geographical Society Contributed Technical Papers, Mexican Archaeology Series*, Vol. I, No. 1. Washington 1940.

— 'Early history of the Olmec problem'. In ELIZABETH P. BENSON (ed.), *Dumbarton Oaks Conference on the Olmec*. Washington 1968: 1–8.

SUAREZ DE PERALTA, JUAN *Tratado del descubrimiento de las Indias y su conquista*. Madrid 1878. (Written about 1580.)

TARAYRE, GUILLEMIN 'Rapport sur l'exploration minéralogique des régions mexicaines', *Archives de la Commission Scientifique du*

Mexique, III. 1867: 173–470.

TAYLOR, WALTER W. *A Study of Archaeology*. Menasha 1948.

TERNAUX COMPANS, HENRI *Voyages, Relations et Mémoires originaux pour servir à l'histoire de la découverte de l'Amérique*, 20 vols. Paris 1837–40.

THAUSING, M. *Quellenschriften für Kunstgeschichte—Dürers Briefe, Tagebücher und Reime*. Vienna 1888.

THEVENOT, MELQUISEDECH *Relation de divers voyages curieux qui n'ont pas été publiés . . .* Paris 1672.

THEVET, ANDRÉ *Les singularités de la France Antarctique*. Paris 1878. (First published Paris 1558.)

THOMAS, CYRUS *Introduction to the study of North American Archaeology*. Cincinnati 1898. (Second edition 1903.)

THOMPSON, J. ERIC S. 'Dating of certain inscriptions of non-Maya origin'. *Carnegie Institution of Washington, Theoretical approaches to problems*, I. 1941.

— 'Maya Hieroglyphic writing'. Introduction. *Carnegie Institution of Washington Publication 589.* 1950.

THOROWGOOD, THOMAS *Jewes in America, or probabilities that the Americans are of that Race . . .* London 1650.

TOMSON, ROBERT 'Viaje a la Nueva España en 1555'. Translated and edited by J. García Icazbalceta, *Boletín de la Sociedad Mexicana de Geografía y Estadística*, Period 2, Vol. I. Mexico 1869: 203–13.

TORQUEMADA, JUAN DE *Monarquía Indiana*. (2nd edn) Madrid 1723. (First published 1615.)

TOSCANO, SALVADOR *Arte Precolombino de México y de la América Central*. Mexico 1944.

TOYNBEE, ARNOLD JOSEPH *A Study of History*. (2nd edn) London 1935.

TOZZER, ALFRED M. 'Summary of the work of the International School of American Archaeology and Ethnology in Mexico'. *American Anthropologist*, new series 17. 1915: 384–95.

— 'Excavation of a site at Santiago Ahuitzotla, D. F., Mexico'. Smithsonian Institution, Bureau of American Ethnology, *Bulletin 74*. Washington 1921.

— 'Time and American Archaeology'. *Natural History*, XXVII. 1927: 210–21.

— 'Alfred Percival Maudslay'. *Boletín del Museo Nacional de México*, Period 5, Vol. 2. 1933: 63–69.

— Maya Research, I. 1934: 3–19.

— 'Prehistory in Middle America'. *Hispanic American Historical Review*, XVII. 1937: 151–59.

TOZZER, ALFRED M. (ed.) 'Landa's Relación de las Cosas de Yucatán'. *Papers of the Peabody Museum of American Archaeology and Ethnography*, Vol. 18. Cambridge, Mass. 1941.

TWEEDIE, ETHEL BRILLIANA *Mexico as I saw it*. London 1901.

TYLOR, EDWARD B. *Anahuac: or Mexico and the Mexicans ancient and modern*. London 1861.

VAILLANT, GEORGE C. 'Chronology and stratigraphy in the Maya area'. *Maya Research*, II, 2. 1935: 119–43.

— 'A correlation of Archaeological and Historical Sequences in the Valley of Mexico'. *American Anthropologist*, XL. 1938: 535–73.

— *Aztecs of Mexico*. New York 1941 and Harmondsworth 1950.

VETANCURT, AGUSTIN DE *Teatro Mexicano . . ..* Mexico 1698.

VEYTIA, MARIANO *Historia Antigua de México*. Mexico 1836.

VILLAGUTIERRE SOTOMAYOR, JUAN DE *Historia de la conquista de la Provincia de El Itzá . . .* Madrid 1701.

WACE, A. J. B. 'The Greeks and Romans as archaeologists'. In HEIZER, 1969.

WAFER, LIONEL *A New Voyage and Description of the Isthmus of America*. London 1699.

WALCKENAER, DE LARENAUDIÈRE and JOMARD *Rapport sur le concours relatif à la Géographie et aux Antiquités de l'Amérique*. Paris 1836.

WALDECK, FREDERICK DE *Voyage pittoresque et archéologique dans la province d'Yucatan pendant les années 1834 et 1836*. Paris 1838.

WALDECK, F. M. and C. E. BRASSEUR DE BOURBOURG *Monuments anciens du Mexique, Palenque et autres ruines de l'ancienne civilization du Mexique*. Paris 1866.

WARD, H. G. *Mexico in 1827*, 2 vols. London 1828.

WAUCHOPE, ROBERT *Lost Tribes and Sunken Continents*. Chicago and London 1962.

WEYERSTALL, ALBERT 'Some observations on Indian mounds, idols and pottery in the Lower Papaloapam Basin'. *Middle American Research Institute Publication* 4. 1932: 23–69.

WHEELER, SIR MORTIMER *Archaeology from the Earth*. Harmondsworth 1956.

WHITE, LESLIE A. and IGNACIO BERNAL 'Correspondencia de Adolfo F. Bandelier'. Instituto Nacional de Antropología e Historia. Mexico 1960.

WILLEY, GORDON R. *An introduction to American Archaeology*, 2 vols. Englewood Cliffs 1966–71.

WILLEY, GORDON R. and JEREMY A. SABLOFF *A History of American Archaeology*. London and San Francisco 1974.

WILSON, ROBERT ANDERSON *A new history of the Conquest of Mexico*. London and Philadelphia 1859.

WINSOR, JUSTIN *Narrative and Critical History of America*, 8 vols. Boston and New York 1887.

WOOLLEY, SIR CHARLES LEONARD *Ur of the Chaldees*. (2nd edn) London 1950.

XIMÉNEZ, FRANCISCO *Las historias del origen de los indios de esta Provincia de Guatemala*. Translated from the Quiché language into Spanish by C. Scherzer. Vienna 1857.

ZAMORA, ALONSO DE *Historia de la Provincia de San Antonio del Nuevo Reino de Granada*. Bogotá 1945. (First published 1701.)

ZAPULLO, MICHELE *Historie di quatro principali citta del mondo . . . Aggiuntovi un compendio dell'istorie dell'Indie, & anche le tavoli astronomiche . . .* Vicenza 1603.

ZARATE, AGUSTIN *Historia del descubrimiento y conquista de la Provincia del Perú*. Mexico n.d. (First published 1555.)

ZAVALA, LORENZO DE 'Notice sur les monuments antiques d'Ushmal'. In *Antiquités Mexicaines*, Vol. I, part 1. Paris 1834: 33–35.

ZAVALA, SILVIO *América en el espiritú francés del siglo XVIII.* Mexico 1949.

Index

Numbers in italic refer to the illustrations